Practical Webix

Learn to Expedite and Improve your Web Development

Frank Zammetti

Apress®

Practical Webix

Frank Zammetti
Pottstown, Pennsylvania, USA

ISBN-13 (pbk): 978-1-4842-3383-2
https://doi.org/10.1007/978-1-4842-3384-9

ISBN-13 (electronic): 978-1-4842-3384-9

Library of Congress Control Number: 2018936351

Managing Director, Apress Media LLC: Welmoed Spahr
Acquisitions Editor: Louise Corrigan
Development Editor: James Markham
Coordinating Editor: Nancy Chen

Cover designed by eStudioCalamar

Cover image by Freepik (www.freepik.com)

Distributed to the book trade worldwide by Springer Science+Business Media New York, 233 Spring Street, 6th Floor, New York, NY 10013. Phone 1-800-SPRINGER, fax (201) 348-4505, e-mail orders-ny@springer-sbm.com, or visit www.springeronline.com. Apress Media, LLC is a California LLC and the sole member (owner) is Springer Science + Business Media Finance Inc (SSBM Finance Inc). SSBM Finance Inc is a **Delaware** corporation.

For information on translations, please e-mail rights@apress.com, or visit www.apress.com/rights-permissions.

Apress titles may be purchased in bulk for academic, corporate, or promotional use. eBook versions and licenses are also available for most titles. For more information, reference our Print and eBook Bulk Sales web page at www.apress.com/bulk-sales.

Any source code or other supplementary material referenced by the author in this book is available to readers on GitHub via the book's product page, located at www.apress.com/9781484233832. For more detailed information, please visit www.apress.com/source-code.

Printed on acid-free paper

This is my ninth book, and with each one it has become more difficult to find people to dedicate them to. This time around, though, it was fairly easy because I realized that I've missed a whole host of people who influenced my life and career in computers in a major way without them even knowing it. So, this one goes out to the following individuals, without whom I'd probably be pumping gas or digging ditches (not that there's anything inherently wrong with those vocations—work is work!):

Ian Williamson, Chris Curry, Jim Westwood, and Clive Sinclair

Steven T. Mayer, Joseph C. Decuir, Jay G. Miner, Douglas G. Neubauer, George McLeod, Ronald E. Milner, Francois Michel, Mark Shieu, Steve Stone, Steve Smith, Delwin Pearson, and Kevin McKinsey

Jack Tramiel, Chuck Peddle, Robert Russell, Bob Yannes, Al Charpentier, Charles Winterble, Yash Terakura, Shiraz Shivji, and David A. Ziembicki

Table of Contents

About the Author

Frank Zammetti is a veteran software developer/architect of nearly 25 professional years and another almost 15 on top of that of nonprofessional development work. He has written eight other technical books for Apress and has served as a technical reviewer for other publishers. Frank is also a fiction writer, though he's still on the hunt for an agent to represent his work. (Hey, if you *happen* to be an agent and you just *happen* to be on the lookout for new talent and you just *happen* to be reading this…just sayin'!)

About the Technical Reviewer

Toby Jee is a software programmer currently located in Sydney, Australia. He loves Linux and open source projects. He programs mainly in Java, JavaScript, TypeScript, and Python. In his spare time, Toby enjoys walkabouts, reading, and playing guitar.

Acknowledgments

I would like to acknowledge all of those who helped bring this book to reality at Apress, among them Nancy Chen, Louise Corrigan, James Markham, and Dhaneesh Kumar (and to anyone else not listed, I heretofore acknowledge you as well). Thanks, folks. I just write the words; in my opinion, you all do the actual hard work!

I'd also like to acknowledge my technical reviewer, Toby Jee. This is actually the first book, if memory serves (which it frequently does not these days, but I'm *pretty* sure about this!), that I haven't had the same tech reviewer (not for any specific reason; it's just the way things go). Toby did, in my estimation, an excellent job throughout on his first tech reviewer job. Thanks, Toby!

Finally, I'd like to acknowledge XB Software, creators of Webix. Aside from creating an excellent product, they helped me a number of times during the writing of this book with issues (Maksim Kozkuhk, Nick Maksimenko, and Tasiana Drozd specifically) and also graciously provided me with a Webix Pro license to use. Thank you, all. I very much appreciate it!

Introduction

Creating a modern web app is tough. There are so many different technology choices, so many different approaches, and so many different architectures, theories, and methods. You can even forego all of that and just use "naked" HTML, CSS, and JavaScript. The decisions can drive even an experienced developer nuts in short order!

I've been doing this exact thing for two decades now (seriously!), so I've seen it all, many times over. One of the key things I've learned is that simplicity is one of the most important considerations. Simplicity is easier to maintain, and writing maintainable software is a key aspect of professional development.

So, when I stumbled upon Webix, I was immediately smitten with its simplicity! It allows you to do some pretty advanced things with a minimum of code. It also doesn't require a big, complex toolchain nor does it require you to learn a bunch of specialized domain-specific languages. It's basic HTML, CSS, and JavaScript against a generally clean API, and that's about it!

In this book, I'll take you through the many capabilities that Webix brings to the table. We'll explore things such as application architecture, the widgets that Webix provides, and the components that you can build a user interface from. Eventually, together we'll build a real application using Webix, but before then you'll have a solid foundation of knowledge from which to build upon.

In keeping with the title of this book, the application we'll build will be very practical, meaning it won't be some grossly simplified, dumbed-down, and contrived example. It'll be a real app, and along the way you'll see many aspects that went into its development, including in some cases the problems I faced in putting it together and the solutions I came up with! In doing so, you'll get solid, hands-on experience with using Webix in a real-world way—a way that will prepare you for building your own apps later.

You'll also learn some things tangential to building the app including how to make it a mobile app using the popular PhoneGap (Cordova) library and how to build a server for the app to interact with. See, it's practical, not just some pointless sample that will leave you wanting for more!

On top of that, you'll get a bonus second app that's drastically different from the first: a game! Yes, we'll build a game together using Webix, if for no other reason than to highlight some other capabilities of Webix that the first app won't necessarily touch on. A game may not be quite as "practical" in a sense, but games sure are fun to make, and a little fun never hurt nobody!

If you were a computer person in the 1980s, then you're quite familiar with typing in 20 small-print magazine pages of machine code to play a game. You certainly could do that with this book, but that would be a lot of typing! So, before you get started, I suggest you head over to the Apress web site, search for this book, and grab the source code bundle from there. That should give you everything you need to follow along without having to type your fingers raw! That said, don't forget that the best way to learn anything is by doing, so definitely get in there and hack at the example code and see what happens when you make changes. I think before long you'll realize that because of the power Webix provides, small changes can make big differences in what winds up on the screen.

So, get ready for what I hope you'll find to be an enjoyable and informative ride through the land of Webix (and other stuff) that will be a rewarding experience!

CHAPTER 1

Better Web Development with Webix

To paraphrase a well-known expression, web development has come a long way, baby!

It's been a long road getting from there to here, from the "dark days," when web development was all about getting the best 15-year-old prodigy you could find to hack HTML for you, to now, where legions of professional developers create advanced, complex apps on the Web.

Before we get to Webix, the pièce de résistance of this book, let's take a quick look back to see where we've been and where we as web developers are in the process of going.

Web Development: The Toddler Years

In the dark ages, many eons ago (you know, the mid-to-late 1990s!), web development was really pretty easy. You had static, unchanging HTML files sitting out on a web server somewhere. These pages linked together via hyperlinks (the *H* in HTML, of course), and that's about all the Web was. Even things like graphics and other media were just starting to hit the scene at that time (raise your hand if you remember when Gopher was the way you accessed content rather than the Web!). For a developer, it wasn't much harder than firing up your favorite text editor, entering some HTML by hand, and pushing it out to the server via FTP or something similar.

Before long, developers realized they needed to introduce some degree of interactivity to the mix. This took several forms to start, but Common Gateway Interface (CGI) was one of the earliest and most famous. This mechanism let the web servers of the day execute small programs on behalf of the client requesting a page. The output from these programs was typically inserted into an HTML document to provide for

© Frank Zammetti 2018
F. Zammetti, *Practical Webix*, https://doi.org/10.1007/978-1-4842-3384-9_1

some portion of it to be dynamic. Maybe that meant inserting markup to show a list of products, how many visitors the page had over the past week, or myriad other things. The big point was that it was the *server* that did the dynamic work. Every time some content had to be generated or some user interaction handled, a request had to be made to the server.

Eventually, the limitations of CGI became apparent (most notably the fact that it was typically a one-request-at-a-time deal and so performance suffered when the number of incoming requests increased too much), so dynamic server languages were created. Things like Microsoft's Active Server Pages (ASP) and Sun's Java servlets came about, among many others whose time mostly came and went quickly.

But, again, that key point remained: the server was doing the work of executing code. The client simply displayed the content that the server created.

Web Development: The Teen Years

At roughly the same time, JavaScript came on the scene. A creation of Brendan Eich (in just ten days, unbelievably!), JavaScript provided developers with the ability to have dynamic elements on their sites without the need for the server to do the work. No longer did you need the server to do all the heavy lifting; the client itself could do some of it by generating content or altering existing content.

There was a lot of experimentation that went on during that time and a lot of lessons learned. One of the biggest that people began to realize quickly was simply that the Web could do more than just simple static web pages or even dynamic content (which, in many ways, still looked like static content to the end user). Developers started to realize that what we had was, in fact, a platform to build *applications* on. There was a fair bit of consternation about this at first and a lot of doubt about whether building *applications* was possible with HTML and JavaScript. There was a lot of debate about whether the classic model of having the server do everything was still better or not either way (and frankly, that debate is still going on today in some circles). There was a lot of testing the limits to see just how far this web app thing could be pushed, and that went on for quite a few years.

Building a complex graphical user interface (GUI) with JavaScript at that point in time was an exercise in frustration and you had to code everything yourself, not to mention all the differences between browsers that you had to cope with. There wasn't the plethora of libraries, frameworks, toolkits, and developer tooling that we have in the

JavaScript world today that dealt with a lot of those details for you. While the situation today can often be overwhelming and overly complicated when you face the plethora of options available, if you lived through the other extreme where you did almost everything yourself, then you realize neither is a perfect world, though the world today is in most respects better for developers.

The key thing is that this period, as developers started to fully realize what the Web was capable of, what could be built on top of it, was a sea change, and it was a big step toward the Next Big Thing.

Web Development: Blossoming Adulthood?

That big thing—something that really altered the landscape and represented a real paradigm shift in web development—was the single-page app (SPA).

This history of SPAs is somewhat difficult to nail down, though the origin of it seems to have been about 2003. Though, people undoubtedly were doing SPAs before then even if they weren't calling them that (or indeed even thinking they were some new, extraordinary architecture). I can say this with complete certainty because in 1999. I wrote an application for my employer at the time that we would recognize today as an SPA. Had I thought I was doing something special, I might have thought to publicize my work and maybe would be a lot richer and more famous than I am (which is to say not really at all on either count!). Unfortunately for me, it simply seemed like the right way to write a complex web app that looked and functioned more like a desktop app of the time than a web site of the time, and I know I couldn't have been the only one doing it around that time.

What makes SPAs so special? Well, one thing is what I just alluded to: they allow you to create a web app that looks, feels, and functions much more like a typical desktop app. When you get to a point where users almost don't realize that they're using a web app at all, then you've reached the ultimate goal where the delivery platform no longer matters; it just becomes an implementation detail.

RIAs are dead, long live RIAs!   Another term you might have heard is *Rich Internet Application* (RIA). This term seems to have fallen out of favor in recent years, but it effectively means what SPA means today. You can generally treat them as synonymous, though you probably won't hear RIA as much anymore.

All of this was made even more difficult by the advent of mobile devices. Nowadays, a web app needs to work on mobile devices as well and across the huge range of such devices that are out in the wild. No longer is it sufficient for your app to work on a desktop PC only. This has proven to be a huge challenge for developers because there are differences that need to be accounted for that are very tricky. Screen size is the obvious one, but just as big is interaction. Mobile devices today are nearly always touch-oriented, whereas desktop PCs are just now starting to incorporate touch as a common feature (and even if you're talking about laptops, where touch is more prevalent, it's still not the primary interaction model most of the time). Writing an SPA that works well on both desktop *and* mobile devices is a tough challenge to deal with and have the results be good for all cases (and all of that ignores devices such as tablets that often straddle the line between mobile and desktop from a development standpoint).

One thing that is critical to allowing for SPA development, especially when the need for mobile exists, is a user interface (UI) toolkit. There are lots of options, including Dojo, ExtJS, jQuery UI, and Angular components, just to name a few. The reason this is so important is it makes developing a modern SPA immeasurably easier. Remember all those years of trial and error and of building everything from scratch yourself that I mentioned earlier? Well, all the lessons learned during that time have evolved into modern UI toolkits, frameworks, and libraries thanks to many smart people who went through that period. These tools provide power and flexibility that's hard to achieve on your own while also mostly abstracting away the ever-present browser differences that can still present huge roadblocks during development.

What's the difference between a library, toolkit, and framework?   This is a frequent question that developers ask, and there isn't necessarily a definitive answer, at least not completely. The difference between a library and a framework is relatively concrete and can be simply described via the Hollywood principle that says "Don't call us, we'll call you." A library, like the ever-popular jQuery, puts your application code in control. You call it to perform functions. A framework, of which Angular is a well-known example, is more like Hollywood in that it calls your code and is essentially in control at execution time. Inversion of control is sometimes invoked to describe the difference too: control is inverted with a framework to the extent that your own code isn't in control (largely); the framework's code is. A toolkit, by contrast, is somewhat nebulous and doesn't have a clear, definitive definition. However, it has nowadays come to be synonymous with the term *UI toolkit*, which basically means a library that is specifically focused on providing UI elements.

Each presents a different way of doing things, sometimes vastly different. Framework7, for example, is a toolkit that takes a web page that contains special markup elements and then parses it on the fly and creates a rich UI from it. You as a developer write HTML, but the actual HTML that the browser renders at runtime is generated by Framework7; your own HTML is transformed into the final HTML in other words. Many toolkits use this model today.

An entirely different model is one that ExtJS is famous for, and that's a model that is very JavaScript-centric. Instead of writing HTML, you write JavaScript in the form, largely, of JavaScript Object Notation (JSON) objects that describe the UI you want and that is then handed off to ExtJS, which uses it to generate the markup required to show the UI you described. You don't end up writing very much HTML yourself with this model.

This UI toolkit area is where Webix comes in.

So, Uh, What Is Webix Exactly?

Simply put, Webix is an HTML5/CSS3-based UI toolkit that helps you build complex and dynamic web apps that are cross-browser and even cross-platform. That means your Webix-based apps will work consistently in virtually any modern browser on virtually any modern platform, including mobile devices. Webix provides a robust set of UI components that provide all the standard things you see in modern UIs including rich form controls, grids, scrolling lists, calendars, charts, layout elements (tabs, accordions, etc.), and so on. Also, it provides a strong collection of more general-purpose functions that are frequently needed when developing SPAs.

Webix is very fast and lightweight, so performance is virtually never a concern.

As if that weren't enough, Webix offers several useful online tools (Skin Builder, Form Builder, and the Code Snippet "playground") as well as integration with many third-party libraries and frameworks.

In short, Webix provides virtually everything you need to build a modern SPA and, as you'll see soon, does so while being incredibly easy to use, with a very low bar to getting started with.

A little history   Webix is the product of IT outsourcing company XB Software in Minsk, Belarus. The initial public release of Webix was in July 2013, and since then, a new version has been released every two to three months, enhancing the library significantly with each release.

Take a look at Figure 1-1. This is your first look at Webix!

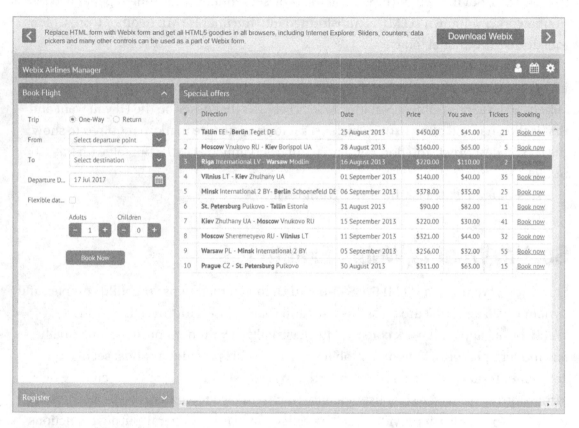

Figure 1-1.   *The Webix airline reservation manager sample app*

This is one of the demos you'll find on the Webix site (webix.com); it's an airline reservation system manager. You can see quite a few things right away, listed here:

- Webix offers a clean, modern look. In fact, one of the best things about Webix is the skinning ability it provides that is easy to work with and customize while providing a lot of flexibility to make your UI look the way you want and need.

- Webix offers all the types of form controls you're used to, plus maybe a few that are less common, and it has robust grid capabilities, which is a staple of modern GUIs.

- Webix provides a layout system that allows you to realize any organizational structure you want. It also provides, optionally, user control (being able to collapse the Register panel on the left, for example).

In Figure 1-2 you can see another example of what Webix can do.

Organizing and managing tabular data can be painless with Webix DataTable widget. Large amounts of related information can be put into easy-to-use tables which provide sorting, filtering and editing features.

Webix trader manager

#	Employee	Customer	Status	Fee	Taxes	Total	Shipping	Payment	Date	
1	Ray M. Parra	Sabrina N. Hermann	new	$12.50	$23.03	$323.38	Shipping A	Credit card	2012-12-20	
2	Lane E. Dion	Bradly N. Mauro	new	$12.00	$6.53	$100.13	Shipping C	Wire transer	2012-12-20	
5	Romaine B. Alley	Amee A. Marshall	new	$12.00	$9.13	$203.64	Shipping A	Wire transer	2012-12-20	
8	Lane E. Dion	Reba H. Casteel	new	$33.00	$54.23	$1,522.63	Shipping B	Cash	2013-01-15	
10	Sudie V. Goldsmith	Bradly N. Mauro	new	$10.00	$12.00	$454.00	Shipping E	Credit Card	2013-01-16	
13	Jolie P. Sparks	Bradly N. Mauro	new	$13.00	$1.00	$255.00	Shipping A	Cash	2013-07-11	
14	Sudie V. Goldsmith	Stephen H. Peachey	new	$63.00	$12.00	$1,522.00	Shipping B	Wire Transfer	2013-07-11	
18	Jamila N. Mccallister	Olimpia C. Whelan	new	$55.00	$13.00	$2,100.00	Shipping E	Credit Card	2013-07-11	
111	Ray M. Parra	Sabrina N. Hermann	new	$12.50	$23.03	$323.38	Shipping A	Credit card	2012-12-20	
112	Lane E. Dion	Bradly N. Mauro	new	$12.00	$6.53	$100.13	Shipping C	Wire transer	2012-12-20	
115	Romaine B. Alley	Amee A. Marshall	new	$12.00	$9.13	$203.64	Shipping A	Wire transer	2012-12-20	
118	Lane E. Dion	Reba H. Casteel	new	$33.00	$54.23	$1,522.63	Shipping B	Cash	2013-01-15	
1110	Sudie V. Goldsmith	Bradly N. Mauro	new	$10.00	$12.00	$454.00	Shipping E	Credit Card	2013-01-16	
1113	Jolie P. Sparks	Bradly N. Mauro	new	$13.00	$1.00	$255.00	Shipping A	Cash	2013-07-11	
1114	Sudie V. Goldsmith	Stephen H. Peachey	new	$63.00	$12.00	$1,522.00	Shipping B	Wire Transfer	2013-07-11	
1118	Jamila N. Mccallister	Olimpia C. Whelan	new	$55.00	$13.00	$2,100.00	Shipping E	Credit Card	2013-07-11	

Figure 1-2. *The Webix trade manager sample app*

This sample app is a trade manager for processing financial trades. In it, you can see a few more features Webix has to offer, listed here:

- More advanced data table capabilities such as real-time filtering (on the Employee and Customer columns) and data ordering (clicking any column header sorts the data)

- A tabbed interface structure, one of the most common layout techniques

I'd like to mention at this point that you should visit the Webix site as soon as possible. As you work with Webix, you'll be visiting it a lot because there are tons of resources to help you, including the API reference, which you'll naturally spend a lot of time looking at. Of course, being a great resource is the aim of this book too, but a good developer uses every resource at their disposal, and the Webix site is one such excellent resource. One of the things you'll find is the nice set of demos showcasing the kinds of things you can do with Webix that I'm showing you here (there are in fact more than I've shown here). It's always nice to be able to play with the demos, though, and see them in action, something that of course isn't possible on the printed page (contrary to what seemingly every sci-fi movie tells us we should have by now!). Despite that technological shortcoming, I'll show you two more of the demos now, starting with Figure 1-3.

Figure 1-3. *The Webix dashboard sample app*

This time, you see a typical dashboard page with features such as the following:

- Charts and graphs (there are many types available)

- A portal-like interface structure

- Icon features and other interface elements such as collapsible sections (which can be applied to many different Webix components in various ways)

Finally, Figure 1-4 shows some features that are available with a Webix Pro pack. (Don't worry, I'll explain what that means in the next section, but for now just understand that it means you may or may not be able to do what this demo shows.)

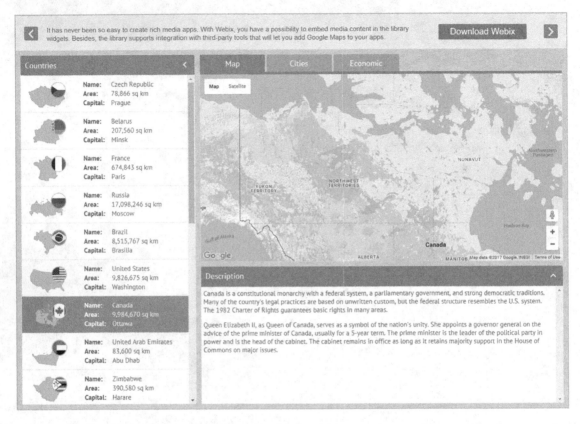

Figure 1-4. *The Webix geo explorer sample app*

Here you can see the map capabilities, which highlight the integration with third-party components that Webix offers (because as good as Webix is, sometimes it isn't enough and you need some help from "outside," and Webix allows for that nicely, as you'll see later).

Ideally, at this point, you're starting to think "Hey, this Webix thing looks pretty cool!" and are starting to think it might be something you want to use (although I assume you already thought that given you bought this book to learn about Webix, but I digress). Choosing a UI toolkit is a decision that has many factors, though, and I'd like to tell you some of the reasons I've chosen Webix for my projects. These are some of the things I personally consider to be among its biggest strengths and the things I've seen that make me such a fan of it.

Why Webix?

With so many choices out there these days, why might you want to choose Webix? Everyone has different priorities, of course, but here are a few that I personally view as being big pluses in Webix's favor:

- There is some excellent documentation available for it. It is well-written (for the most part) and covers all the bases. Need a guide for using a particular component? That's available. Want to look up methods available for a given component? There's a robust API guide for that. Want a more learning-oriented lesson on how to do something a little more general, say, communicating with a server? Webix has you covered! It's all organized extremely well and is easy to find and navigate on the Webix web site.

- It's simple. This will be a recurring theme throughout this book because I've worked with many libraries, frameworks, and toolkits over the years, and Webix is truly one of the easiest I've ever used. It's incredibly simple to get started with (which you'll see shortly!) and easy to work with. An essential part of this is that it nearly always works like you expect it to; there are minimal surprises when working with Webix. There's also a fantastic consistency to its API, which means that even if you aren't sure how to do something, given a little experience you'll frequently be able to guess the answer because you've seen something similar with Webix before. Once again, few surprises! I've had this experience many times while using it:

  "Hmm, how do I *X*?" (Maybe *X* is "tell if a button is visible.")

  Then a few seconds of head-scratching later...

  "Oh, I bet it's *Y*." (And *Y* is "a method named isVisible().")

  Then a few seconds of typing later...

  "Yep, it was *Y*, just like I guessed!"

  Especially if you haven't had a lot of experience using lots of different libraries, then you may not realize how unusual such a conversation with yourself is, but I promise you, it doesn't happen as often as you'd hope with all JavaScript libraries.

- It has *proper* mobile support. One of the problems I've have dealt with over the years is writing an app that works well on desktop and mobile devices. If you have any experience at all with that, then you too will know that it frequently means having to write a whole lot of separate code, some targeted to the desktop and some to mobile, essentially doubling your development effort. The advent of responsive design has alleviated some of that pain, but there's still plenty of it, especially for more robust web apps. An excellent aspect of Webix, though, is that a UI written with it will, for the most part, work well on mobile as well as desktops. Now, to be fair, you do still sometimes have to do some branching and writing some amount of "duplicate" code to get everything just the way you want. But, Webix has developed all its components to work on mobile *and* desktop equally well, so a single UI can mostly be written that works on both with a minimum of duplication of effort. Frankly, few competitors I've ever seen can make that claim, and it's a big advantage for Webix in my view.

- It is comprehensive. There's a debate raging these days about whether a single library is sufficient or whether a polyglot "choose whatever is needed and combine it with everything else" approach is best. I've frankly worked both ways, and as a result, I've become convinced that one monolithic library is better. However, realizing that vision is extremely difficult because few libraries are comprehensive enough to cover all the bases, or enough of them at least to make that vision work. In years past, the number of choices that met this criterion was small enough that you could count them on one hand, but these days there are more good options, and Webix is one of them. Aside from the rich set of UI components it offers, Webix has enough "helper" functions that you probably won't need to go outside of it very often. As I mentioned earlier, there are some integration capabilities that Webix offers, both to bring in other libraries and use them within Webix and also to use Webix within larger frameworks like Angular, so you certainly can when needed go outside Webix. But, my experience tells me that the amount you truly need to go outside Webix will generally be less than with many other options out there, and I view that as a big plus when it comes to long-term maintenance, something professional developers worry a great deal about.

I presume you're convinced now that Webix is an excellent choice! So, what offerings are available exactly?

Multiple Editions to Choose From

Webix is available in several editions, or *packs* in Webix parlance. Here is an instance where I'm going to be a bit lazy: Figure 1-5 shows what the Webix web site says about the available packs.

Figure 1-5. *The Webix editions table*

The big differentiator in the packs, aside from the obvious of cost, is how many developers your license covers. Another difference is which of the complex widgets (which you'll look at in the next chapter, but for now think of them almost as applications unto themselves) you have access to (if any) and what type of support you have access to. (for the Individual License pack, you don't get any complex widgets by default; they need to be purchased separately if you want them.) The Unlim Pack also offers a few additional services such as live support chat and integration auditing.

In addition to these packs, Webix is offered for free as Webix Standard (as opposed to any of the paid licenses, which are considered "Webix Pro") and is covered under the GPLv3 open source license. Standard lacks some things that the Pro packs provide, and again, I'll let the Webix site show that; see Figure 1-6. (Note that the details on the site

13

can and do change with each subsequent version as new components are added. In fact, I can no longer find this information on the Webix web site as this chapter went to print, but as far as I can tell, it's still fundamentally valid.) Also note that the Webix web site does not list the Standard version alongside the Pro licenses, and you have to dig around the site just a little bit to find it. (This is a company after all, and its raison d'être is to make money, so that's to be expected.) At the time of this writing, you'll find an Open Source section below the table shown in Figure 1-5 (which you can access by clicking the Pricing link on the site) that leads to the Standard download link.

Webix PRO and Webix Standard

What is the difference between Webix versions? We support free software and publicly provide you two types of Webix based on commercial and open source purposes.

	WEBIX PRO	WEBIX STANDARD
License	Developer License Agreement	GNU GPLv3
Widgets and controls	84	63
Data table functionality	✓	—
Complex widgets support	✓	—
Saving and restoring application state	✓	—
Extra styling and customization	✓	—
Localization ?	300 locales	9 locales

Figure 1-6. *Open source (Standard) versus Pro versions*

As you can see, the number of widgets and controls you get with Standard is reduced, and you get none of the complex widgets or additional data table functionality. You also cannot save and restore application state, which means that when the user resizes components, if your design allows that, you can't save those customizations and restore them when your app is relaunched. Note that this does *not* have anything to do with the ability to work with data; that is entirely intact in Standard. Pro also offers additional capabilities regarding styling and customizing your app as well as additional localization support.

What do you *really* **miss out on by not going Pro?**   So, what *exactly* do you lose by not having a Pro license? Well, in terms of widgets and controls, you lose these 21 (as of the time of this writing): `barcode`, `bullet graph`, `check suggest`, `data view suggest`, `date range`, `date range picker`, `date range suggest`, `excel viewer`, `gage`, `grid suggest`, `maps`, `multicombo`, `multiselect`, `multisuggest`, `multitext`, `organogram`, `PDF viewer`, `portlet`, `range chart`, `treemap`, and `query builder`. You know what some of these are I'm sure, but don't worry if you don't because you'll see them over the next two chapters.

Regarding lost data table functionality, with Standard, you can't use the following: advanced filtering, area selection, colspan and rowspan, grouped columns, header menu, subrows/subviews, and vertical/rotate headers.

At the time of this writing, there were five complex widgets that you can't use with standard: `pivot`, `kanban`, `file manager`, `scheduler`, and `spreadsheet`.

Finally, as far as those additional styling and customization features go that you only get with Pro, those are custom scrollbars and formatted text inputs.

As you can see, there's a good bit that Pro provides (and don't forget the added support, which is a must for "professional" development). But, Standard still gives you more than enough for a significant number of purposes, so if you don't mind the GPLv3 caveat, then you can save some money for sure.

In fact, for the purposes of this book, or at least the purposes of developing the application in Chapters 4–8 (and the second app in Chapter 9), Standard is all that is needed. In Chapters 2 and 3, I'll show you many of the things you get only with a Pro license, but these won't be necessary for the remainder of the book.

Online Tools

In addition to what you get with Webix physically, meaning when you download the Webix code to use in your project, Webix offers several online tools. These tools are always available to anyone for free. In fact, they are an excellent way of experimenting with Webix without having to download anything, install anything, or purchase anything.

One of the tools I especially think is one you'll find yourself using in many cases is the first one we're going to look at now: Code Snippet.

Code Snippet

Code Snippet is an online playground of sorts that lets you mess around with Webix code without having to download anything and without having to do all the boilerplate code that goes along with any kind of web development. Figure 1-7 shows what Code Snippet is all about.

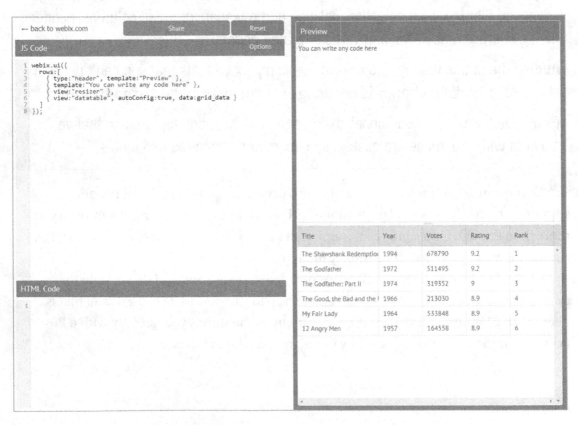

Figure 1-7. *Online tool Code Snippet*

When you first launch Code Snippet, this is what you'll see. As a helpful starting point, it even gives you a snippet of code that works! To use Code Snippet, you enter JavaScript code in the upper-left section and HTML (optionally) in the lower left. Then, on the right, what you enter is interpreted in real time, and the UI you specify is produced. Code Snippet even provides some preconfigured data sources that can be used with the components that display data, as in the data table shown here (clicking the Options button there provides a list of the data sources available).

Note that what you see on the right is a *real* UI at this point, meaning you can interact with it fully. As you make changes to the code, the UI is automatically rebuilt, so you don't even need to publish or click a build button or anything like that (any time you stop typing for a few seconds it automatically refreshes). You can even change the skin that is used, so if you want to see what your UI will look like using the Android-inspired Material skin, you can do that with a simple click of the Options button.

Also, Code Snippet gives you the ability to change how the UI is initialized, meaning if you prefer to define your UI with XML, you can do so, as you can see in Figure 1-8.

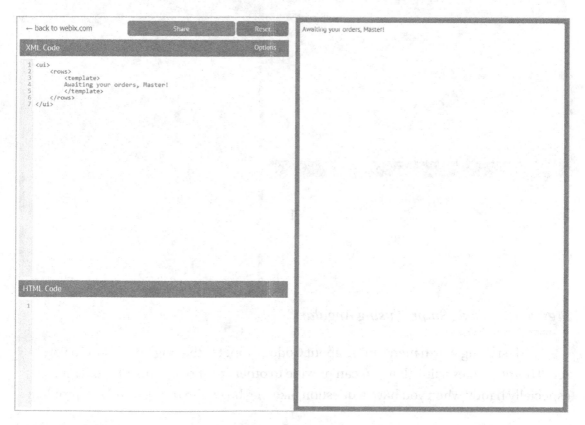

Figure 1-8. *Code Snippet using XML to describe the UI*

I've never used the XML `init` method, and I personally think it's not the most elegant way to use Webix, so I won't be going into it in more detail in this book. However, I wanted to make you aware of the option if it's something you want to explore later on your own.

If that weren't enough, you can also use Code Snippet to test using Webix with the popular frameworks Angular and Backbone. In Figure 1-9 you can see an example of the Angular `init` method, which also demonstrates what happens when you need to enter HTML code (it also shows a different skin, though that might be difficult to discern on the printed page).

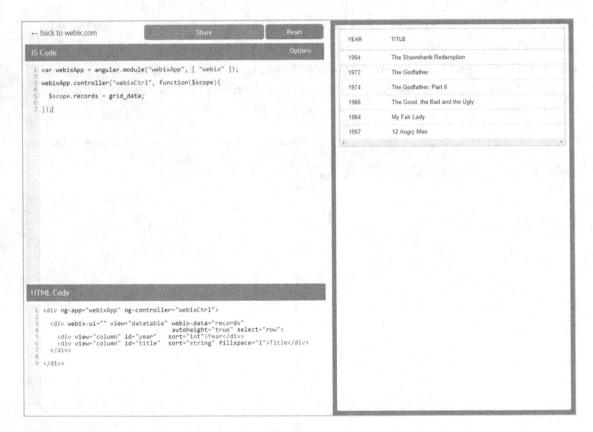

Figure 1-9. *Code Snippet using Angular*

The last thing worth mentioning about Code Snippet is that big Share button you see. This generates a link that you can provide to others to show your snippet. This is especially handy when you have a question, like maybe you're trying to solve a problem and want to post it to the Webix support forums. Being able to link to a snippet that demonstrates the issue you're trying to solve is very handy indeed!

Form Builder

Another great online tool that Webix offers is the Form Builder. This makes creating forms with Webix a snap. In Figure 1-10 you can see an example of Form Builder.

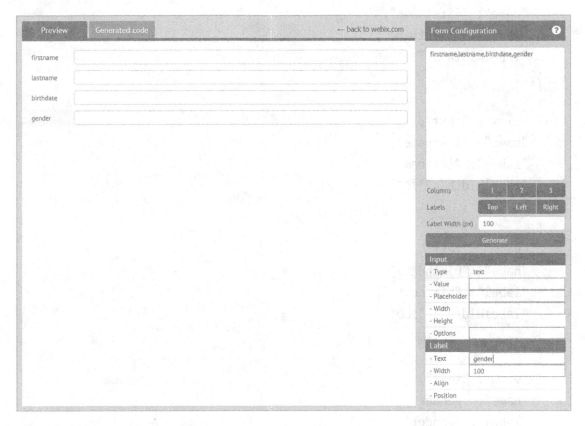

Figure 1-10. *Form Builder*

You simply enter a comma-separated list of field names and click the Generate button. You can also adjust the number of columns you want the form to be laid out in and how wide the field labels should be. You'll then get to see the form on the left. From there, you can click any field to see its properties on the bottom right and refine them further. When you're happy with how it all looks, you just need to click the Generated

Code tab and then click the Generate button and you'll be given the code for your form!
Here's an example:

```
{
  "view": "form",
  "elements": [
    {
      "view": "text",
      "name": "firstname",
      "label": "firstname",
      "labelWidth": "100"
    },
    {
      "view": "text",
      "name": "lastname",
      "label": "lastname",
      "labelWidth": "100"
    },
    {
      "view": "text",
      "name": "birthdate",
      "label": "birthdate",
      "labelWidth": "100"
    },
    {
      "view": "text",
      "name": "gender",
      "label": "gender",
      "labelWidth": "100"
    }
  ]
}
```

Don't worry about understanding that right now; it's just enough to know right now
that Form Builder is a no-hassle way to create forms visually and not have to worry about
writing the code from scratch by hand.

Skin Builder

The last online tool that Webix has in its toolbox is the Skin Builder. As I'm sure you can guess, it's what you can use to create new skins to use with Webix. Figure 1-11 shows the Skin Builder.

Figure 1-11. *Skin Builder*

It may look complicated at first, but in reality it's not. The first thing you do is choose one of the available sample apps (some of which you saw earlier) so that you can see your skin in real time. Then, you select one of the prepackaged skins to use as the basis for your new skin. From there, you access the Colors, Fonts, or Sizes sections to adjust the various facets of the skin. Once you have everything looking just the way you want, click the Download button, and you'll get an archive that contains your skin (as a single CSS file) along with some useful information for using it. Like with Code Snippet, you can share a link to your skin as well.

These three tools go a long way to making Webix a pleasure to work with. I encourage you to play with them now to see what else they can do. Note that because of the nature of the project, the rest of the book deals with building. I won't be touching on these tools again, so get in there and play a bit!

Getting Started

Now that you've seen what Webix is all about and what it can do for you, let's talk about what is required to get started coding with Webix. There are two approaches that you can take, and while I'll show you both, for the purposes of this book I recommend using the latter, for no other reason than it doesn't assume you have anything installed already and doesn't ask you to install anything in terms of development tooling. Given that one of the primary things I like about Webix is its simplicity, I'd like to keep necessary tooling to a minimum to keep with that simplicity train of thought. However, if you're more comfortable with the (ever so slightly) less simple approach, then you're more than welcome to go that route, of course. Especially if you're already familiar with it (in which case you can skip the next section; just know that webix is the NPM package name), then it's not at all a bad option.

The NPM Way

In the world of modern JavaScript development, it's not unusual to start a new project with Node Package Manager (NPM). If the packages you need are present in the NPM repository, then it's as simple as running a few basic commands at a command prompt, and you're off to the races. As it happens, Webix *is* available in the repository. So, if you're NPM inclined, all it takes to start a new project is to choose a directory to be the home of your project and then run the following command:

```
npm init
```

Naturally, this assumes you already have NPM installed, which is typically installed as part of Node.js (or just Node for short), so if you don't have that installed already and want to try this approach, then head over to nodejs.org and install the version appropriate for your system.

Once you run that command, you'll find a `package.json` file has been created in the directory you run the command from. This file describes your project and, while it's somewhat Node-oriented, that doesn't stop it from working fine for a Webix app.

For example, that command for me created a `package.json` file that looks like this:

```
{
  "name": "test",
  "version": "1.0.0",
  "description": "test",
  "main": "index.js",
  "scripts": {
    "test": "echo \"Error: no test specified\" && exit 1"
  },
  "author": "",
  "license": "ISC"
}
```

Your version might look different depending on what version of Node/NPM you have installed and of course what choices you made during the interactive running of the previous command, but it should look similar.

To now get Webix into the mix, a new element has to be added, as shown here:

```
"dependencies": {
  "webix": "*"
}
```

That can be added anywhere, as long as it's at the same level as all the other elements. This tells NPM that you want Webix to be imported in your project, and you want it to be the latest version available (that's what * means).

With that added, go back to a command prompt and execute the following:

```
npm install
```

Now, you'll find that a `package-lock.json` file has been created. This is the file NPM uses to store information about what was generated by its various commands. For the purposes here, it doesn't matter (other than the fact that you should simply leave it be). In addition, and more relevantly, is that a new directory, `node_modules`, has been created. This is where the modules you list in `package.json` and that NPM downloads for you are stored (as well as any additional modules that the specified modules depend on; NPM takes care of all of that for you, but in the case of Webix, there are no dependencies). You'll find that inside of it is a single directory, unsurprisingly named `webix`. You now have Webix available to your project in this directory!

The "Direct" Way

The other way to get started with Webix, without needing Node and NPM installed, is to simply head over to the Webix web site and download the Webix package. Really, that's it! Once you do that, just unzip the zip file you downloaded (there's a big Download Webix button right there on the front page that you land on) in a directory that will be the home to your project, and you're all set! Note that unzipping the file puts the content in the current directory, so you'll probably want to unzip to a `webix` subdirectory instead.

This book assumes you'll use this method to get started. One difference you'll find between these two approaches is that when you go the NPM route, you *do not* get all the samples that you do when you grab the zip file from the Webix web site. You will get only the necessary code for Webix itself, which essentially is the contents of the `codebase` directory that is present in the zip file alongside the `samples` directory.

To put it more simply, when using NPM to set up a Webix project, you'll only get what you actually need in order to use Webix. When you get Webix from the Webix web site, you'll also get samples.

Fisher-Price's My First Webix App

Regardless of which route you took to get here, Webix should be ready to start building an app with. Let's throw together a basic Webix app so you can get a first look at Webix in action. In the directory you created for your project, create an `index.html` file and in it put the contents from Listing 1-1.

Listing 1-1. A Simple Webix App to Pique Your Interest (the Code)

```
<!DOCTYPE html>

<html>

  <head>

    <title>My First Webix App</title>

    <link rel="stylesheet" type="text/css" href="../webix/codebase/webix.css">
    <script type="text/javascript" src="../webix/codebase/webix_debug.js">
    </script>

    <style>
      .col1 { background-color:#ffc0c0; }
      .col2 { background-color:#c0ffc0; }
      .col3 { background-color:#ffffc0; }
    </style>

    <script>

      webix.ready(function() {

        webix.ui({
          view : "layout", type : "wide",
          rows : [
            /* Row 1 */
            { type : "header", template : "Hello" },
            /* Row 2 */
            { template : "Greetings, human!" },
            /* Row 3 */
            { gravity : 2,
              cols : [
                { css : "col1", template : "Webix" },
                { view : "resizer" },
                { css : "col2", template : "Is" },
                { view : "resizer" },
```

```
                        { css : "col3", template : "Cool" }
                      ]
                    },
                    /* Row 4 */
                    { type : "header", template : "Goodbye"  },
                    /* Row 5 */
                    { height : 50,
                      cols : [
                        { template : "Farewell thee well!" },
                        { view : "button", width : 150, type : "iconButton",
                          Icon : "users", label : "Click for fun",
                          click : function() {
                            webix.message({ type : "error", text :
                            "See?<br><br>Wasn't that fun?!" });
                          }
                        }
                      ]
                    }
                  ]
                });

              });

          </script>

        </head>

        <body></body>

      </html>
```

Once that's done, fire up your browser of choice, load this file, and bask in the glory that is Webix! Ok, I may be overselling things, but I think you'll agree that although what you see on the screen (shown in Figure 1-12) isn't all that complex, neither is the code that gets you there.

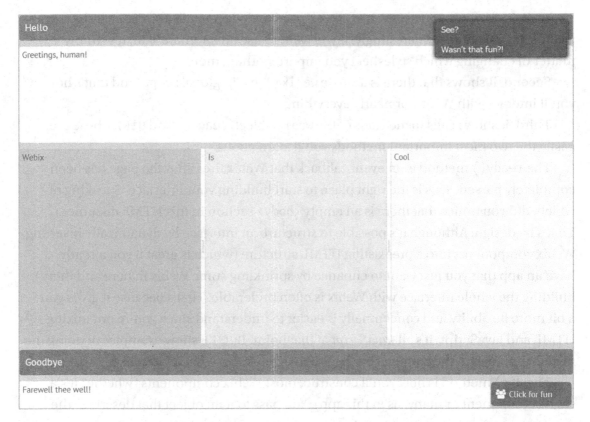

Figure 1-12. *A simple Webix app to pique your interest (the result of the code)*

Don't forget those paths!   Remember that you may have to adjust the paths to point to where Webix is relative to this directory since you'll need to download Webix separately from the source for this book, or if you decide to type this in yourself manually.

Did you see an error?   You will likely see an error in the upper-right corner when you try this indicating you can't do this using the `file://` protocol. That's not exactly true because it *does* work. However, to avoid that error, you can switch to using `webix.js` instead of `webix_debug.js`, or you can put this source code on a web server and access it using `http://`, but that is left as an exercise for you. You can, for the purposes here, simply ignore the message.

As simple as this example is, it, in fact, shows quite a bit.

First, it shows that to use Webix, all you need to do is include a single stylesheet and a single JavaScript file. Interestingly, if you want to use an alternate skin, it's simply a matter of changing which stylesheet you import, nothing more.

Second, it shows that there is a single `webix` object in global scope, and that's how you'll interact with Webix for nearly everything.

Third, it shows calls to methods of the `webix` object, `ready()` and `ui()`. These are easily the two most important methods you'll learn about.

The `ready()` method is an event callback that Webix fires after the page has been completely parsed. This is the right place to start building your interface. Speaking of which, did you notice that there is an empty `<body>` section in this HTML document? That's by design! Although it's possible to structure an interface by dynamically inserting Webix components into a preexisting HTML structure (which is great if you already have an app that you just want to enhance by sprinkling some Webix in here and there), building the whole interface with Webix is often preferable. That's because it gives you a bit more flexibility and conceptually is easier to understand since you're not mixing HTML and JavaScript; it's all *JavaScript* at that point. But, I'll show examples of doing the mixed approach in the coming chapters so that you know what it looks like.

The `ui()` method is how you'll construct most Webix components (whether it's a single component or many, as in this app). You pass to it an object that describes the component you want to construct. In most cases, you'll specify the type of component by setting the `view` attribute (in Webix, the term *view* essentially means the same as widget or component in other toolkits). Here, I'm constructing a layout component (which is also the default `view` attribute value if you don't specify one as I've done here), which is a ubiquitous component that allows you to construct a grid-based layout. The layout can be as simple or as complex as you need. In this app, I've created a typical border layout that gives north, south, east, west, and center areas for the app's content, but also I've added a header row above the north and south areas, so really, it's five rows in total. The third row is split into three columns, and the fifth row, the conceptual south region, is divided into two columns. So, to think about this all another way, it's five rows, with the second row containing three columns and the fifth row containing two columns.

As you can see, you specify the layout by creating `rows` and `cols` arrays as attributes of elements. The top-level component is the layout itself, which has a `rows` array (and if your layout is more columnar in nature, you can specify `cols` instead, or don't specify either, and then you'll have a layout that fills the screen). There are five elements in this array, each a row in our layout. The third element, the third row, has a `cols` attribute, which is again an array where each element is a column in that row. Note that there is no explicit size for these. Webix will divide the available space evenly between them. The fifth row similarly has a `cols` attribute, this time with two elements. In this case, the second element has an explicit width set, so Webix will size it as specified, and then the first element, the first column, will fill the remaining horizontal space. The elements of these arrays, which you can nest other `rows` and `cols` arrays in as much as you like, combine to define the grid structure.

This layout also has a `type` of `wide`, which shows how you can further define the attribute of a component (making the space between the child components a little wider in this case).

You should also have noticed the `gravity` attribute on that third row. Usually, Webix will divide the space available for a given component equally. So, for example, if that `gravity` attribute weren't present, then the five rows would be sized equally by dividing up the available vertical space. Well, to be more accurate, the second, third, and fifth rows would be, but the first and fourth wouldn't because those are defined as `header` types, and `header` components define a height based on pixels. So, they would be sized to a fixed height, and then Webix would divide the *remaining* space between those three rows. Well, to be *even more* accurate, only the second and third rows would be automatically sized because the fifth row has a `height` in pixels explicitly specified. Anything sized explicitly like that is always laid out first, and only then does anything that gets sized automatically get sized, within the *remaining* space. But, the `gravity` attribute allows you to control this and size things relative to others. In this case, the third row will be sized to be twice as large as the second because of that `gravity` value of 2. The default value is 1, but larger or smaller values tell Webix how to size that component relative to the rest.

Fourth, this app shows you how you can put content in the areas of a layout. There are two approaches demonstrated: using the `template` attribute and making other Webix components children of the layout.

With the `template` attribute, you can insert arbitrary HTML content. Here, it's just some plain text, but you can insert anything you like and get as fancy as you like.

You can also directly create other Webix components as children in a layout. For example, in the fifth row, there are two columns. The first is an ordinary element with some HTML as you've seen before, but the second is a button. There are many types of buttons in Webix, as you'll see in the next chapter, but here you can see that an `iconButton` is one that has an icon and some text. The icons can be specified several ways, but one of the easiest is to use the many types available in the Font Awesome package that Webix includes. Take a look at `http://fontawesome.io/icons` to see what's available, but be forewarned: there's *a lot*, and you may be there for a while! You can also see how event handlers can be attached to components; here a `click` event is used to handle when the user clicks (or taps, if on a mobile device) the button.

Fifth, in the button's `click` handler you can see one of the methods Webix provides for giving feedback to the user; in this case, a simple `webix.message()` call gets you a small message that appears in the upper-right corner and, after a time, slides away (or when it's clicked by the user). You can configure these messages in various ways, and in this example, I've made it red to stand out by setting its `type` to `error`.

Sixth, in the third row, you may have noticed that I've been saying there are three columns, but in fact there are five. Between the three "primary" columns are two columns with a `view` value of `resizer`. This is another Webix component that provides the little lines you can see in Figure 1-12. This allows the user to resize these columns by dragging on these resize handles. You can put them between almost any components you want, which makes for a compelling capability to let the user lay out the interface to their liking and needs.

Seventh, the `css` attribute applied to the three primary columns in the third row shows how you can apply a CSS class to a Webix element. This lets you do things such as change the background color, as I've done here. This gives you a ton of flexibility because whatever Webix generates for the browser to display can be further altered and enhanced with the CSS methods you already know and (maybe) love.

Finally, it's important to note that launching this example on a mobile device more or less works fine. I say "more or less" because some elements don't resize as you'd ideally want, but note that things *do in fact* resize on the fly! You've got a (roughly) responsive layout here with no effort, and Webix does it for you automatically! Moreover, things like the button interaction work as expected. This is a critical point because most things in Webix are like this; they'll work basically as you'd expect whether you're on a mobile device with a small screen or on a powerful desktop with a huge monitor. You'll need to worry about being cross-platform very little with Webix in terms of things just working, though you still may have to take into consideration reorganizing the layout based on available screen real estate. But, that's par for the course with cross-platform development (and Webix has some help for you there too, as you'll see in later chapters).

Summary

In this chapter, I talked about the evolution of web development, from simple, static pages to the inclusion of scripting and to the modern age of rich SPAs. I then discussed Webix a bit, what it is, how it came about, and what it has to offer at a high level. You learned about the online tools it provides to make your development more efficient. You looked at the various editions that are available, the differences between them, and why you might choose one over the other.

You then took some first steps to getting started with Webix. You looked at the NPM approach as well as the "old-fashioned" approach of "just go download it!" You then built a small sample app that demonstrates many basic aspects of Webix, and you explored that code to get your feet wet in the world of Webix.

In the next chapter, you'll start diving into Webix in more detail and really see what it can do for you. Hold on to your hat; it's going to be a wild ride!

CHAPTER 2

Getting to Know Webix

In Chapter 1, you looked at web development in general and a brief history of it, all the way into the age of the SPA. Then you took a high-level look at Webix itself and started to see some of the ways that it helps you develop SPAs. In this chapter and the next, you'll take more of a deep-dive into Webix and start to become familiar with its core concepts. You'll look at the specific components it offers to build user interfaces.

The first topic that I'll touch on is something that isn't necessarily specific to Webix because it's something that you would have to consider with any SPA development, and that's how to structure your application and the code that comprises it.

How to Structure a Webix App

Modern JavaScript development is quite a bit different from what came before. There was a time when you would, as I did as an example in Chapter 1, just create a single HTML file that would contain all your code, all your CSS, and everything. In fact, in an odd turn of events, we in a sense created SPAs long before the real concept of what they were came about!

However, the limitations of that approach become apparent quickly. For starters, having one long source file to look at can be very unwieldy. Of course, the idea of code reuse is made more difficult when you take this approach. Another issue is that if you want to use a modern IDE or even just an advanced text editor, you typically run into difficulties with a single source file because now you've got various types of content mixed together (HTML, CSS, JavaScript). As a result, the IDE or editor can't always do things like syntax highlighting and coloring and autocomplete quite as well as you might like (modern IDEs are pretty amazing and can usually manage OK, but not always). Plus, the speed of these tools is often impacted negatively when the file starts to get too long.

There may be other reasons, but even at this point, it should be obvious that there must be a better way!

33

© Frank Zammetti 2018
F. Zammetti, *Practical Webix*, https://doi.org/10.1007/978-1-4842-3384-9_2

Indeed, there is: break your application into manageable pieces. The thing is, there's no definitive guide on how you do this. However, at the lowest level, it usually means separate CSS and JavaScript files, separate from the HTML files. Even just that level of decomposition brings benefits.

Webix specifically is quite unopinionated about this. Some libraries and frameworks are *very* opinionated, some to the point of outright *requiring* you to organize your code in a certain way for it to work at all, but Webix isn't like that. Webix gives you a lot of flexibility but also a lot of responsibility.

That said, it's a good idea to have at least a basic application structure, or code organization. The Webix documentation does offer a suggested organization, and it's one I agree with, though perhaps with some minor embellishments.

Let's take the simple example app from Chapter 1 and refactor it with better code structure in mind. Let's start with the `index.html` file, which with just some minor changes now looks like this:

```
<!DOCTYPE html>
<html>
  <head>

    <!-- Webix itself. -->
    <link rel="stylesheet" href="webix.css" type="text/css" media="screen"
    charset="utf-8">
    <script src="webix.js" type="text/javascript" charset="utf-8"></script>

    <!-- Your application code. -->
    <link rel="stylesheet" type="text/css" href="styles.css">
    <script type="text/javascript" src="ui.js"></script>
    <script type="text/javascript" src="app.js"></script>

  </head>

  <body></body>
</html>
```

You've already examined the basics of this in Chapter 1, so there shouldn't be any surprises here. The few changes I've made to implement the new structure are the `ui.js`, `app.js` and `styles.css` imports. Put simply, this is where the code and styles of your application will live.

Note   For your purposes here, you don't need anything in the `styles.css` file.
I always like to include it just to remind myself to put my CSS definitions in there
when and if the time comes.

Why two JavaScript files, though? The goal is to separate your actual UI from the
logic that backs it up. As you saw in Chapter 1, Webix works by constructing UI objects
via code (at least in one mode of operation, the mode I'll primarily be using throughout
this book). If you look back at that first example app, you'll notice that the function
that gets executed when the button is clicked is embedded in the JSON that defines the
UI. Usually, it's better to separate these two things. From a conceptual standpoint, it's
better because it keeps related things together, meaning the code that defines the UI
layout is separate from the actions that the UI can perform (usually via user interaction,
though not exclusively). It's also better from a code organization standpoint because you
can focus in on the construction of the UI or its operation separately. It also opens up the
possibility of easily changing the UI without altering the operational code, or vice versa,
which means the code overall is more flexible.

So, to restructure things, the `ui.js` file is where you have code to define the UI. If you
take the example app from Chapter 1 and re-architect it with this pattern, your `ui.js` file
would look like this:

```
const uiDefinition = {
  view : "layout", type : "wide",
  rows : [
    /* Row 1 */
    { type : "header", template : "Hello" },
    /* Row 2 */
    { template : "Greetings, human!" },
    /* Row 3 */
    { gravity : 2,
      cols : [
        { css : "col1", template : "Webix" },
        { view : "resizer" },
        { css : "col2", template : "Is" },
        { view : "resizer" },
        { css : "col3", template : "Cool" }
```

```
      ]
    },
    /* Row 4 */
    { type : "header", template : "Goodbye"  },
    /* Row 5 */
    { height : 50,
      cols : [
        { template : "Farewell thee well!" },
        { view : "button", width : 150, type : "iconButton",
          icon : "users", label : "Click for fun",
          click : buttonClick
        }
      ]
    }
  ]
};
```

The difference is that instead of passing a JSON object directly to the webix.ui()
function (which you'll recall is the one-stop shopping function, so to speak, that allows
you to construct most Webix components), you instead hold that JSON in a variable.
That's because in the app.js file you'll now do this:

```
webix.ready(function() {
  webix.ui(uiDefinition);
});
```

Note   The Webix documentation suggests putting this code in the body of the
index.html file. This advice is usually given so that the parsing of the page
isn't blocked and your code will execute only once that parsing has finished.
However, using webix.ready() effectively makes this redundant since it won't
execute the function you pass to it before that anyway, so I suggest not doing this.
Putting *all* your JavaScript in a .js file to me makes more logical sense, and any
performance hit is going to be so negligible with this amount of code that it's worth
paying in return for having a cleaner (in my eyes) structure.

That essentially separates the definition of the UI from the code that builds it. But, what about that button click handler function? Notice in the `ui.js` file the function is no longer present and instead a reference to something called `buttonClick` is present. You know this must be a function, but it hasn't been defined yet. So, you add it to your `app.js` file, shown here:

```
function buttonClick() {
  webix.message({ type : "error", text : "See?<br><br>Wasn't that fun?!"
});
}
```

Again, you separate the definition of the UI from its interaction logic. That's the clean separation we're going for.

The final piece of the puzzle is an embellishment I suggest on top of the core idea that Webix itself suggests, and that's encapsulation of your code. What I mean is that you'll notice that the `buttonClick` function is in global scope here, as is the call to `webix.ready()` and also the `uiDefinition` variable. While the `webix.ready()` call isn't a big deal because it doesn't put anything in global scope, the other two could be issues since not polluting global scope any more than you have to is a fundamental guideline in JavaScript development to help avoid conflicts. So, my suggestion is to create an object for your application code to live in and let *that* be the only thing in global scope. With that in mind, the final `app.js` file would look like this:

```
const MyApp = {

  init : function() {
    webix.ready(function() {
      webix.ui(this.uiDefinition);
    }.bind(this))
  },

  buttonClick : function() {
    webix.message({ type : "error", text : "See?<br><br>Wasn't that fun?!"
});
  }

};
MyApp.init();
```

Now, what happens when `index.html` is loaded? After Webix and the `styles.css` file are loaded and parsed by the browser, `app.js` is loaded and parsed. This results in the creation of an object named `MyApp` in global scope. This object has two functions, `init()` and `buttonClick`. Right after the definition of `MyApp` is a call to that `init()` function, which itself calls the `webix.ready()` function referencing the `this.uiDefinition` member (but remember that the function passed to `webix.ready()` won't execute at this point, so it doesn't matter that `this.uiDefinition` is currently undefined). That function needs to be bound to `MyApp`, though, which it wouldn't be within an explicit call to `bind()`. This matters because without `bind()` there, you would need to reference `MyApp.uiDefinition`, which means if you ever want to change the name of the `MyApp` variable, then you'd need to change any code that uses it too. The `bind()` call allows you to avoid that by ensuring the `this` reference points to what you need it to point at.

Next, `ui.js` is loaded and parsed, which results in `uiDefinition` now having the appropriate JSON data defining the UI. Now, once the DOM is ready, Webix calls the function passed to `webix.ready()`, which then builds your UI as defined in `uiDefinition`.

Critically, though, all the code related to your application is now encapsulated within `MyApp`, and `MyApp` is the only thing in global scope. That includes the function that responds to the button click event. If you build out this application further, you would continue to add members to `MyApp`, keeping global scope clean. That way, if you wanted to bring in additional libraries or perhaps code from another team, you wouldn't have to be (as) worried about naming conflicts in global scope.

Note   If you prefer ES6 syntax, then there's nothing wrong with creating a `MyApp` class and then instantiating it and calling `init()` as shown here. However, classes are perfect for when you may need to instantiate multiple instances of an object, but in this case, there's only ever going to be one canonical object associated with the application, so to me it makes more sense to make it a simple object (and I prefer it being a constant as well). But that's an implementation detail that's up to you. The whole point here is to encapsulate your application code in some form— that's what matters.

It's important to remember, though, having looked at this approach, that there is no right or wrong way necessarily to structure a Webix application (or an SPA generally). There certainly are ways that most developers view as better or worse than others, but nothing truly canonical. Many frameworks define an approach that they think is better, some more rigidly than others. In keeping with most things with Webix, nothing truly rigid exists. However, Webix does offer something else, another approach, to help define a "good" application structure, and that's Webix Jet.

Webix Jet

Webix Jet is referred to as a *microframework*. That term sometimes means different things to different people (and in different contexts!), but in terms of Webix, it means a minimal framework for an application structure that allows Webix to take on some repetitive, boilerplate tasks from your application code. In short, it means (in theory at least) having to write less code yourself and having a logical, consistent application architecture.

Note   Webix Jet could really have its own chapter, but because I've chosen to not use it for this book beyond this chapter, I'm going to give you an overview here only. If you find that Webix Jet meets your needs and mental model, then you'll find much more detail in the Webix documentation, and you should have a foundation to build on from this section with it. My goal here is to give you just the basics so that you can reasonably make that determination on your own. Importantly, though, be aware that most, if not all, of the Webix concepts that will be talked about in this book apply whether using Webix Jet or not, so virtually everything after this section will be completely relevant and mostly unchanged with or without Webix Jet.

Webix Jet works by breaking an app into multiple views. These views are contained in .js files stored in a views directory under the root of your app. These views are UIs built like any other Webix UI. You then navigate to the various views by changing the URL of the app. Well, to be more accurate, you change a portion of the URL, specifically the part after the hashbang.

In other words, say you have an app with three views: mainmenu, userlist, and activities (perhaps it's an app that allows you to see what users are logged into your server and what activity they're performing). Each of these views would be defined in its own .js file in the views directory named mainmenu.js, userlist.js, and activities.js. The .js file for the mainmenu view (views/mainmenu.js), for example, might look like this:

```
define([
  "app"
], function(app) {

  var menu = {
    view : "menu", id : "menu", select : true,
    template : "#value#",
    data : [
      { value : "User List", href:"#!/userlist" },
      { value : "Activities", href:"#!/activities" }
    ]
  };

  return { $menu : "menu" };

});
```

As you can see, using Webix Jet requires you to define your UI a little differently. But, it's still the same sort of UI definition you've seen before: the object returned here will eventually be fed to `webix.ui()` to construct the view as you define.

First, the menu component is exactly what you'd expect; it's a component that shows a list of items that the user can select from (a menu in other words!). This type of component accepts data to display, which is why it has a `data` attribute. Exactly what the objects passed to this attribute are depends on the specific component, but you'll see the `data` attribute like this many times throughout this book. In this case, you pass an array of objects, with each object having two attributes: `value`, which is the text to display, and `href`, which is the URL to go to when the item is selected.

Before I talk about that, though, I need to discuss that `template` attribute. You've seen that before, of course, but here is something new: using variables within a template. When you pass data to a component, the attributes of those data objects become available within the template string using the #xxx# syntax. In this way, you can make each item in the menu (or whatever component you're dealing with) display the data in whatever fashion you need and the values of each data object will be inserted for the #xxx# strings.

Finally, when using Webix Jet, you need to return the UI definition from the `define()` function's callback, which here you do by referencing the ID assigned to the menu component.

Now, when you want to navigate to the userlist view, you need to change the URL of the page, which the menu component allows you to do without writing any code. Webix Jet monitors the URL changes (the URL is the portion after the hashbang). When it sees it (assuming the URL is one it recognizes as a view), then the page location won't actually be changed. Instead, Webix renders the specified view. So, the user list will be displayed when you click that menu item, or the list of activities they're performing will be displayed when you click the second item.

Note the benefits here. You don't need to write that navigation code, nor do you have to deal with what it means to change views (meaning tearing down the existing UI and the main menu and building the user list of activities with list UIs). The downside, of course, is that you must adhere to the structure that Webix demands, as well as any limitations it may impose. You're giving up control in other words, and whether that's worth it or not is a decision only you can make.

Speaking of adhering to a structure, Webix Jet also requires that you have a models directory (if you're dealing with data, which most apps do). In this directory, you'll find data models, which are JavaScript files that provide the data your components (the ones that deal with data at least) display. With a menu, as you saw, there's no real point to this, so you just specify the data inline as discussed. Although if your menu needs to be dynamic, then there might well be a reason to have a model associated with it. However, let's take the list of users as a better example of something that is going to deal with something other than static data. For that, you might create a file named users.js in the models directory like so:

```
define([], function() {

  var users = new webix.DataCollection({
    url : "getUsers.php"
  });

  return { data : users };

});
```

Here, you have a DataCollection object, which is another Webix component that stores a collection of nonhierarchical data. You can imagine it like a data table but without a UI. It's a place to store data that other components know how to work with. Here, a request to a PHP page (on the server, presumably) is made, and that will return some JSON that provides records, one for each user. With that available, you might now display those records in a data table, another Webix component, in the userlist.js view file.

```
define(["models/users"],function(records) {

    var ui = {
      view : "datatable", autoConfig : true
    };

    return {
      $ui : ui,
      $oninit : function(view) {
        view.parse(users.data);
      }
    };

});
```

This view will now build a datatable component using the data retrieved and populated in the users model. The object returned from here tells Webix Jet how to build the UI, by referencing the ui variables, as well as providing a function to execute when Webix Jet initializes this view. Here, it hands the data from the users model off to the view.parse() function, which takes care of inserting the data into the data table. In this way, you keep your data separate from your presentation but bind it all together at runtime thanks to Webix Jet doing a lot of the work for you behind the scenes, which is the whole point of Webix Jet (plus providing a standardized structure to your application).

As you can see, Webix Jet allows you to skip writing some generally boilerplate code at the cost of having to adhere to a relatively strict application structure. It also, to my eyes, makes people write code in a slightly more convoluted way. But again, the question you need to ask yourself is whether any of the perceived negatives (which you may not even consider negatives at all!) are worth the benefit. As I mentioned earlier, I won't be using Jet from this point on, if for no other reason than I feel it requires a little more rigidity than I'd like, and I also think that it will make learning Webix a little tougher if for no other reason than some details will be hidden from you, and thus you won't get quite as deep an understanding. At the end of the day, Webix Jet is essentially a layer that sits on top of Webix, so I think that learning Webix without that layer in the way will be more beneficial for you.

But Webix Jet certainly has a good story to tell, so if at the end of this book you decide that it's the way you want to go, you'll hear no argument from me! Best of all, you'll have a solid foundation with Webix on which to build with Webix Jet and really gain benefits from it.

Widgets, Controls, Complex Widgets, and Extensions

With an idea of how to structure an application at a high level now churning around in that brain of yours, let's dive into the components that are available for you to build UIs with and how you actually lay those components out on the screen. Before doing that, though, let's talk some terminology.

In the world of Webix, several terms all mean similar things or are subsets of another term. Typically, you'll deal with a couple of terms.

- Components
- Widgets
- Specialized widgets
- Complex widgets
- Controls
- Extensions
- Layouts

Let's take a brief look at each of these categories.

Components

At a high level, you have the term *components*, which is a generic concept that encapsulates all the others. A widget is a component, a control is a component, a layout is a component, and so on. A component is simply a UI element that you can ask Webix to create and put on the screen.

Widgets

Then you have *widgets*, which are components that have a visual element to them, meaning something the user sees and can usually interact with. Widgets include things such as data tables, lists, trees, grids, charts, and so on. Widgets tend to be a little "bigger" in terms of what they do than controls, which you'll look at soon, and widgets tend to serve specific purposes such as the following:

- Visualizing data

- Managing data

- Working with dates and times

- Organizing other widgets and controls (layout, which you'll get to soon as well)

Widgets are, simply put, what you build UIs from.

Specialized Widgets

Specialized widgets (which the Webix documentation calls *specific widgets*) are a subset of widgets that serve a specialized purpose. For example, the barcode widget is specialized to create barcodes. The `colorboard` widget is specialized to allow the user to choose a color from a palette. The `query builder` widget is specialized to allow the user to dynamically create a query that can grab specified data from a collection. While plain old widgets tend to be fairly general-purpose, specialized widgets are more focused on some specific task.

Complex Widgets

Complex widgets are another subset of widgets and are differentiated by them being, well, more *complex*! This means they look almost like full applications themselves and in fact like they include other widgets as part of them, if not literally including them. Some examples of these are the `pivot`, which is an advanced spreadsheet-like widget, the `file manager`, which is like Windows Explorer in Windows or Finder in Mac, or the `Kanban board`, which presents a lane-oriented interface typically seen in Agile development progress-tracking contexts.

Controls

Controls are a subset of widgets as well in the sense that they have a UI and are interactive, but they're different in that they tend to be smaller and more focused on a specific user interaction. Controls are mainly for dealing with user events and are typically seen in forms (though not exclusively). Controls cover things such as buttons, check boxes, text boxes, sliders, radio buttons, selects, and labels (and labels show that controls don't always need to be interactive because while labels *could* be coded to interact with events like clicks, they typically aren't).

Extensions

Extensions are something that doesn't fall neatly into the other categories, or, more precisely, they may cross boundaries between a few. Extensions typically have a UI like everything else, but they frequently provide integration with some other library or facility. For example, the text editor extension allows you to easily use some third-party editors like TinyMCE, Mercury, and CKEditor in your Webix app and makes it look like any other complex widget. The map extension provides the ability to show a map in your app backed by Google, Yandex, Here, or OpenStreet, again acting like a complex widget.

So really, you could think of extensions as complex widgets that usually provide some form of integration with something else, be it another library or some online API (though not always: the sidebar extension, for example, is just a widget with no integration, and it's only an extension because it isn't included with Webix itself and must be pulled down from the Webix GitHub repo at `https://github.com/webix-hub/components`).

Layouts

Layouts are the final group, and they too are a subset of widgets (and thereby components as well), but layouts serve a unique purpose: they help you organize your interface and lay out other components. Layouts are an important topic, so you're going to look at that in a little more detail now.

Let's not rewrite the docs, m'kay?   This chapter, and the next, is meant to give you an overview of what Webix can do and start to introduce some Webix concepts here and there. What it's *not* intended to do is to replicate the Webix documentation. As such, understand that not every available configuration option will be explored, and not every event hook, method, or styling option will be demonstrated. My intent is to call out some of the items that I suspect you'll use most often, but I will in no way, shape, or form be trying to cover every last detail. As such, these chapters aren't meant as an API reference, they're meant as a code-level overview and to start getting your feet wet with Webix code and concepts.

The Basics of Layout

In the sample app in Chapter 1, you saw some of the basics of layouts, specifically the `layout` widget. This is the default widget that you get if you don't specify one via the `view` attribute, which I mentioned in Chapter 1. The `view` attribute is how you tell Webix what component you want to create, but because creating a layout is such an integral task, Webix considers that the default if you don't supply a `view` attribute (though you can say `view:"layout"` if you want to be explicit).

The basic `layout` widget allows you to create arbitrary structures using rows and columns. As you'll recall, you can specify the `rows` and `cols` attributes, nesting them as you want, to create a grid structure into which you can put HTML content (using the `template` attribute) or other Webix components. The cells (which is the generic term for a row or column in a layout) of this grid have borders between them, though you can control that with the `type` attribute.

- `line`: Cells with borders (this is the default)

- `clean`: Cells without borders

- `wide`: Cells with borders and extra-wide space between siblings

- `space`: Cells with borders and extra-wide space between siblings, plus padding from the parent container

- `head`: Cells with borders and small space between siblings

- `form`: Cells without borders and with padding around all of them

Figure 2-1 shows what each of these looks like.

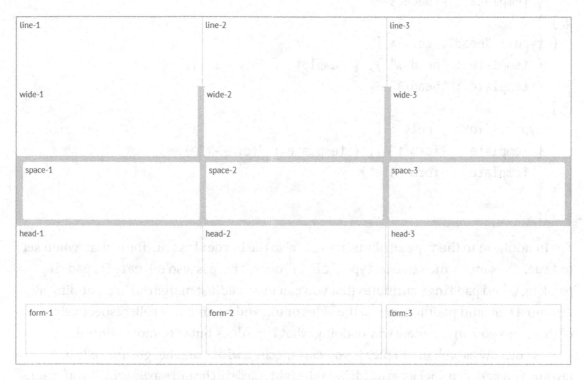

Figure 2-1. *The various type attribute values, all in one place*

Listing 2-1 shows the code that produces this.

Listing 2-1. All the Layout Types on Parade

```
webix.ui({ type : "clean", rows : [
  { type : "line",
    cols : [ { template : "line-1" }, { template : "line-2" },
    { template : "line-3"  }
  ] },
  { type : "wide", cols : [
    { template : "wide-1" }, { template : "wide-2" },
    { template : "wide-3"  }
  ] },
  { type : "space", cols : [
```

```
      { template : "space-1" }, { template : "space-2" },
      { template : "space-3"  }
    ] },
    { type : "head", cols : [
      { template : "head-1" }, { template : "head-2" },
      { template : "head-3"  }
    ] },
    { type : "form", cols : [
      { template : "form-1" }, { template : "form--2" },
      { template : "form--3"  }
    ] }
  ] });
```

In addition to the type attribute, there is also the borderless attribute that, when set to true, does much the same as type: "clean" does. There is also the margin, padding, paddingX, and paddingY attributes that you can use to adjust margin sizing, padding all around a cell, and padding on just the sides or top and bottom of a cell, respectively. All of this gives you an alternate way of doing what type does but with more control.

As you saw as well in Chapter 1, you can specify a width and height for cells in a layout. You can also specify minWidth, minHeight, maxWidth, and maxHeight if you want, which tell Webix the minimum and maximum sizes to allow the cells to be when the browser window is resized.

One of the other things you saw in Chapter 1 is that you can specify a type of header, resulting in a header element being created on a cell. This is in contrast to headerlayout, which is the first layout widget other than layout of a few that I'll discuss. These layout widgets produce specific types of layouts that are common in applications. While it would probably be possible to produce these layouts with just layout and some coding on your part, they're such common patterns that Webix supplies them for you. The headerlayout is one that can produce a horizontal or vertical layout (not an arbitrary grid like layout does) with an optional header (though given its name it's reasonable to think that you usually will have headers on the cells), and the cells can be collapsed by the user.

Take a look at Listing 2-2 to see how this is coded.

Just the facts, ma'am!   For most of the examples in this chapter, I'm going to show only a snippet of code to save some space. Understand, though, that these snippets are all executed from `webix.ready()`, and the HTML files they are in (which you can, of course, find in the code package for this book) are complete HTML documents, nearly identical to the earlier sample app (not the refactored version; there's no need for that type of structure for simple examples like these, where it's better to keep it all in one file so you can look at it holistically).

Listing 2-2. A Simple headerlayout Example

```
webix.ui({ view : "headerlayout", cols : [
  { header : "Column 1", body : "Hello from column 1", width : 200 },
  { header : "Column 2", body : "Hello from column 2", width : 300 },
  { header : "Column 3", body : "Hello from column 3" }
] });
```

The `view:"headerlayout"` specifies the type of widget you want as always, and this example produces a horizontal layout, so you want a series of columns. For each, a `header` attribute specifies the header text, and this widget requires you to use a `body` attribute rather than `template`. (I'm jumping ahead a little bit, but it uses these attributes because `headerlayout` is based on the `accordion` widget, which is a container for `accordionitem` components, and those use these attributes, so thanks to the object-oriented nature of Webix, this is also true of the items inside a `headerlayout`). In addition, you can optionally specify a `width` for the columns as I've done here (the third column will fill the remaining space). Figure 2-2 shows what this looks like, and note that I've collapsed the second column to show that's possible with this widget.

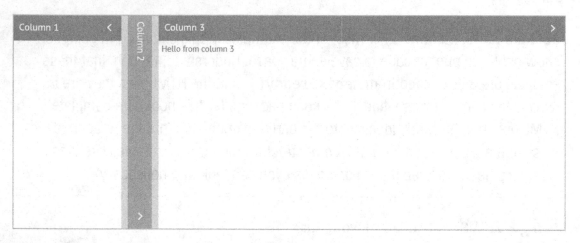

Figure 2-2. *The headerlayout in action*

I should note at this point that you absolutely can nest this widget within another, as is true for all the layouts. For example, let's create a two-column layout that has a headerlayout on the left and then just a couple of plain cells on the right. Listing 2-3 shows this code.

Listing 2-3. A (Slightly) More Complex Layout Using Nested Layouts

```
webix.ui({ type : "wide", cols : [
  { view : "headerlayout", type : "wide", width : 200, rows : [
    { header : "Row1", body : "Row1" },
    { header : "Row2", body : "Row2" },
    { header : "Row3", body : "Row3" }
  ] },
  { type : "wide", rows : [
    { template : "Row-1" },
    { template : "Row-2" },
    { template : "Row-3" },
    { template : "Row-4" }
  ] }
] });
```

I've specified type:"wide" everywhere so that you can see the borders nicely. The first column has view:"headerlayout" specified, so Webix creates that widget for you and inserts it into that first column, which I've also specified a width for. The second column contains four rows, which are just plain old cells with some text in them. Note that because that first column is itself a layout and one that allows its cells to be collapsed, you can, of course, do that, as you can see in Figure 2-3.

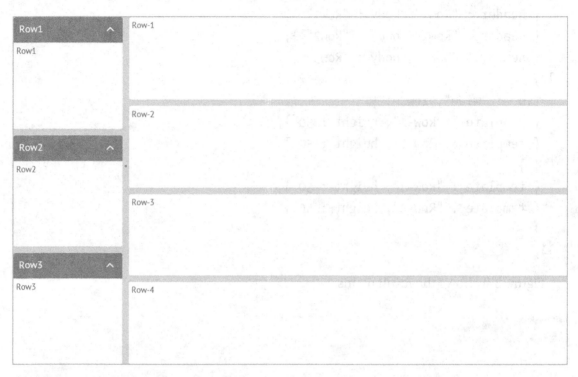

Figure 2-3. *That slightly more complex layout in all its, uh, glory*

You may have noticed that none of the cells in these layouts can be resized (not counting being able to collapse the cells of a headerlayout). As you'll recall from Chapter 1, if you specify view: "resizer" for a cell, then that creates a widget, the resizer, that knows how to allow the user to drag it and adjust the sizes of its neighbors.

The final layout concept I will talk about is resizer. This is a widget like resizer that serves a special purpose. Let's say you want to put a space between rows 1 and 2 and rows 3 and 4 in Figure 2-3. Moreover, you want to specify heights on the existing rows, let's say 50 pixels, and you want that space in between to take up whatever is left. The spacer widget allows you to do this, as you can see in Listing 2-4.

Listing 2-4. The Spacer Widget

```
webix.ui({ type : "wide", cols : [
  { view : "headerlayout", type : "wide", width : 200, rows : [
    { header : "Row1", body : "Row1" },
    { header : "Row2", body : "Row2" },
    { header : "Row3", body : "Row3" }
  ] },
  { type : "wide", rows : [
    { template : "Row-1", height : 50 },
    { template : "Row-2", height : 50 },
    { },
    { template : "Row-3", height : 50 },
    { template : "Row-4", height : 50 }
  ] }
] });
```

Figure 2-4 shows the result of this.

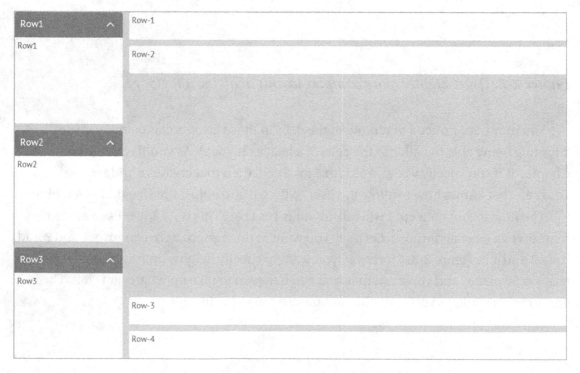

Figure 2-4. *The spacer creates...wait for it...space!*

Notice in the code that { } is all it takes. Optionally, you can do { view : "spacer" } if brevity isn't your thing (to paraphrase The Dude from *The Big Lebowski*). Because there are no rows and cols specified, Webix makes this a spacer rather than a layout, as is usually the default value of view. It makes sense if you think about it. If there are no rows and cols, then all a layout could do is take up all the available space, which is what a spacer does!

The spacer is handy when you need to align things in certain ways. For example, if you want to have two buttons and you want to have one on the left of a cell and one on the right, then all you need to do is something like this:

```
{ cols : [
  { view : "button", value : "button1" },
  { },
  { view : "button", value : "button2" }
] }
```

Of course, I'm giving you a little preview of the button widget, but I think you can handle it! The important part is that spacer. The result is similar to Figure 2-4, but horizontally instead of vertically, meaning each button gets "pushed" as far as it can from the center of the cell this configuration is specified in, and assuming it's a row like in Figure 2-4, that means each button will be on the far left and far right of the row (which also tells us that spacer works both horizontally and vertically, of course).

Specific Layout Components

As I mentioned earlier, there are several what I would call "canned" layout widgets that produce certain types of common layouts, with headerlayout being one of them. Let's take a quick look at the others now.

abslayout

The abslayout, which is available only with a pro Webix license, is perhaps the easiest to understand of all the layouts (though interestingly is probably the one you'll use the least). First, take a look at Listing 2-5 to get a sense what it looks like.

Listing 2-5. The abslayout

```
webix.ui({
  view : "abslayout", width : 200, height : 200, css : "container",
  cells : [
      { template : "UL", top : 5, left : 5, width : 30, height : 30,
      css : "corner" },
      { template : "UR", top : 5, left : 165, width : 30, height : 30,
      css : "corner" },
      { template : "LL", top : 165, left : 5, width : 30, height : 30,
      css : "corner" },
      { template : "LR", top : 165, left : 165, width : 30, height : 30,
      css : "corner" },
  ]
});
```

The idea here is to define an area of the screen, 200 pixels wide and 200 pixels tall, and then within it place four elements, one at each corner of the container area. As you can see, each of the four inner items has a top attribute and a left attribute that functions just like top and left in CSS, defining the X and Y locations of its upper-left corner, all relative to the container, which is the abslayout itself. Figure 2-5 shows the result of this.

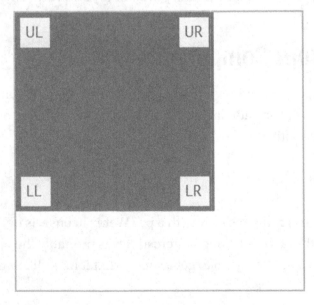

Figure 2-5. *The abslayout*

New Concept: Component Styling

A new concept here is the ability to specify a `css` attribute on most Webix components. This lets you apply styles to the component, in this case based on a preexisting CSS class. If you run the example, you'll see that the container `abslayout` component has a red background, and the four inner components have a yellow background, all thanks to the `container` and `corner` CSS classes.

accordion

The `accordion` layout is a layout that allows you to create either vertical or horizontal panes where (usually) one and only one is expanded while the others are collapsed. This expansion/collapsing is controlled by the user. Listing 2-6 shows the code for this.

Listing 2-6. The accordion Layout

```
webix.ready(function() {

  webix.ui({
    view : "accordion", type : "wide",
    rows : [
      { header : "Babylon 5", body : "Sheridan<br>Delenn<br>Garibaldi<br>
      G'Kar<br>Londo" },
      { header : "Star Trek", body : "Kirk<br>Sisko<br>Archer<br>Picard<br>
      Janeway", collapsed : true },
      { header : "Stargate SG-1", body : "O'Neill<br>Danial<br>Carter<br>
      Teal'c", collapsed : true }
    ]
  });

});
```

Figure 2-6 shows the result of this code. In it, you'll see that the Babylon 5 pane is expanded, while the Star Trek and Stargate SG-1 panes are collapsed (as it should be since Babylon 5 is the best!), with the arrows on the right indicating that by pointing either up or down. The user can click the header of a pane to expand or collapse it. When clicking a collapsed pane, it expands, while all others are collapsed. Clicking an expanded pane collapses it and expands, well, something! The truth is that in this case I've seen some unexpected results, but some pane is always expanded.

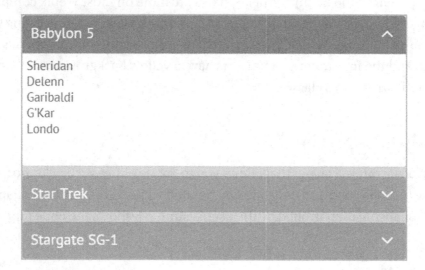

Figure 2-6. *The accordion layout*

Note that when you create an `accordion`, you also implicitly create one or more `accordionitem` components. Webix does this for you automatically; you don't need to do it explicitly, but every pane of the `accordion` is an `accordionitem` component. In some ways, this isn't terribly important when using the `accordion`, but it can matter when you need to find a property in the documentation. For example, if you want to alter the height of the headers for each pane, you won't find what you need if you look up `accordion` in the documentation. But, look up `accordionitem`, and you'll find a `headerHeight` option that does what you want.

There are a few interesting configuration options available for an `accordion`, including `animate`, which tells Webix whether to animate the expansion and collapse of panes. This seems to not be implemented, but it's available because of the object-oriented nature of Webix components in that they extend base classes and thereby get the features present in them. I mention it because my expectation is that this will be implemented in a future version of Webix, and it's an option that you'll see on many components, so it's good to know about. This can be a simple Boolean to enable or disable animation, or it can be an option that defines the type of animation you want. Then there's `collapsed`. When set to `true`, it initially collapses all panes (it defaults to `false`). The `disabled` option you'll see on most components, and its function is pretty obvious: set it to `true` to disable the component, and set it to `false` to enable it (which is the default). Finally, `multi` allows multiple panes to be open at once when set to `true`. This in effect makes an `accordion` *not* an accordion in the classic sense, but it's an option you might want in some situations.

New Concept: Methods

One of the questions you may have right now is "OK, it's nice that I can set `disabled` to `true` when I define a component, but what good is that? Why create it if it's always going to be disabled? I need to be able to enable/disable it dynamically!" And of course, you're right! So far, I've been talking about configuration options exclusively (or *properties*, as the Webix documentation refers to them as), but there's a whole other aspect to components, and that's methods. After all, a component is also a JavaScript object, and JavaScript objects frequently have methods associated with them (and remember, a method is just a function that's a member of an object).

However, as you know, calling a method requires you to have a reference to an object. So, how do you get a reference to a Webix component? There are two ways.

```
var myComponent = webix.ui({ template : "Hello" });
```

The variable `myComponent` now holds a reference to the component that code creates (remember, that's the default component Webix creates if you don't specify a `view` attribute). Now, you can call methods on that reference as you would any other JavaScript object reference. For example, to disable that layout, you can use this:

```
myComponent.disable();
```

Now, that works fine if you only need a reference to the component being created and you remember to catch the return value from `webix.ui()`, which is always a reference to the top-level component created, but what happens if there are nested components so that more than one is created? For example, what if you do this:

```
var myComponent = webix.ui({
  rows : [
    { template : "row1" }, { template : "row2" }
  ]
});
```

Here, you've really got three components being created: the outer view and the two inner views, one for each row. What if you want to disable that first row only? The variable myComponent is a reference to the outer view, not the row you want to disable, so doing myComponent.disable() disables the wrong thing (well, it *does* actual disable the *right* thing, but it *also* disables other things, and that you don't want). One way you can handle this is to use the getChildViews() method that all views expose. That will return an array, in this case with two elements, and then you can do the following:

```
myComponent.getChildViews()[1].disable();
```

However, that's a little verbose and also error-prone. What if you add a row between 1 and 2? Now the code would disable the wrong thing! A better way is this:

```
var myComponent = webix.ui({
  rows : [
    { id : "row1", template : "row1" }, { id : "row2", template : "row2" }
  ]
});
```

Notice the new id attributes on each row? Now, you can use a helper function that Webix makes available to you to get a reference to the second row.

```
var myRow2 = $$("row2").disable();
```

The $$() function allows you to get a reference to a Webix component by ID. You can define an ID for any component, though you don't have to, and in fact you usually will only do so when you know you will need to get a reference to it later (Webix will create an ID automatically if you don't, so every component does, in fact, have a unique ID even if you do nothing). Then, you can call methods on the reference returned by $$() like usual with JavaScript objects.

This is something you'll see a lot of throughout this book, but this is the basic pattern that I wanted to make you aware of now.

carousel

The carousel layout is a component commonly seen on web sites. Typically they are used to show images, though they don't have to. A carousel layout provides some form of user control that allows them to move from one item to another, back and forth, as they see fit. The code for a carousel is like any other layout, as Listing 2-7 shows.

Listing 2-7. The carousel Layout

```
webix.ui({
  view : "carousel", width : 400, height : 300,
  cols : [
    { css : { "background-color" : "#ff0000", "color" : "#ffff00" },
    template : "Gilligan" },
    { css : { "background-color" : "#00ff00", "color" : "#000000" },
    template : "Professor" },
    { css : { "background-color" : "#0000ff", "color" : "#ffffff" },
    template : "Mary Ann" }
  ]
});
```

This provides you with three castaways...er, items...that the user can navigate between using the arrow buttons, as shown in Figure 2-7.

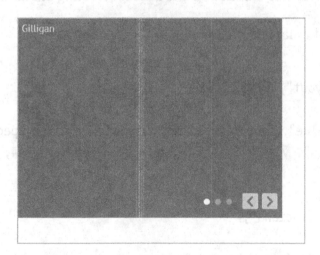

Figure 2-7. *The carousel*

The dots to the left of the buttons show which item is showing out of the whole set. One interesting thing about the carousel is that navigating between the items is by default animated; you'll see a nice little slide animation as you click the arrows. You can, of course, disable this animation (or change the animation style) with the `animate` option you saw earlier. Also, you can control the speed of the animation with the `scrollSpeed` attribute (it defaults to 300ms).

New Concept: Inline CSS

Something else of note in this example is the new way to use the css attribute. Recall earlier that you saw that you could specify an existing CSS class here. It turns out that you can also define your styles inline by making the value of the css attribute an object, where each attribute of the object is a CSS setting. Which you use is entirely up to you and the use case you have.

datalayout

The datalayout is another component that is available only with a Pro license, and its goal is to allow you to create more complex layouts that use data, including things such as sublists, multipage forms, and binding several data components together. Although data is something you've seen a little bit of and it's something you'll dive into more details about in the next chapter, I wanted you to get a look at this layout now since I'm talking about layout. Listing 2-8 shows some code for creating this kind of layout.

Listing 2-8. The datalayout

```
webix.ui({
  view : "datalayout", type : "wide",
  rows : [
    { name : "$value", type : "header", template : "Alien species: #name#" },
    { name : "data", view : "list", template : "Eyes: #eyes#, Arms: #arms#" }
  ],
  data : [
    { name : "Krelmacians",
      data : [
        { eyes : "2 (at adulthood)", arms : 2 },
        { eyes : "1 (at birth)", arms : 2 }
      ]
    },
```

```
  { name : "Gentooans",
    data : [
      { eyes : 4, arms : 8 }
    ]
  }
 ]
});
```

This one is a bit harder to visualize just by looking at the code, so Figure 2-8 shows you what this code does, and as you can see, there's more to it than usual!

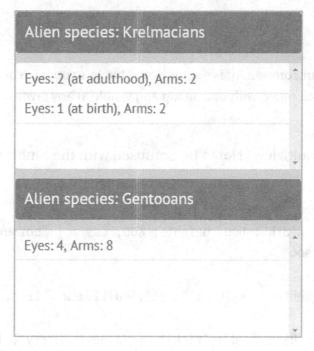

Figure 2-8. *The datalayout*

You start by defining either rows or cols for the layout, as you do with virtually all layouts. Each row, in the case of this sample, represents part of a template for an item to be displayed. The name attribute for each row tells Webix what part of the data attribute to pass to the view (remember, a row is a view). For the first row, the name $value is a special key that tells Webix to pass the entire data object to the view, and it will decide what to do with it. The second row specifies data, which means that the data attribute (the one within the object that is the value of the data config option of the datalayout itself) will be passed to the view. The first view for row 1 then uses the #name# string as a replacement token that Webix replaces with the value of the name attribute from the data. Likewise, the second row uses #eyes# and #arms# to get at those data elements. Webix knows that there is more than one element in the data array for the Krelmacians item, so it repeats the second row, so both items are displayed.

The datalayout is clearly a much more complex component than the other layout types, but that complexity brings lots of power and flexibility for displaying data. You'll meet the list component later, which is conceptually similar, and it's the one you'll probably use most for displaying a list of data, but keep the datalayout component in mind should your needs be more advanced.

multiview

The multiview layout component is a simple one that lets you have multiple layers of content on top of each other, with one on top and visible at any given time. See Listing 2-9 for an example here.

Listing 2-9. The multiview (Not to Be Confused with the Multiverse from Physics!)

```
webix.ui({
  type : "clean", width : 600, height : 400, css : { "border" :
  "2px solid #ff0000" },
  rows : [
    { view : "segmented", value : "left", multiview : true,
      options : [
        { value : "Rick", id : "rick"}, { value : "Morty", id : "morty" }
      ]
    },
    { cells : [
      { id : "rick", template : "Alcoholic<br>Science Genius<br>Father of
      Beth" },
      { id : "morty", template : "14 years old<br>Mortiest Morty<br>Sidekick" }
    ] }
  ]
});
```

This example also shows the segmented component, which has some special wiring available to allow it to control a multiview. Figure 2-9 shows what all of this looks like.

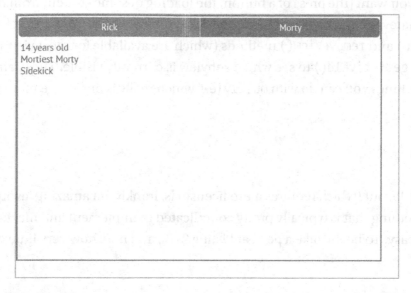

Figure 2-9. *The multiview*

When you click either Rick or Morty up top, the associated content slides into view (you can, of course, disable that animation). To do this, you first create a basic layout, using your friend the css attribute to show a border around it. Then, you define two rows, with the first containing the segmented component. The multiview attribute, when set to true, is what enables that special logic I mentioned and makes the component control the multiview. The key is that the multiview cells and the segmented cells must have the same IDs. As long as that's true, you don't need to write any code to allow this switching.

Now, one thing you may be wondering is why you don't see view:"multiview" on the component containing the cells attribute. If you added it, you would find that everything looks and works the same. The trick here is that when that component is inside of a segmented component that has multiview:true on it, the view type of the component with the cells is implicitly set to multiview. You could have a multiview component outside of a segmented, in which case you would have to specify view:"multiview" yourself (and you of course would then not have the automatic navigation plumbing that a segmented gives you—you'd have to build that yourself and switch between multiview cells programmatically).

Alternatively, if you don't want to use a `segmented`, you can use the `setValue()` method, passing it the ID of the subview to show. You can trigger that through any interaction you want (the press of a button, the loading of some content from the network, whatever). You can dynamically add and remove views from a `multiview` using the `addView()` and `removeView()` methods (which are available for most views in fact). You can call `getActiveId()` to see which subview is currently visible. These are just some of the things you can do with `multiview`, which really is one of the more useful layouts!

portlet

The `portlet` layout (which requires a Pro license) is, frankly, an amazing layout because it takes something that is typically pretty complicated to implement and makes it shockingly easy. To begin, take a peek at Listing 2-10, and note how very little code there actually is.

Listing 2-10. The portlet Layout

```
webix.ui({
  type : "space",
  cols : [
    { view : "portlet", body : { template : "Portlet #1" }},
    { view : "portlet", body : { template : "Portlet #2" }},
    { view : "portlet", body : { template : "Portlet #3" }},
  ]
});
```

Figure 2-10 shows what this looks like when Webix renders it. Well, that's not *entirely* true. What's shown is what Webix renders *and* what it allows me as the user to do.

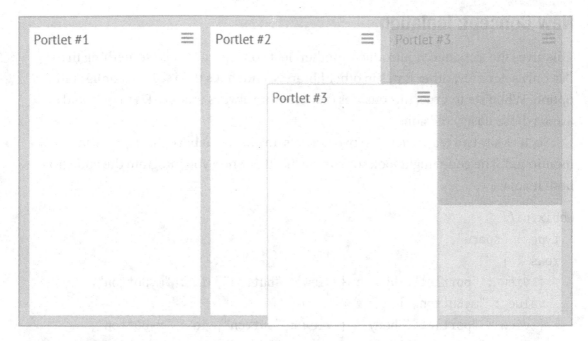

Figure 2-10. *The portlet layout*

See how Portlet #3 is floating on top? That's a result of me dragging the little handle in the upper-right corner to drag the whole Portlet #3 around. You can see where it started on the right; its "ghost" remains there. Now I can drop that anywhere I like! If I want it between Portlet #1 and Portlet #2, I can drop it there. If I want it to be half as tall and just take up the top of the third column, I can do that too. This layout gives complete control to the user to arrange the UI how they see fit and all without you writing really any code to support it! This sort of portal UI usually takes more effort to create (trust me, I know from experience!), but with Webix it's a piece of cake!

Portlets can contain any content, as specified in the body attribute, so you can build arbitrarily complex UIs in them (yes, that can be HTML content, as shown here or other Webix components) and then move them around how you want.

However, if you've ever worked with actual portals, then you may be wondering about a problem that's easy to run into, and that's the problem of ID collision. Frequently, portals are built by multiple teams working separately. As such, it's easy for two teams to use the same IDs for things, and this is a problem. Just like in plain HTML where DOM IDs must be unique across the document, Webix IDs need to be unique across the app. That's only logical. If I have two buttons with an ID of myButton, how does $$("myButton") know which you want?

New Concept: Isolation

This gives me a chance to introduce another neat concept in Webix, something that I've only seen a few other times in other libraries, and that's the `isolate` configuration option. When set to `true`, this ensures that there are always unique IDs in play and avoids those nasty collisions.

So, let's say two teams develop two portlets. In each, you have that `myButton` I mentioned. The code might look something like this when you integrate the code from both teams:

```
webix.ui({
  type : "space",
  rows : [
    { view : "portlet", body : { view : "button", id : "myButton",
    value : "myButton" }},
    { view : "portlet", body : { view : "button", id : "myButton",
    value : "myButton" }}
  ]
});
```

First, if you execute this, you'll see that Webix gives you an error message in the upper-right corner or a page that says: "Non unique view id: myButton." First, thank you, good guy Webix, that's very helpful (and I don't mean that sarcastically!). Note, however, that this is true only if you use `webix_debug.js`. When using the "production" `webix.js` file, you will *not* see this message.

Second, if you try to do $$("myButton"), which button do you get a reference to? It's a good bet it isn't the one you want at least 50 percent of the time!

Thanks to Webix's excellent debug message, you know exactly what the problem is, but how do you fix it?

One thing you could do is assign a code to each team and tell them they have to prefix their IDs with it. So, maybe you wind up with the following:

```
webix.ui({
  type : "space",
  rows : [
    { view : "portlet", body : { view : "button", id : "team1_myButton",
    value : "myButton" }},
```

```
  { view : "portlet", body : { view : "button", id : "team2_myButton",
    value : "myButton" }}
 ]
});
```

Sure, that'll do the trick, but it's kind of annoying and means you have to coordinate with both teams. That isn't always easy in the modern development world with teams geographically separate, even in different time zones. Plus, if they forget anywhere, which is easy to do in a more complex portlet than this, then the risk of collision is introduced.

So, Webix provides you with an elegant answer in the form of the `isolate` attribute.

```
webix.ui({
  type : "space",
  rows : [
    { view : "portlet", isolate : true, id : "portlet1",
      body : { view : "button", id : "myButton", value : "myButton"
    }},
    { view : "portlet", isolate : true, id : "portlet2",
      body : { view : "button", id : "myButton", value : "myButton"
    }}
  ]
});
```

I've added `isolate:true` to both of the portlets, and I've also assigned an `id` to each portlet. While the latter isn't strictly speaking necessary (because Webix assigns a unique ID internally if you don't explicitly), without doing that it becomes harder to do this:

```
$$("portlet1").$$("myButton").disable();
```

See what I did there? I can now get a reference to `portlet1`, and from that, I can ask for a reference to `myButton`, and Webix knows which button I mean, even though it has the same `id` as the button in the other portlet. I've disambiguated things thanks to `isolate`!

You can use `isolate` in virtually any context where a naming conflict might arise and anywhere that you think it makes sense to have two components with the same `id` that you may still want to address individually. `isolate` is *not* specific to portlets, layouts, or anything else.

tabview

The `tabview` layout is a common layout that provides for a tabbed interface that lets the user jump between multiple panes of content at the click of a button (or touch of a finger on a touch display). Listing 2-11 shows the code for a `tabview`, which is just like most of the others you've seen (there's that simplicity and consistency I've mentioned a few times now).

Listing 2-11. The tabview

```
webix.ui({
  view : "tabview", width : 400, height : 300,
  cells : [
    { header : "Entry", template : "Some form controls here", css : "entry" },
    { header : "Results", template : "Show results of the data entry here",
    css : "results" }
  ]
});
```

Figure 2-11 shows what you get when this code is processed by Webix.

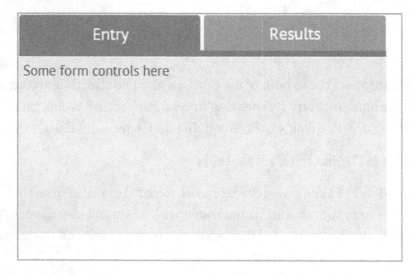

Figure 2-11. *The tabview*

Here, two tabs are presented, and the user can jump between them as they see fit. The tabview has most of the same options as multiview does, along with some from the accordion (again owing to the object-oriented nature of Webix, which the Webix documentation does a good job calling out via the "Based on" line that accompanies the high-level explanation of pretty much all Webix components).

toolbar

The next layout component to discuss is arguably not a layout component at all, but that's the way the Webix documentation classifies it, so I won't argue! This component is used for creating a toolbar as seen in most applications, and you define it just like most other components, as Listing 2-12 shows.

Listing 2-12. The toolbar

```
webix.ui({
  view : "toolbar", height : 50,
  cols : [
    { view : "button", label : "New", width : 90, type : "iconButton",
    icon : "file" },
    { view : "button", label : "Open", width : 90, type : "iconButton",
    icon : "folder-open" },
    { view : "button", label : "Close", width : 90, type : "iconButton",
    icon : "window-close" }
  ]
});
```

Now, there's something new here that applies to many Webix components, so after you gaze longingly at Figure 2-12, I'll talk about those icons.

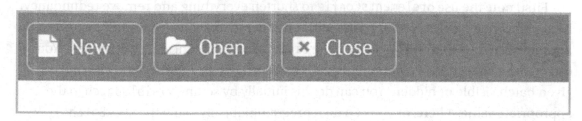

Figure 2-12. *The toolbar*

Webix ships with the Font Awesome collection of font-based icons, and they are used throughout Webix, but they are available for your use as well. In typical fashion, Webix makes this easy. Simply specify the `icon` attribute and the name of the Font Awesome icon you want (the list of which you can find at `fontawesome.io/icons`), and you're done! Well, not quite; in the case of a button, you have to specify its `type` as `iconButton`. Otherwise, a button just shows text. But, I'm getting ahead of myself a bit as you'll look at buttons later.

A `toolbar` is always horizontal, but not to worry, there are other components for doing what a `toolbar` does vertically that I'll get to later. For now, a few interesting config options to mention include `elementsConfig`, which allows you to define attributes for all the child elements of the toolbar. For example, if you want all buttons to be `iconButton` types, you can use `elementsConfig:{type:"iconButton"}` and not have to specify the type for each button.

New Concept: Visibility Batching

I'll introduce one new concept before I finish with the layout components. Look at this bit of code:

```
webix.ui({
  view : "toolbar", height : 50, visibleBatch : 1,
  cols : [
    { label : "New", icon : "file", batch : 1 },
    { label : "Open", icon : "folder-open", batch : 2 },
    { label : "Close", icon : "window-close", batch : 1 },
    { label : "Save", icon : "save", batch : 2 }
  ],
  elementsConfig : { view : "button", width : 90, type : "iconButton" }
});
```

First, note the use of `elementsConfig` to shorten everything and remove redundancy. Nice, right? But, more important, when this is rendered, only the New and Close buttons are shown. Why is that? It's because of the `visibleBatch` and the `batch` attributes. You can create a collection of components, calling them a batch, and then you can make a given batch visible or hidden. You can do this initially by setting `visibleBatch` to the appropriate value, 1 here, or you can do it programmatically using the `showBatch()` method on the container (the `toolbar` here). This gives you a clean way to hide and show groups of components as needed during the lifetime of your application. Note that you can name a batch anything you like, it doesn't have to be a number. Want to call it "buttons that are only needed after the user logs in"? You can do that! It's all up to you!

Summary

In this chapter, you looked at a great many Webix components and saw many core Webix concepts in action. You became familiar with a lot of what Webix offers and saw the code that goes into using it. Ideally, you feel like you have a decent grasp on the basics and a good idea of the types of UIs you can build with Webix.

In the next chapter, you'll continue looking at the rest of the Webix widget set, including those that deal with data entry and data, which you'll of course look at in more detail. You'll also look at some more advanced types of UI interactions that Webix supports.

CHAPTER 3

Getting to Know Webix Even More!

In the previous chapter, you started getting to know Webix by looking at some core concepts such as application structure, layout, and component interaction. You then started surveying many of the components that Webix offers you as a developer.

In this chapter, you'll continue that exploration, and you'll be introduced to some new concepts and new widgets, continuing to build on the foundational knowledge you'll need to build the real applications that the remainder of the book will deal with.

This chapter starts with something that you've seen a little bit of but that is a larger topic, namely, forms.

Forms and Data Entry Controls

Let's discuss data entry. In the interest of killing fewer trees, I'll present a single unified example here, in Listing 3-1, and then cover the individual pieces. This example contains every data entry control covered in this chapter, so as you go through the rest of the chapter, please refer to this listing and the associated figure as I discuss each component. (Note that I left out some surrounding code in the interest of keeping a long chapter from getting any longer, but rest assured, this is the part that matters for this chapter.)

Listing 3-1. All Form/Data Entry Control Widgets in One Place (the Code)

```
let dataObj = [
  { id : "1", value : "Dream Theater" },
  { id : "2", value : "Kamelot" },
  { id : "3", value : "Circus Maximus" }
];
```

© Frank Zammetti 2018
F. Zammetti, *Practical Webix*, https://doi.org/10.1007/978-1-4842-3384-9_3

```
webix.ui({
  view : "form", id : "form1", width : 1000, height : 820,
  css : { "border" : "2px solid #000000", "margin" : "10px" },
  elementsConfig : { labelWidth : 120 },
  elements : [ {
    cols : [
      /* Column 1 */
      { width : 420, rows : [
        { view : "button", label : "button" },
        { view : "checkbox", label : "checkbox" },
        { view : "colorpicker", label : "colorpicker" },
        { view : "combo", label : "combo", value : "2", options : dataObj,
                required : true },
        { view : "counter", label : "counter" },
        { view : "datepicker", label : "datepicker" },
        { view : "dbllist", height : 200, value : "1,3",
          css : { "margin-top" : "10px!important" }, data : dataObj
        },
        { view : "label", label : "This is a label, and below is an icon",
                align : "center" },
        { view : "icon", icon: "envelope", align : "left" },
        { view : "fieldset", label : "Pro-Only Widgets",
        body : { rows : [
            { view : "daterangepicker", label : "daterangepicker" },
            { view : "multicombo", label : "multicombo", value : "1,3",
                    options : dataObj },
            { view : "multiselect", label : "multiselect", value : "2,3",
                    options : dataObj },
            { view : "multitext", label : "multitext" }
          ] }
        }
      ] },
```

```
      /* Column 2 */
      { },
      /* Column 3 */
      { width : 520, rows : [
        { view : "radio", label : "radio", value : "1", options : dataObj },
        { view : "rangeslider", label : "rangeslider" },
        { view : "richselect", label : "richselect", value : "2", options :
                dataObj },
        { view : "richtext", label : "richtext", height : 150 },
        { view : "search", label : "search" },
        { view : "segmented", label : "segmented", value : "3", options :
                dataObj },
        { view : "select", label : "select", value : "1", options : dataObj },
        { view : "slider", label : "slider" },
        { view : "text", id : "myText", name : "myText", label : "text",
          validate : webix.rules.isNumber,
          invalidMessage : "Must be a number", bottomPadding : 20,
          on : {
            onBlur : function() { $$("form1").validate() }
          }
        },
        { view : "textarea", label : "textarea", height : 220 },
        { view : "toggle", onLabel : "toggle ON", offLabel : "toggle",
          width : 100, align : "right"
        }
      ] }
    ]
  } ]
});
```

Of course, a code listing wouldn't be complete without a screenshot to go along with it, and that's exactly what Figure 3-1 is. There will be a few other figures later for things that I couldn't show in this one, but for the most part, this is the one you'll need to look back at during the subsequent discussions.

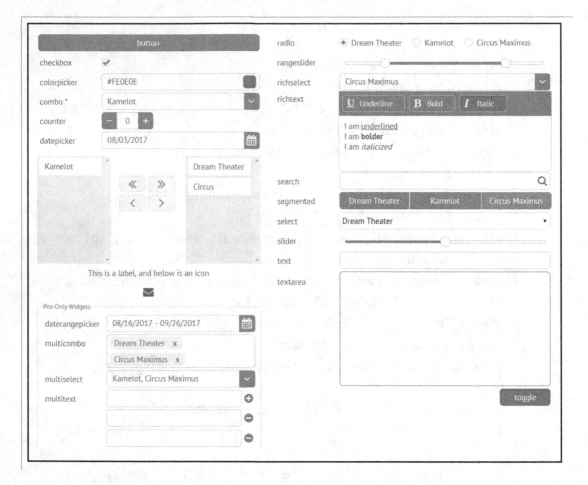

Figure 3-1. *All form/data entry control widgets in one place (the screenshot)*

Now, let's break down what you see here so you can begin to understand what each element is, starting with the container for all of this, the form component.

form

In the HTML world, data entry usually means forms, and that's what it by and large means in the Webix world too (which, of course, ultimately *is* the HTML world after all!). Webix provides a form component that can host a, uh, *host* of data entry controls. It's similar to the plain HTML <form> element, though it provides extra capabilities that its plain HTML brethren does not.

A Webix `form` component inherits from the Webix `view` component, so you can do all the same sorts of layout tricks you can otherwise, using `rows` and `cols`. However, forms also have an `elements` attribute, which effectively acts like the `rows` attribute does in that it lays out your elements in a vertical arrangement. For all the features of the `form` component to work, though, all your data entry controls need to be children of the `elements` attribute. But, you can use `rows` and `cols` within `elements` just fine, so you can lay out forms as you want; you just need to nest everything within `elements`.

The `form` component provides convenience methods for setting and getting values: the aptly named `setValues()` and `getValues()` methods. To use `setValues()`, ensure that every element in the form has a `name` attribute and then just pass the method an object where the attributes are those names. Conversely, `setValues()` returns to you an object in that form. You can also get the value of a single field by using `$$("<form_id>").elements.<field_name>.getValue()`, or if you give an `id` to an individual entry control, then you can use `$$("<control_id").getValue()`.

Speaking of values, Webix also enhances a plain form by keeping track of which fields have been changed and which haven't; this then allows the `form` component to provide the `getDirtyValues()` and `getCleanValues()` methods to get the fields that have been changed and those that haven't, respectively.

New Concept: A Brief Introduction to Events

Components in Webix, in addition to having lots of configuration properties you can adjust, attributes you can look at after creation, and methods to interact with them, also provide a robust event model. You've seen a little bit of this already in the form of the `click` handler attached to buttons. What events a given component exposes can vary greatly, so you'll need to check the documentation to look them up.

Some events you can configure when the component is created, as with the `click` handler for buttons. Other times, you may need to hook into them after the call to `webix.ui()` completes. Once that's done, the component exists, and you can then do the following:

```
$$("myButton").attachEvent("onItemClick", function(id, event) {
  // Do something useful!
});
```

The attachEvent() method is available for virtually all components, and all you need to do is pass it the type of event you want to listen for (as determined from the documentation) and then pass it a function to execute when that event happens. The arguments to that function are also determined by the documentation because they are different for every type of event.

Alternatively, you can define event handlers "inline" by using the on attribute during construction. The value you provide will be an object where the keys are event names, and the values are the functions to execute. So, the previous code could look like this instead:

```
{ id : "myButton", view : "button", label : "My button",
  on : {
    onItemClick : function() {
      // Do something useful!
    }
  }
}
```

For form fields, you can also attach events, for example, to do something when the value of a text field changes.

```
$$("<form_id>").elements["<field_name>"].attachEvent("onChange",
function(newVal, oldVal) {
  webix.message(`Value changed from ${oldVal} to ${newVal}`;
});
```

One thing that often comes up in event handlers for form fields is needing access to the form within the event handler. You can certainly use $$() to get a reference to it, but you can also do this.getFormView() within the event handler because this will reference the control.

htmlform

Before you get to the actual data entry controls, let's look at something that's kind of a helper widget, so to speak, the htmlform. To demonstrate this, I need to show an entire HTML document; see Listing 3-2.

Listing 3-2. Using htmlform to Wrap an Existing Plain HTML Form (the Code)

```html
<!DOCTYPE html>

<html>

  <head>

    <title>htmlform</title>

    <link rel="stylesheet" type="text/css" href="../webix/codebase/webix.css">
    <script type="text/javascript" src="../webix/codebase/webix_debug.js">
    </script>

    <script>
      webix.ready(function() {

        let frm = webix.ui({ id : "myFormView", view : "htmlform", content
        : "myForm" });
        frm.setValues({ firstname : "Frank", lastname : "Zammetti" });

      });

    </script>

  </head>

  <body>
    <div id="myForm">
      <div>
        <label for="firstName">First Name</label><br/>
        <input type="text" name="firstName" placeholder="Required"/>
      </div>
      <div>
        <label for="lastName">Last Name</label><br/>
        <input type="text" name="lastName" placeholder="Required"/>
      </div>
    </div>
  </body>

</html>
```

The purpose of htmlform is to take an existing plain old HTML <form> element and wrap it in a Webix form component, thereby giving it all the features a Webix form provides as previously discussed. To use it, all you need to do is specify the HTML ID of the <form> element when constructing the htmlform component as the value of the content attribute. You wind up with what you see in Figure 3-2.

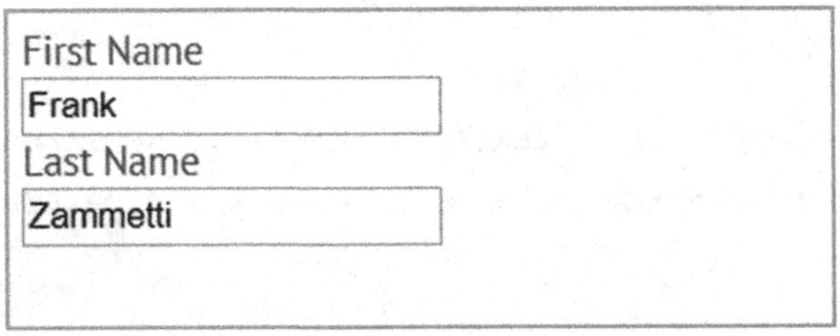

First Name
Frank
Last Name
Zammetti

Figure 3-2. *Using htmlform to wrap an existing plain HTML form (the screenshot)*

If that doesn't look much different from the plain <html> form, you're right! In fact, there's a *slight* styling difference, but it's easy not even to notice it. (If you try the sample code there, you can see it switch over quickly when the page loads if you watch carefully enough.) But, the point of this is that now you can do things such as using the setValues() method, which of course isn't available with an HTML <form> element.

Also note that when Webix wraps the original form in an htmlform component, the field names become lowercased. Note that in the original form, the fields are named firstName and lastName, but when setValues() is called, firstname and lastname must be used. I frankly am not able to tell whether this is a bug or a feature, but I can find no reference to it in the documentation. It's just something to be aware of either way.

In my opinion, it's usually better to build Webix UIs entirely in code, so this component wouldn't get much use in my mind. But, I did want to point it out because if you're trying to just add a little bit of Webix to an existing app, then this might be something that you find useful.

Now, let's move on to the actual data entry components that you see in Figure 3-1, starting with one you've seen several times already: the button.

button

C'mon, you know very well what a button is! You push it and something happens. That's it!

What you may not know, though, is that Webix offers a wide variety of forms a `button` component can take. You can see a plain `button` in Figure 3-1, and you've seen buttons with icons a couple of times. All of the various types are specified with the `type` attribute when you construct a `button`. No `type` attribute gives you a plain `button`, and `iconButton` gives you one with an icon to the left. You can also do `iconButtonTop` to put the icon on the top, or `iconTop`, which is the same except without a border. Then there's `type form`, which gives you a plain `button` that's green, and `danger`, which gives you a red `button`. There are also `prev` and `next`, which give you buttons with left or right edges that are arrows, respectively.

You can specify `type image`, which then requires you to supply an `image` config option that points to an image file. (Just like an icon `button`, an image `button` can have text, but it doesn't have to; you can put the image on the left or top as you want.)

A `type` of `htmlbutton` creates a `button` that you define with HTML and CSS. (The `css` attribute works as always, and the `label` attribute provides the markup to show in the `button`.)

Buttons can also have badges, which are little circles that typically show numbers for things such as unread e-mails in your inbox, for example. In point of fact, any `button` type can have a badge; you just need to provide a value for the `badge` attribute.

Naturally, a `button` without a `click` handler isn't going to be of much use, and as you've seen already, that's just a function you supply. Also, as you've seen, buttons can be sized with `width` and `height` like most components. Buttons also support an `autowidth` option that when `true` will size the button to its content automatically.

checkbox

A `checkbox` widget allows the user to make a binary yes/no choice.

Usually, a `checkbox` has its label to the left, but you can put the `checkbox` itself on the left and the label on the right by setting `labelRight` to `true` during construction.

When you get the value of the `checkbox`, what value do you actually get for either state? By default, you'll get 1 for checked and 0 for unchecked, but you can change that by setting one or both of `checkValue` or `uncheckValue`.

Finally, most of the time, the skin you're using in your application (where skinning is something I'll discuss more in the next chapter) defines what a `checkbox` looks like. However, if you want to force Webix to render it as a plain HTML check box, then you can set `customCheckbox` to `false` (it defaults to `true`).

toggle

The `toggle` component is conceptually a lot like a `checkbox` in that it's used to allow a user to make an either-or decision. It's essentially a different presentation of a yes/no or on/off type of choice.

By default, the `toggle` component appears like a button, but when clicked, its appearance changes to indicate that it is pressed, and it stays pressed. It's "sticky" in a sense—a stuck button! However, `toggle` supports several presentations by altering the `type` property, and the available values mimic the plain button: `iconButton`, `image`, `imageButton`, `imageTop`, `imageButtonTop`, `next`, and `prev`. Also like a button, you can specify an `icon`, and you can, of course, set the `label` text. In addition, toggle offers an `onIcon` and `offIcon` configuration option that works like `icon` does but will change the icon depending on whether the toggle is on or off.

As a matter of opinion, I suggest only ever using the `toggle` widget in its image variants. The reason is that, to my eyes, the default toggle look is too subtle to be usable. However, also note that this can be impacted by what skin you choose, so take this advice with a grain of salt, and decide for yourself, but take the time to make the comparison and base your decision on it. That's the key!

colorpicker

The `colorpicker` widget is kind of a special drop-down element where what drops down is a color swatch palette that the user can choose a color from.

Try the example code in Listing 3-1 and click the box next to the `colorpicker` label and you'll get a box below it with a bunch of colors in it. Clicking one sets the value of the component, which you can retrieve like any other.

There really isn't much in the way of options or methods for a `colorpicker`; it's a pretty simple component.

combo

The `combo` component combines a drop-down select component with a text edit box. This allows the user to either enter a value directly or select one from the list.

You specify a list of options to display in the drop-down portion (you can do this statically as a value to the `option` attribute, or you can do this with a collection of `data`, as the example shows), and you can optionally specify some text to show in the edit portion when the user hasn't entered anything by specifying a value for `placeholder` during construction.

New Concept: Required Fields and Form Validation

In Figure 3-1, you may notice that there is a little asterisk next to the combo field. That's because it has been marked `required:true`. You can mark any form field as required. This affects form validation: a form will be considered valid or invalid based on whether all its required fields have values.

In addition, you can define some rules for fields on your form by adding a `rules` attribute to your form definition. These rules then play into whether the form is valid or not. The value will be an object along these lines:

```
rules : {
  "email" : webix.rules.isEmail,
  "firstName" : webix.rules.isNotEmpty,
  "hasChildren" : webix.rules.isChecked,
  "age" : webix.rules.isNumber
}
```

Each property of the rule object must match the `name` attribute of a form field, and the value is one of these four rules that Webix supplies. The first ensures the entry is in the form of an e-mail address. The second checks if the field is empty or not. (This is redundant with the `required` option, though `required` gives you the asterisk to indicate the field is required, whereas just defining a rule does not; that's the key difference.) The third checks to see whether a `checkbox` field is selected (which is kind of pointless frankly). Finally, the fourth ensures the entry is numeric in nature.

With these rules and the `required` option in play, you can then call `validate()` on the form at any time and get back a Boolean that tells you if the form is currently in a valid state according to these rules or not.

You can also define these rules on a per-field basis by setting the `validate` property and giving it one of the same four rule values shown here. Listing 3-1 shows that done on the `text` field. Note too that validation won't work if the field doesn't have a `name` defined.

These four rules are actually functions, and it's entirely possible for you to add your own; you aren't limited to just these four. You'll see an example of this in a later chapter.

Form fields also allow you to specify an error message to show when the value isn't valid by setting the `invalidMessage` attribute, as you can see that I've done for the `text` field. If you do this, you'll need to ensure there's space below the field to show the message in. That's the reason I added `bottomPadding:20` to the text field definition.

Finally, as with the `text` field, you'll probably want to perform validation on each field as the user moves through them. To do this, you need to attach an event handler to the field, most probably in response to the `onBlur` event that fires when focus leaves the field. In the example, you can see where I've done this, and the function executed for that event calls the `validate()` method on the form. If you type some letters into the text field and then tab out of it, you'll see the field turns red and the `invalidMessage` appears below it because I've attached the `isNumber` rule to it.

counter

The `counter` control is for entry of numbers within a defined range and is sometimes referred to as a *spinner*. It's a small text box with a plus and minus button on the left and right sides (at least with the Webix version; with other UI toolkits they are frequently arrows and are together on the right side). The user can click the buttons to increase or decrease the value, or they can enter a number manually.

With the `counter` widget, you can set `min` and `max` values to define the upper and lower limits, and you can also change the `step` to tell it how much the value changes with each click of either button (defaults to 1).

Aside from those three, this component really doesn't offer any other special configuration options or methods, just the typical ones available to most components and data entry controls.

datepicker

The `datepicker` component is a text field with a calendar icon next to it that when clicked shows a calendar for the user to select a date from. Figure 3-3 shows what this looks like when the user clicks the calendar icon.

Figure 3-3. *The datapicker component*

The user can enter a date manually if `editable` is set to `true` (it defaults to `false`), but by default clicking anywhere in the field, not just the calendar icon, triggers the calendar drop-down. As you can see, the user can select a month and year, either by scrolling through them with the left and right arrows or by clicking the month/year displayed, which brings up an alternate display for them to select from, shown in Figure 3-4.

Figure 3-4. *Selecting a month/year, alternate view*

A few interesting config options are available for this component. The `format` attribute sets the date format and uses a Java-like format specifier such as %d-%M-%Y, for example. The documentation lists all the specification values available, and there are quite a few, so you can get whatever format you need. The `timepicker` option allows you also to support the entry of time. When this is set to `true`, you get a small clock icon and the time in the bottom left of the calendar (on the same row as Today and Clear, which are clickable items the user can use to quickly select the current day or clear the current value, respectively). Figure 3-5 shows what happens when you click that icon or the time.

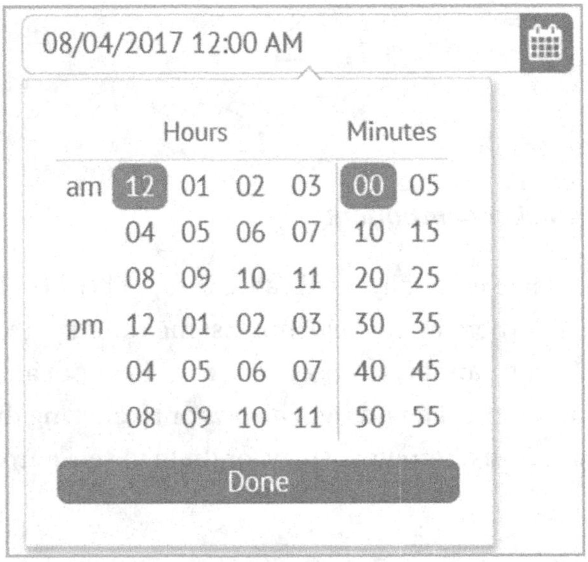

Figure 3-5. Selecting a time with the datepicker

As you can see, the date is displayed in the text field portion and is subject to formatting via the `format` specification. Additionally, you can use the `timeIcon` attribute to specify a different Font Awesome icon to show on the calendar to trigger time entry if you want.

Finally, as far as methods go, there's nothing really specific to this component. However, I'll use this opportunity to point out the `setBottomText()` method, which is available for most form controls. This allows you to put a small bit of static text below the control, similar to a validation failure message, but it is by default a slightly gray, small bit of text, not red like a validation failure message is. It's good for setting things like hints and tips for a field.

daterangepicker

The daterangepicker, which is available only with a Pro license and which you can see in Figure 3-6, is probably best described as the datepicker component on steroids.

Figure 3-6. *Don't do drugs kid! No need for steroids, get swole naturally! (Oh yeah, and this is the daterangepicker.)*

If you need your users to select two dates to indicate a range, then this is the component for you. It does all the same things the datepicker does, including allowing for time input, but it presents two calendars together and displays the date as a range in the text box. It also highlights the range in the calendar, as you can see. This is a convenient and obvious way for users to select a date range.

There doesn't appear to be any methods of config options specific to this component, but everything that the datepicker can do, this can do too.

dbllist

The `dbllist` component is sometimes called a swapper, a list builder, a shuttle, or a swap list (I've even seen it called a slushbucket!). Point being, there's no official name for this, so Webix calling it a `dbllist` is as good as any.

You most certainly know what it is, though. You've got two boxes next to each other (or on top of each other perhaps), and you can move items from one list to the other, either by dragging and dropping or by clicking buttons. There are usually buttons to move a single selected item as well as buttons to move all the items between the lists. The point, generally, is to take a list of possible items and construct a list that is usually a subset (but doesn't have to be) that the application then uses for some purpose. In my example, I'm able to move some of my favorite bands between the lists, and perhaps I'll take the list on the right and order tickets when a button is clicked, for example.

To use it, you need to supply `data`, and as I'm sure you've noticed, all the components that use data in this example use the same data collection. You can specify an initial `value`, which for a `dbllist` since more than one item can be selected, can be a comma-separated list. Those items are initially put over on the right, which Webix treats as the "target," meaning the list you're going to do something with ultimately.

This component actually supports both interaction models, meaning drag-and-drop as well as buttons. Interestingly, I don't see a way to disable either form of interaction directly; it seems you get both whether you want them or not. (In a case like this, you might be able to intercept some events and effectively cancel them, the drag-and-drop events specifically, though I don't see a way to do that, so it might be in this case that you're getting drag-and-drop functionality whether you like it or not!)

The buttons in the middle are something you *can* change, though, by using the `buttons` config attribute. Setting it to `false` hides the buttons entirely (which, hey, gives you a way to disable *that* interaction model at least!). Alternatively, you can supply a template to change their appearance.

```
buttons : `<button class='dbllist_button'>Select</button>
           <button class='dbllist_button'>Remove</button>`
```

Aside from that, the most important method you'll need is `getValue()`, which returns to you a comma-separated string that is a list of the IDs of the items in the box on the right.

fieldset

The fieldset component isn't a data entry control per se, but it's included in the list because it's very much related to data entry. This component is what provides the border with the text *Pro-Only Widgets* in the example. That is its only purpose: to group components together in a visual way. It has no impact on data entry otherwise and as such has really no config options, methods, or events beyond the basics that every component has.

icon

The icon component is exactly what you think. It's a static icon image, nothing more. You can provide a click handler to make it active to perform some function. Similarly, you can provide a popup attribute, which is the ID of an existing pop-up component, and Webix will automatically show the pop-up when the icon is clicked, allowing you to skip writing your own click handler. As with most components, you can also provide a tooltip attribute that is text to display in a tooltip when the control is hovered over. Beyond that, like the fieldset component, this is a simple one that doesn't offer much beyond the basics that all components provide, plus these few that I've mentioned here.

label

The label component is, like fieldset and icon, a simple component that just displays something statically with little configuration or methods available, this time displaying some static text. In fact, beyond the label attribute, which is the text to display, and the inputWidth attribute, which defines the width of the component, the only interesting option is the align attribute, which defines how the text is aligned with relation to the parent container. The possible values are left, right, and center, and I'm going to go out on a limb here and assume you can guess what they do!

multicombo

The multicombo control, another Pro-only widget, is an interesting one. What it does is provides a drop-down that you can choose options from (via check boxes), and then it displays those options in a box as what are frequently called *chips*. These chips can be removed with an X icon. It's a neat way to allow a user to select multiple options and be able to remove them later if necessary.

For the most part, you configure a `multicombo` just like a `combo`, but with some additional features. Setting the `keepText` option to `true` (which happens to be the default) means that when you select an item, it stays in the list (and shows up as selected, as you can see in Figure 3-7. Setting it to `false` means the items are removed from the list when selected (and they'll return to the list if removed with the X icon).

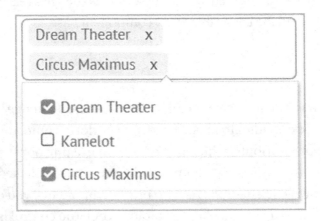

Figure 3-7.   *The multicombo (when just one combo won't do!)*

The `getValue()` method returns to you a comma-separated string of the selected items. When you set initially selected values by supplying a comma-separated list for the `value` attribute, you can use something other than a comma to separate your items by setting the `separator` config attribute (so `value:"1-2"` works if you also set `separator:"-"`, for example).

The `multicombo` also performs a suggest feature, meaning that as you type in the text box portion, it will try to find a match from the options below. By default, what you enter must match one of the options, but if you set `newValues` to `true`, then what the user enters will remain as an option represented by a chip, thus allowing values not in the list to be entered.

multiselect

Keeping with the theme of Pro-only components (as well as "multi" components), you now have the `multiselect` component. This component is like `multicombo`. In fact, when you click it, you'll see the same sort of drop-down that you see in Figure 3-7. The only real difference is that while `multicombo` shows you the selected items as chips, `multiselect` instead shows them as a comma-separated list.

This component also does suggest like `multicombo` does; however, `multiselect` doesn't allow the user to enter arbitrary values like `multicombo` does.

multitext

The final "multi," Pro-only widget to look at is `multitext`. This component allows the user to enter an arbitrary number of arbitrary items, meaning they can enter any string they want, and they can enter as many as they want. The control has a plus icon next to it and each press of it adds a new text entry field below it (expanding its container, it should be noted). Each row has a minus icon next to it, allowing the user to remove that row.

For all practical purposes, this control is just like the plain `text` component you'll see shortly, so it doesn't have much in the way of extra features. The only thing of note is the `subConfig` attribute. This allows you to define characteristics of each added row, such as the `label` to show for each. Also note that adding rows expands the container the `multitext` is in, which is something you may want to take into consideration as you design your interface.

radio

A `radio` widget, sometimes called a *radio button*, is a group of mutually exclusive options from which the user is expected to choose (only) one. You simply supply it with a list of `options` to display and optionally an initial `value` for which is selected, and that's it.

By default, `radio` will lay its options out horizontally, but setting `vertical` to `true` switches to a vertical layout with each option going down in a column. Like the `checkbox`, which had a `customCheckbox` config option, `radio` has a `customRadio` option that you can use to switch to a plain HTML radio button rather than a skinned one according to the theme currently in effect.

segmented

Like the `radio` component, the `segmented` component is a way for a user to select one and only one choice from a group of choices. Technically, a `segmented` is a collection of `button`s, but they are `button`s that toggle their appearance (a color change) when one is selected.

As shown when the `multiview` was discussed, there is special plumbing built into the `segmented` to connect it to a `multiview` to let the user switch between the views by setting the `multiview` config option on the `segmented`. As you can see from the example code, the `options` attribute is how you define the labels for each of the buttons.

The `segmented` widget provides a `showOption()` method and a `hideOption()` method that accepts an ID to hide and show options (segments) dynamically.

This component is especially good for touch-based interfaces since it provides a bigger touch target and so is generally easier to use with that form of interaction than a `radio` is.

select

The `select` component basically mimics the plain HTML `<select>` element in that it presents a list of options in a drop-down for the user to choose from. This widget does *not* allow arbitrary entries, so the user must always select an option from the list. This widget also does *not* allow multiple selections.

As with most components that require data to populate the available options, you set the `options` attribute to define them, and you can select an initial value by specifying the `value` attribute during construction. Beyond that, there aren't any special config options or methods for this component, but all the usual suspects are there: `bottomLabel`, `bottomPadding`, `css`, `id`, `label`, `tooltip`, `validate`, `required`, `enable()`, `disable()`, `getValue()`, `show()`, `hide()`, and `setValue()`, to name just the most commonly used.

richselect

The `richselect`, for the most part, looks and works like `select` does, but the big difference is that with `richselect`, the drop-down portion is a `popup` component. As such, you can create a richer display in the drop-down by specifying the `template` attribute and tell it how to render each option. It can be as simple or as complex as you want, including images next to each item as one example. You can also specify a `labelHeight` value as part of an object that is the value of the `type` attribute to adjust the height of each item in the list.

Aside from those few, there aren't really any other `richselect`-specific options or methods. If you've seen one `select`, you've seen 'em all, even the rich variety essentially!

slider

The `counter` component that you saw earlier allows the user to select a numeric value from a defined range and do so in discrete steps. The `slider` component does the same, but with a different presentation: a horizontal line with a knob that the user drags to change the value.

Like the `counter` widget, you can define `min`, `max`, and `step` values to define the range and how the value changes as you move the knob.

At present, a `slider` cannot be vertical, nor can you allow values other than numbers (some sliders in other toolkits allow you to define string values for each position, but Webix does not as of this writing).

Those things aside, a `slider` has essentially the same set of properties, methods, and events that the `counter` does. It really is almost the same control, just with a different look and of course a different way for the user to interact with it. Which you use depends on your use case. A `slider` is usually better when there's a wider range of values, but it takes up more space, so you should consider that. (You can, of course, define its width, so you can make it as small as you want, but if it gets too small, then interacting with a `slider` becomes difficult, so you have to consider that as well.)

rangeslider

Like the difference between a `datepicker` and a `daterangepicker`, the `rangeslider` allows you to select a range, a starting number, and an ending number. It does this by simply presenting a slider with *two* knobs that can be dragged instead of just one with the `slider`. The value you get back when you call `getValue()` is a comma-separated string listing the starting and ending values if you set the `stringResult` attribute to `true`. Otherwise, it'll be an object with the start and end values as attributes (the latter is the default).

As the user drags the knobs, they can never cross each other, so the one on the left is always the starting value, and the one on the right is the ending value (they *can*, however, occupy the same space and hence the same value).

As far as config options, methods, and events go, they are identical to those of the slider.

text

The text widget is simply a one-line field where a user can enter text. You can optionally provide a placeholder value during construction to show a label inside the field, which is primarily what distinguishes this from the plain HTML <input type="text"> field.

You can also, like the HTML version, specify a type attribute and give it a value of text (which is the default), password (which masks the input as the user types), or email (which specifies the entry is to be in the form of an e-mail address).

In addition, you can supply a pattern config option that defines a formatting pattern. The value of this option is an object with two attributes: mask and allow. The mask attribute defines a pattern using the # symbol and pattern symbols such as hyphens, periods, and spaces. This allows the field to format the value as the user types. The allow attribute allows you to define a regular expression to limit what the user can input. Using these two together allows for some powerful entry fields that limit user errors greatly. Webix also supplies a few patterns itself, and they are defined as webix.patterns.phone, webix.patterns.card, and webix.pattern.date. These are objects that define the appropriate mask and allow values, so you can reference them as the value of your pattern attribute.

search

The search component is really nothing more than a text component with a search icon integrated into it. This is such a common pattern that Webix supplies a special component for it. There isn't any extra functionality beyond what the plain text component offers, though. It really is just the addition of the search icon that makes this different! You can change the icon shown using the icon attribute like for many other controls, but beyond that, there really isn't much to say about this component frankly.

textarea

The textarea widget is just like its <textarea> plain HTML brethren, but in Webix clothing. It has all the same options and methods as a text component does, but of course, you'll need to specify a width and height for this one since it allows for multiple lines of text to be entered. A scrollbar will appear when the user enters more than can fit in the box as initially sized.

Like search, there isn't much more to say on this one. It's just a big text component that allows multiple lines. Otherwise, its API is identical to the text component.

richtext

The final component to look at is another text entry component called the richtext. This one is similar to textarea, so is of course similar to text as well, but the big difference here is that richtext allows you to do some formatting of entered text, specifically bold, italic, and underlining. It does this by providing three buttons at the top. When you click them, whatever text is selected will have the appropriate style applied (or removed if it already had it set since the buttons are toggles).

You might imagine that there are a lot of extra config options and methods available for this widget, but in fact, there aren't. Its API is pretty much the same as the other three text entry ones.

forminput

The final data entry component to look at is one that in a sense isn't a data entry component, at least not like the others you've seen. The forminput component is instead a component that allows you to take other Webix components and use them as form components. Check out Listing 3-3 to see what the code for this looks like.

Listing 3-3. The forminput Widget

```
let myDataTable = {
  view : "datatable", height : 200,
  columns : [
    { id : "name", header : "Employee Name" },
    { id : "position", header : "Position" },
    { id : "phone", header : "Phone Number", fillspace : 1 },
  ],
  data : [
    { name : "Jack", position : "Dillon", phone : "111-222-3333" },
    { name : "Susan", position : "Everest", phone : "444-555-6666" },
    { name : "Charlie", position : "Jackson", phone : "777-888-9999" }
  ]
};
```

```
webix.ui({
  view : "form",
  elementsConfig : { labelWidth: 120 },
  rows : [
    { view : "text", width : 300, label : "Manager ID" },
    { view : "forminput", label : "Employees Grid", body : myDataTable },
    { view : "button", value : "Save", inputWidth : 200, align : "right" }
  ]
});
```

What I've done here is created a datatable component, which is a component you'll look at in the next chapter, but in essence, it's like an HTML <table> and is used to display columnar data. But, critically, it isn't a component you can usually put in a Webix form. However, once you wrap it in a forminput, then you can, as Figure 3-8 shows. 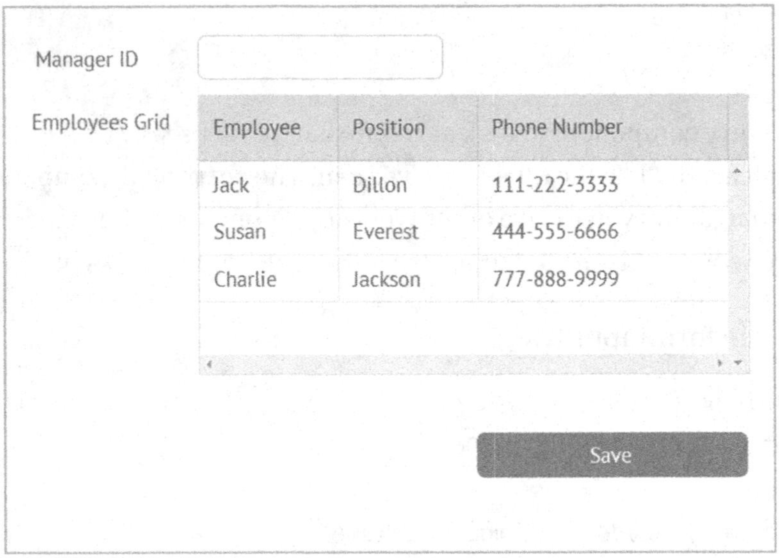

Figure 3-8. *Beware datatables in forminput's clothing*

All you really do is add a component with a view:"forminput" to the form and then specify another component as the body (and yes, this can be a Webix view that contains any number of components; it doesn't have to be just one). Then, as long as the components that forminput wraps has a name attribute, they'll show up in the form's values when you call getValues(), and you can use most of the form logic config attributes on them—things such as `required` and `validate` and all that. Of course, what values you get from various components, especially when it's a group of components, can be an object with a complex structure, but that's the price you pay for being able to use widgets that aren't ostensibly data entry controls in a form!

The Basics of Data

In this chapter, you'll be looking at many data-aware components, though you've already seen some in the previous chapter. And, as part of seeing those, you saw that for many components you can supply a `data` attribute when you construct the component to provide data to it. This is, in a broad way, the basics of using data, and for many applications, it'll be all you need. However, there's more to data with Webix than that, as you have probably guessed!

Loading Data from an External Source

First, you aren't required to provide the data "inline" via the `data` attribute; you can also load it from an external source, and you can do that with the `url` config option. As the name implies, this is a URL to a resource that the component will retrieve and parse as data to feed to the component. By default, it is assumed that the resource returned is in JSON form, so if you had a file on your server named `data.json`, then you might do `url:"http://myserver.com/data.json"` to load the data. The contents of `data.json` would look just like what you provide to the data attribute, perhaps this if it was returning a list of users:

```
[
  { id : "user1", numberOfLogons : 3 },
  { id : "user2", numberOfLogons : 5 }
]
```

Of course, you absolutely can specify the URL of a dynamic resource, perhaps a JSP or PHP file, which produces the JSON on the fly. The response doesn't even need to be JSON, though that's the default. If you want to use XML instead, for example, then you just need to provide a `datatype` attribute in addition to `url` and specify one of the supported values: `json`, `xml`, `jsarray`, or `csv`.

Dynamic Data Loading

Of course, loading data when the component is constructed isn't always what you want. Sometimes you'll need to load data later, maybe in response to some user action. That's easy to do by calling the load() method on the component. There are three arguments to this method: the URL of the data to load, the data type (which can be omitted if it is JSON), and a callback function to call when the data loads (which is also optional). So, in simplest terms, you can just pass the URL to load to the load() method and, as they say, thy will shall be done, and the data will be loaded into the component!

If you want to load some data that *doesn't* come from an external source or maybe does come from an external source but you prefer to write your code to retrieve and load it, then the parse() method is your friend. This takes in a string of JSON or a JavaScript object (like you would specify for the data attribute), and parses it and adds the records to the component. Note that it does, in fact, add them to any existing data in the component, so if you want to replace the data entirely with the new data, then you need to call the clearAll() method on the component before calling parse().

DataStore

Now, the clearAll() method is interesting because it's not a member of data-aware components directly; it is, in fact, a member of something called DataStore, which is something that Webix creates behind the scenes when dealing with data. In fact, if you specify a data attribute for a data-aware component, you'll find after the component is constructed that the value of the data attribute is now a Webix DataStore object and is no longer the plain JavaScript object you provided!

A DataStore is a collection of records, which are themselves just JavaScript objects. The two users in the previous data.json example are examples of records.

The DataStore provides a host of data-related functionality, besides that clearAll() method, including things such as filtering of data via the filter() method, sorting of data via the sort() method, and even getting the data in the DataStore as a JSON object via the serialize() method. The importData() method allows you to copy the data from one DataStore to another, so to copy the data from a list component named myOtherList to a list component named myList, you might do the following:

```
$$("myList").data.importData($$("myOtherList")
```

Note that the importData() method is called on the data property of the component, and that's because of what I previously said: Webix has created a DataStore object for you and assigned it to the data reference, replacing whatever you might have specified there when the component was configured.

With a DataStore, you can also retrieve a count() of records in it, and you can perform an operation on each record by using the each() method and providing it with a function to call for each record. You can search for a record with the find() method by providing it with a function that determines whether a record matches the criteria you set out. You can also get records from a DataStore by specific ID using getItem(). You can, of course, add and remove (with add() and remove()) items to a DataStore, and by extension the component using it, and you can update an existing item using updateItem() too.

Remember, the operations you perform on a DataStore that mutate data are immediately reflected in the component using that DataStore. That's the key concept here and is what makes the Webix data API that this is all part of so powerful.

Proxies

The final data topic I want to talk about is proxies. Proxies are JavaScript code that knows how to read a particular type of data or read data in a certain kind of way and provide it to a DataStore. In essence, proxies provide addition loading logic to a DataStore.

The way you specify a proxy is by means of a prefix to the value passed to the load() method or the value of the data attribute. As an example, let's say you want to store your data for a datatable component (which you'll see in the next section, but for now just imagine it like an HTML table that is aware of how to use data from a DataStore) in IndexedDB in-browser storage. (IndexedDB is a low-level API for client-side storage of significant amounts of structured data, including files/blobs.) When you construct the datatable, you need to tell it this with a prefix to the url attribute:

```
{ view : "datatable", id : "myDatatable", url : "indexdb->myDB/
myCollection" }
```

The indexdb-> prefix tells Webix that you want to use the indexdb proxy to load (and save) data for this datatable. If you want to load the data after component construction, you can do the same with the load() method.

```
$$("myDatatable").load("indexdb->myDB/myCollection");
```

To support saving data back to the database, you need to specify the save config option, using the same value as the url option.

Of course, this won't do much good if you don't create that database first, so Webix provides a means to do that via the proxy API.

```
webix.proxy.indexdb.create("myDB", {
  myCollection : [
    { id : 1, firstName : "Luke", lastName : "Skywalker", jedi : true },
    { id : 2, firstName : "Han", lastName : "Solo", jedi : false }
  ],
}, null, function() { });
```

The first argument is the name of the database; the second is an object that contains data for a collection (or multiple collections if you need to). The third is the database version, though the Webix documentation says to typically not bother with this and just pass null, and the fourth is a callback that is called once the data has been loaded. If you do this before constructing a component like the datatable described, then the component will display the data from the database (assuming the browser supports IndexedDB, of course).

Webix supports a number of proxies out of the box, including the following:

- offline and cache: For offline support of applications that use server-side data

- local: For saving component data into a browser local storage and working with it

- connector: For saving data via a server-side connector

- rest: For working with a server in the REST mode

- post: For loading data in a POST request (GET by default)

- sync: For loading data via a synchronous Ajax request (by default, loading is performed by an asynchronous request)

- indexdb: For working with IndexedDB in-browser database storage

- `faye`: For enabling live data update on all clients currently using the application

- `binary`: For loading and reading files as `arraybuffer`

- `json`: For sending JSON data to a server via RESTful "save" requests with the `application/json` content type

Given the wide variety in these, I won't be covering each one, but they all function similarly to the `indexdb` proxy as far as how you deal with it goes. Of course, you also have the ability to create your own proxy if needed; Webix provides extension points for doing that.

Specialized Data Components

With the basics of data in Webix covered, it's time to move on to specialized data components, or data-aware components. Specialized data components are those components that are specifically designed to deal with a collection of data. They display data, visualize it in some way, and, in some cases, allow the user to interact with or even edit that data. Let's look at these components now.

chart

The `chart` component is without a doubt the most flexible data component Webix offers. It allows you to visualize data in a wide variety of ways, some of which will be familiar to you, some maybe not. For example, given this bit of data, all of the types of charts shown in Figure 3-9 can be produced:

```
let chartData = [
  { count : 65, dollars : 130, color : "#ff0000", type : "AA" },
  { count : 120, dollars : 280, color : "#00ff00", type : "BB" },
  { count : 50, dollars : 98, color : "#0000ff", type : "CC" },
  { count : 90, dollars : 110, color : "#ffff00", type : "DD" }
];
```

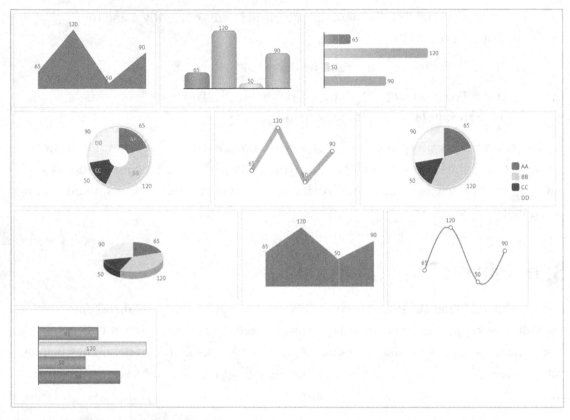

Figure 3-9. *A ton of beautiful charts, if you're in to that sort of thing*

Not all charts use all the elements of the data, but that's fine because Webix will just ignore the data elements that a given chart type doesn't need. Listing 3-4 shows the code to produce this display, which includes the ten charts you see as well as the layout they all fit into (in order to have space between them).

Listing 3-4. The Code for Lots of Different Types of Charts

```
webix.ui({
  rows : [
    { height : 10 },
    /* Row 1 */
    { cols : [
      { width : 10 },
      /* Area chart. */
      { view : "chart", type : "area", value : "#count#", label : "#count#",
```

```
            width : 300, height : 200, data : chartData
        },
        { width : 10 },
        /* Bar chart. */
        { view : "chart", type : "bar", value : "#count#", label : "#count#",
                barWidth : 100,
            radius : 10, gradient : "3d", width : 300, height : 200, data :
                chartData
        },
        { width : 10 },
        /* Horizontal bar chart. */
        { view : "chart", type : "barH", value : "#count#", label :
                "#count#", barWidth : 20,
            gradient : "falling", width : 300, height : 200, data : chartData,
                padding : 40
        },
        { }
    ]},
    { height : 10 },
    /* Row 2 */
    { cols : [
        { width : 10 },
        /* Donut chart. */
        { view : "chart", type : "donut", value : "#count#", color : "#color#",
                label : "#count#",
            shadow : 20, data : chartData,
            pieInnerText :
                "<span style=\"color:#82c0ff;font-weight:bold;padding:10px;\"
                    >#type#</span>",
        },
        { width : 10 },
        /* Line chart. */
        { view : "chart", type : "line", value : "#count#", label : "#count#",
            width : 300, height : 200, data : chartData,
            line : { color : "#ffa0d0", width : 10 }
        },
```

```
      { width : 10 },
      /* Pie chart. */
      { view : "chart", type : "pie", value : "#count#", color : "#color#",
        label : "#count#",
        shadow : 20, data : chartData,
        legend : { width : 90, align:"right",
          values: [
            { text : "AA", color : "#ff0000" },
            { text : "BB", color : "#00ff00" },
            { text : "CC", color : "#0000ff" },
            { text : "DD", color : "#ffff00" },
          ]
        }
      },
      { }
    ]},
    { height : 10 },
    /* Row 3 */
    { cols : [
      { width : 10 },
      /* 3D pie chart. */
      { view : "chart", type : "pie3D", value : "#count#", color :
        "#color#", label : "#count#",
        data : chartData
      },
      { width : 10 },
      /* Stacked area chart. */
      { view : "chart", type : "stackedArea", value : "#count#", label :
        "#count#",
        width : 300, height : 200, data : chartData
      },
      { width : 10 },
      /* Spline chart. */
      { view : "chart", type : "spline", value : "#count#", label :
        "#count#",
```

```
        width : 300, height : 200, data : chartData
      },
      { }
    ]},
    { height : 10 },
    /* Row 4 */
    { cols : [
      { width : 10 },
      /* Stacked horizontal bar chart. */
      { view : "chart", type : "stackedBarH", value : "#count#", label :
        "#count#",
        radius : 10, gradient : "falling", width : 300, height : 200, data
                : chartData
      },
      { }
    ]},
    { }
  ]
});
```

Overall, this is a simple layout that is four rows with seven columns in the first three
and three columns in the final row. (You can see some spacers in there, specifically as
the last column in each row, as well as for a fifth row to fill out the page completely.)
Each chart is one of the columns in a given row.

Each chart, as you'd guess, has its own specific config options available depending
on the features of a given chart type, but they all have the same basis, so you'll find the
all-important data attribute on each. They all have the same type and chart, and the
type attribute defines the type of chart you want.

Because there's quite a variety of charts and options available for each, I won't
go into describing each here and instead leave that job to the documentation. For
the most part, though, I think you'll find this code fairly self-explanatory. Even if you
aren't familiar with a given chart type, I suspect you can make sense of how a chart is
constructed pretty easily.

datatable

A datatable component is what most other libraries and UI toolkits call a grid. It's a tabular form of data and in the case of the Webix datatable also allows for editing the data (optionally, of course). A datatable provides functionality such as sorting, filtering, pagination of large data sets, and more. Figure 3-10 shows what a basic datatable looks like.

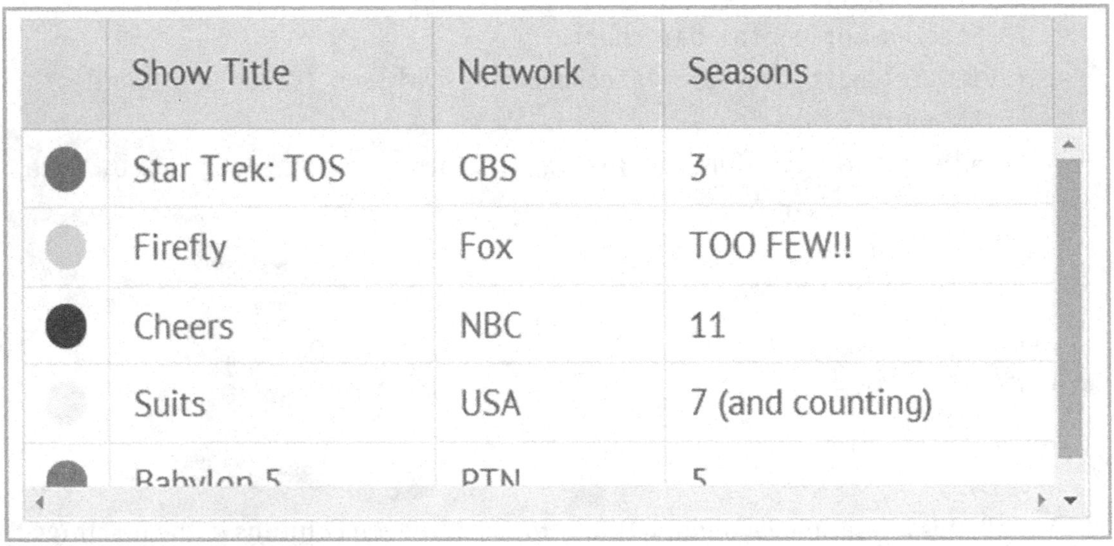

	Show Title	Network	Seasons
●	Star Trek: TOS	CBS	3
●	Firefly	Fox	TOO FEW!!
●	Cheers	NBC	11
	Suits	USA	7 (and counting)
●	Babylon 5	PTN	5

Figure 3-10. *A simple datatable*

In this example, I've sorted the data on the Show Title column by clicking the column header. This feature is enabled by default for every datatable you create. How do you create one, you ask? Listing 3-5 answers that question!

Listing 3-5. Not a Coffee Table, But a datatable

```
webix.ui({
  view : "datatable", width : 460, height : 216, editable : true,
  css : { margin : "10px" }, borderless : false,
  columns : [
    { id : "marker", header : "", width : 38, editor : "color",
```

```
      template : function(inObj) {
        return "<span style=\"background-color:" + inObj.marker +
          ";border-radius:20px;padding-right:10px;\">  </span>";
      }
    },
    { id : "title", header : "Show title", width : 140, sort : "string" },
    { id : "network", header : "Network", width : 100, editor : "text" },
    { id : "seasons", header : "Seasons", fillspace : true }
  ],
  data : [
    { marker : "#ff0000", title : "Star Trek: TOS", network : "CBS",
      seasons : 3 },
    { marker : "#00ff00", title : "Firefly", network : "Fox", seasons :
      "TOO FEW!!" },
    { marker : "#0000ff", title : "Cheers", network : "NBC", seasons : 11 },
    { marker : "#ffff00", title : "Suits", network : "USA", seasons : "7
      (and counting)" },
    { marker : "#ff00ff", title : "Babylon 5", network : "PTN",
      seasons : "5" }
  ]
});
```

As you can see, you define the columns that your datatable will provide. The id attribute for each column must match the name of an attribute in your data collection. For each column, you can specify column header text. You can also optionally specify a template that will generate the HTML for the header text if you need to do something more complex, as I've done here, to show a colored circle based on the marker color specified in the data. You can also specify the type of sorting a column provides when the user clicks the header by specifying a sort value from one of int (for numeric sorting), date (for date sorting obviously), string (for textual sorting), or string_strict (which is a case-sensitive version of string sorting). The fillspace option, when set to true, indicates that the column should stretch to fill the remaining horizontal space of the container the datatable is in, if any.

A column can also specify that its `data` can be edited by adding an `editor` attribute and specifying the type of editor the column provides. Webix offers a number of editors (and you can create your own too), including the following:

- `text`: A simple text editor box

- `password`: A text editor box that masks its input

- `inline-text`: A more advanced and customizable version of text (for example, allows you to supply a template to format the entry with)

- `select`: Just like an HTML `<select>` element

- `combo`: A `select` that the user can also edit the text of and thereby can enter values not in the list

- `richselect`: A `select` that allows more customization of its display

- `multiselect`: Only available in Webix Pro, allows for selecting multiple values from a select list

- `checkbox`: A simple check box

- `inline-checkbox`: A more customizable check box (for example, if you want to have a Boolean selection that toggles between the words *yes* and *no*)

- `color`: Allows the user to select a color from a palette

- `date`: A pop-up calendar for date entry

- `popup`: Allows virtually any type of input you care to code since you provide the code for what the editor shows in essence

The `datatable` widget is extremely rich and provides many other options. There are too many to go into all of them, but some of the most interesting include `headermenu` that, when set to `true`, provides a menu when you right-click a column header that then allows you to hide or show columns. There's also `topSplit`, which defines the number of rows, if any, that you want to freeze, meaning they won't scroll out of view as the user scrolls through the rest of the data in the `datatable`. The `leftSplit` option does the same but allows you to freeze columns on the left. The `blockselect` option allows the user to select a block of rows and columns. Similarly, setting `multiselect` to `true` allows the user to select multiple noncontiguous cells in the `datatable` (which the `getSelectedItem()` method lets you get; it returns an array of objects for each selection if there is more than one).

The `datatable` provides a rich API in terms of methods that allow you to manipulate virtually every aspect of the component. You can even group your data by calling the `group()` method and passing it an object that defines how you want the data grouped. Then there's `collectValues()`, which returns to you an array of unique values for the specified column. You can get the `count()` method of currently visible data items, and you can use the `eachColumn()` or `eachRow()` method to iterate over the visible columns or rows in the table (both require you to supply a function to be executed for each column or row, respectively). You can use `freezeRow()` to fix a row to the top of the datatable on the fly. Finally, you can move rows around using `moveBottom()`, `moveTop()`, or `move()` to reorganize your list.

The `datatable` is one of the most robust widgets Webix offers and will likely meet any need you have to display data in a tabular form, though that's not the only widget that provides this capability, as you'll see.

dataview

The `dataview` component is another widget that displays data in a tabular format, but unlike a `datatable`, this one doesn't explicitly have rows and columns. Instead, the data items it displays get laid out in what winds up being a grid, which of course is *effectively* rows and columns, but you aren't explicitly defining them as such in your code as you do with a `datatable`.

Figure 3-11 shows a `dataview` in all its non-rows-and-columns-but-still-kinda-rows-and-columns glory, listing some of my favorite video games (well, mine *and* my mom's—she's the Ladybug fan!).

Pitfall	Pick Axe Pete	Ladybug	Altered Beast
Year: 1982	Year: 1982	Year: 1981	Year: 1988
System: Atari 2600	System: Odyssey2	System: Colecovision	System: Sega Genesis
Halo	Crash Bandicoot	Guitar Hero	
Year: 2001	Year: 1996	Year: 2005	
System: Xbox	System: Playstation	System: Playstation 2	

Figure 3-11. A dataview component for kids who spend too much time indoors

As you can see, it does kind of look like there are rows and columns, but there really aren't, not explicitly at least. The display of the individual items, however, is entirely under your control as the programmer via a template, as you can see in Listing 3-6.

Listing 3-6. The Code Behind the dataview

```
webix.ui({
  view : "dataview", xCount : 4, type : { height : 100 }, width : 640,
  height : 250,
    borderless : false, css : { margin : "10px" }, select : true,
    multiselect : true,
    template : "<div class=\"webix_strong\" style=\"background-color:#ffeaea;\">" +
            "#title#</div> Year: #year#<br>System: #system#",
    data : [
      {  title : "Pitfall", year : 1982, system : "Atari 2600" },
      {  title : "Pick Axe Pete", year : 1982, system : "Odyssey2" },
      {  title : "Ladybug", year : 1981, system : "Colecovision" },
      {  title : "Altered Beast", year : 1988, system : "Sega Genesis" },
      {  title : "Halo", year : 2001, system : "Xbox" },
      {  title : "Crash Bandicoot", year : 1996, system : "Playstation" },
      {  title : "Guitar Hero", year : 2005, system : "Playstation 2" }
    ]
});
```

Well, I'm kind of fibbing here, aren't I? As you might guess, the xCount config attribute does in a sense define columns to the extent that it tells the dataview how many items across you want to display. However, still, it's not defining columns per se, so I'll stick with what I said! Note that there is also a yCount option available that of course does the same for the vertical direction.

As alluded to earlier, the template attribute defines the HTML that will be generated for each data item. Note that there are some built-in classes that Webix provides, such as webix_strong that I've used here, though it's entirely optional whether you use them or not; you can, of course, create your own.

A dataview allows the user to select items if you set select to true and even allows them to select multiple items by holding select while they click when multiselect is set to true. You can even handle these clicks if you like by specifying a function to call for the onClick or onDblClick config options (the latter if you want to handle double-clicks).

The `dataview` component provides a number of interesting methods. One is `showItem()`, which will scroll the `dataview` to make a given item visible. You can move items around using `move()`, `moveBottom()`, `moveTop()`, and `moveSelection()`, which allows you to move an item in any direction. Of course, you have `getSelected()` to find out what's selected, and even `isSelected()` if you just want to tell whether an item is selected or not. Finally, `exists()` can be used to tell if an item in the `dataview` is selected based on ID.

As usual, this is just a sampling of the options, events, and methods available for this component; there's a fair bit more that the official Webix documentation lists.

list

The `list` component is a bit of a workhorse in that it's probably the most common component you'll use when developing mobile apps, especially to display a list of data items. Although it works perfectly fine for nonmobile applications too, it really is designed for mobile devices, especially devices with touch screens (which doesn't *necessarily* mean mobile anymore!). Figure 3-12 shows a basic `list`.

Figure 3-12. A true workhorse component: the list

This example uses some data that the Webix examples that you'll find on the Webix documentation site uses (which is why you can't yell at me for the typo on line 10 there; I didn't create the data!) and displays it in a simple list. I haven't shown all the data because it's rather large, but it's not all that important for this example frankly, the code for which is shown in Listing 3-7.

Listing 3-7. The List Example Code

```
webix.ui({
  rows : [
    { height : 10 },
    { cols : [
      { width : 10 },
      { view : "pager", id : "moviePager", animate : true, size : 10 },
      { }
    ] },
    { cols : [
      { width : 10 },
        { view : "list", width : 500, height : 360, borderless : false,
          template : "#rank#. #title# (#year#)", select : true,
          multiselect : true,
          scroll : false, pager : "moviePager", data : big_film_set
        },
      { }
    ] },
    { }
  ]
});
```

Skip the pager component for now; I'll circle back around to that in a moment. The list component configuration below that is pretty straightforward. You can supply a width and height like for most components, and the template attribute provides the information the list needs to know how to display each item. The data is of course referenced by the aptly named data attribute, and you can allow or disallow user selection of options by setting the select attribute, and you can further allow multiple selections by holding Control when they click by setting `multiselect` to `true`. In this example, I've also directed the list to not scroll by setting `scroll` to `false`, but by default that's `true` since most of the time you want a list to allow scrolling.

New Concept: Data Paging

Now, let's go back to that `pager` attribute and component, shall we?

For many data components, you can provide a paging mechanism to allow the user to navigate through a large data set. When you provide a value for the `pager` option, this points to a `pager` component that you've defined elsewhere, as I've done here above the list. The `pager` is just another Webix component, of course, (you know this because there's a `view` attribute), and for it, you describe how many items should be in each group by specifying the `size` attribute. So here, you'll see ten movies per group, and the `pager` will then take care of providing buttons for as many groups as there are. In addition to `size` to specify the number of records per page, you can specify how many buttons you want with the `group` option (the default seems to be five). As the user clicks the buttons, they will be renumbered accordingly. (Picture it as a number line, and as the user clicks a button to the right, they are scrolling down the number line, so to speak.)

As I mentioned, you can use a `pager` with many data components, though whether it actually makes sense to do so is something you'll need to decide on a case-by-case basis. It's the object-oriented nature of Webix that allows it to work seamlessly with a variety of components.

grouplist

A `grouplist` component is nothing but a list that...wait for it...allows grouping! Take a look at it in Figure 3-13 to see how this presents itself.

Figure 3-13. *Grouping a list with grouplist*

Being based on the list component means the API for grouplist is very similar, as the code in Listing 3-8 demonstrates. You could, in fact, change the view to list, and it would work (although probably not in as useful a way as you might hope given what the grouplist does for you).

Listing 3-8. The grouplist Example Code

```
webix.ui({
  view : "grouplist", scroll : true, width : 300, height : 100, borderless
  : false,
  css : { margin : "10px" },
  data : [
    { value : "Movies", open : true, data : [
      { value : "Star Trek", open : true, data : [
        { value : "The Motion Picture" },
        { value : "The Wrath of Khan"},
        { value : "The Search for Spock"}
      ]},
      { value : "Star Wars", open : true, data : [
        { value : "A New Hope" },
        { value : "The Empire Strikes Back"},
        { value : "Return of the Jedi"}
      ]}
    ]},
    { value : "Books", open : true, data : [
      { value : "Harry Potter", open : true, data : [
        { value : "The Sorcerer's Stone" },
        { value : "The Chamber of Secrets"},
        { value : "The Prisoner of Azkaban"}
      ]},
      { value : "The Dark Tower", open : true, data : [
        { value : "The Gunslinger" },
        { value : "The Drawing of the Three"},
```

```
        { value : "The Waste Lands"}
      ]}
    ]}
  ]
});
```

This provides for grouping the data *and navigating through it* based on the hierarchy of the data. Starting with the top-level items in the list, Movies and Books in this example, these form the first groups you see. Then, as the user clicks one of them, the user in effect drills down into the data, navigating through the subgroups. This example shows that I've drilled down into movies, and I'm now at the second-level grouping showing *Star Trek* and *Star Wars*, the next level of data under Movies. If I were to click either of those, then, of course, I'd see the movies below them, three in each group. The component also draws group headers above the data that can be clicked to go back up the hierarchy tree.

Virtually all of the config options available for `list` are available for `grouplist`, and the same is true of its methods and events. The group headers can be specified with the `templateGroup` attribute (this is a template string like you've seen elsewhere), and the same is true for the group headings that signify going back up the data tree by using the `templateBack` attribute.

New Concept: Filtering

The `grouplist`, as well as most other data-oriented components, allows you to call its `filter()` method to filter the data presented. For example, assuming you catch the reference returned by `webix.ui()` in the variable `grpList`, you could do the following:

```
grpList.filter("#value#", "Books");
```

This would, of course, result in only the data from the Books branch of data being shown. As I said, this isn't unique to the `grouplist` component; almost any that uses data can have `filter()` called on it. You simply pass it the field from the data records to filter on as the first argument and the value to allow as the second, and you're good to go.

unitlist

The `unitlist` component is essentially a `list` where the items are grouped based on some function that you specify. Figure 3-14 shows what this looks like.

Figure 3-14. *Those who work with The Doctor, the UNITlist*

As you can tell, I've grouped these songs by the first letter of their title. What does the code for this look like? Listing 3-9 is your answer!

Listing 3-9. The unitlist Example Code

```
webix.ui({
  view : "unitlist", width : 300, height : 280, type : { height : 30 },
  template : "#title#",
  borderless : false, css : { margin : "10px" },
  uniteBy : function(inObj) {
    return inObj.title.substr(0,1);
  },
  data : [
    { id : 1, title : "Images and Words (Dream Theater)" },
    { id : 2, title : "Dark Side of the Moon (Pink Floyd)" },
    { id : 3, title : "Jagged Little Pill (Alanis Morrissette)" },
    { id : 4, title : "Ten (Pearl Jam)" },
    { id : 5, title : "The Stranger (Billy Joel)" },
    { id : 6, title : "Thriller (Michael Jackson)" },
    { id : 7, title : "21 (Adele)" }
  ]
});
```

As you can see, this looks an awful lot like code for a `list` but with the addition of the `uniteBy` config option. This function takes in each object and returns a value that is used for grouping. In other words, every time this function is called, once for each data record, some value is returned. All the similar values are grouped together (after the data has been sorted). You could return anything here, maybe a rating for each song, for example, or whatever makes sense for your data.

Although the API of `unitlist` looks a lot like `list` since it's based on `list`, there are some differences. For one, you can get an array of the groups by calling the `getUnits()` method. You can also call `getUnitList()`, passing it the name of one of the groups, to get an array of record IDs for that group. For example, calling `getUnitList("T")` on the example returns [`4, 5, 6`].

property

The `property` widget is used to build what is usually referred to as a *property sheet*, which is a display of two columns where the first column is the name of a property and the right is its value, usually editable in some way. This is typically seen in IDEs to describe the properties of an object. In Figure 3-15, the objects are baseball players.

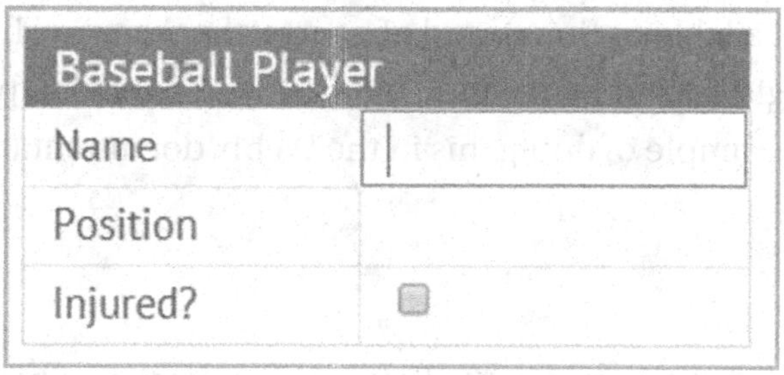

Figure 3-15. *Hey you kids, get off my property!*

In the first column, you have some properties of baseball players: their name, position, and whether they are currently injured. The `Name` property is a text field as you can see, and the injury status is a Boolean, so a check box makes sense there. What you can't see is that if you click into the Position box, you'll get a drop-down list of positions. Listing 3-10 shows the code behind this example.

Listing 3-10. The Property Sheet Example Code

```
webix.ui({
  view : "property", width : 260, height : 112, nameWidth : 120, borderless
  : false,
  css : { margin : "10px" },
  elements : [
    { label : "Baseball Player", type : "label"},
    { label : "Name", type : "text" },
    { label : "Position", type : "select",
      options : ["1B", "2B", "3B", "LF", "CF", "RF", "SS", "C", "P" ]
    },
    { label : "Injured?", type : "checkbox" }
  ]
});
```

Each field displayed in a property sheet takes a type, which must be one of the following: color (a colorboard used to select a color), text (a plain old text editor), password (a masked text field), select (like an HTML <select> control), combo (like select, but also editable like a text field), richselect (like a select but allowing for richer display of the available options), and of course checkbox as shown in the example. It's also possible to register your own editor, but then you'll need to provide the code for that (you can find an example of doing this in the Webix documentation).

tree

Like the grouplist, the tree component allows for the display of hierarchical data, but this time as a series of nodes where each can be expanded or collapsed by the user. You've no doubt seen plenty of trees in many different applications, but if not, Figure 3-16 shows one.

Figure 3-16. *Swaying in the wind: an example tree component*

A tree starts with a root node, Songs here, and then below it are branches for bands or artists and then the songs for each. The plus/minus symbols next to each branch allow it to be expanded or collapsed so the user can drill down into the data. Being essentially just a grouplist in a different form, the code for a tree is quite a lot like the grouplist, as Listing 3-11 shows.

Listing 3-11. The Tree Example Code

```
webix.ui({
  view : "tree", select : true, borderless : false,
  css : { margin : "10px" }, width : 240, height : 200,
  data : [
    { value : "Songs", open : true,
      data : [
        { open : true, value : "Metallica",
          data : [
            { value : "Enter Sandman" },
            { value : "Ride the Lightning" },
            { value : "Hero of the Day" }
          ]
        },
        { value : "Billy Joel",
```

```
        data : [
          { value : "Movin' Out" },
          { value : "Piano Man" }
        ]
      }
    ]
  }
]
});
```

The data here is just like `grouplist` in that each node can have a data element that contains further nodes. This time, you can specify an `open` attribute to tell Webix if the node should be opened (expanded) or not when initially shown.

A `tree` can be filtered by calling its `filter()` method, and they can be sorted by calling the `sort()` method, to which you supply a callback to make the comparison between each set of nodes passed into it (or use the default sort provided).

New Concept: Extending Webix Components

The tree widget also has the capability to allow editing. However, this isn't built in. To do this, you need to extend the tree component. For this, Webix provides the `webix.protoUI()` method. This merges several objects together and creates a new one. To create an editable tree, you can do the following:

```
webix.protoUI({ name : "edittree" }, webix.EditAbility, webix.ui.tree);
```

The first argument is the destination object. Here, you want to create a new component, and components have a `name` property, so you define that. The arguments after that are the objects you want to merge into the destination. Here, you, of course, want to start with the basic tree component, and into it, you want to merge the `webix.EditAbility` object. This is an object that Webix supplies that implements common edit interactions. The result of doing this is that Webix will now know what an `edittree` component is, which means you can alter the example code to specify `view:"edittree"` now. However, that won't be enough: you also have to tell Webix that this tree is editable. Fortunately, that's easy. Simply add the following to the tree's definition:

```
editable : true, editor : "text", editValue : "value",
```

Once that's done, you'll find that a single click of any item in the tree allows you to edit it. This sort of component extension is a great capability to have at your disposal because it means that even when Webix doesn't exactly meet your needs, there is a mechanism at the ready that allows you to extend it to do so.

treetable

The treetable component is an extended tree widget and is a bit of a hybrid in that it combines a datatable with a tree, as you can see in Figure 3-17.

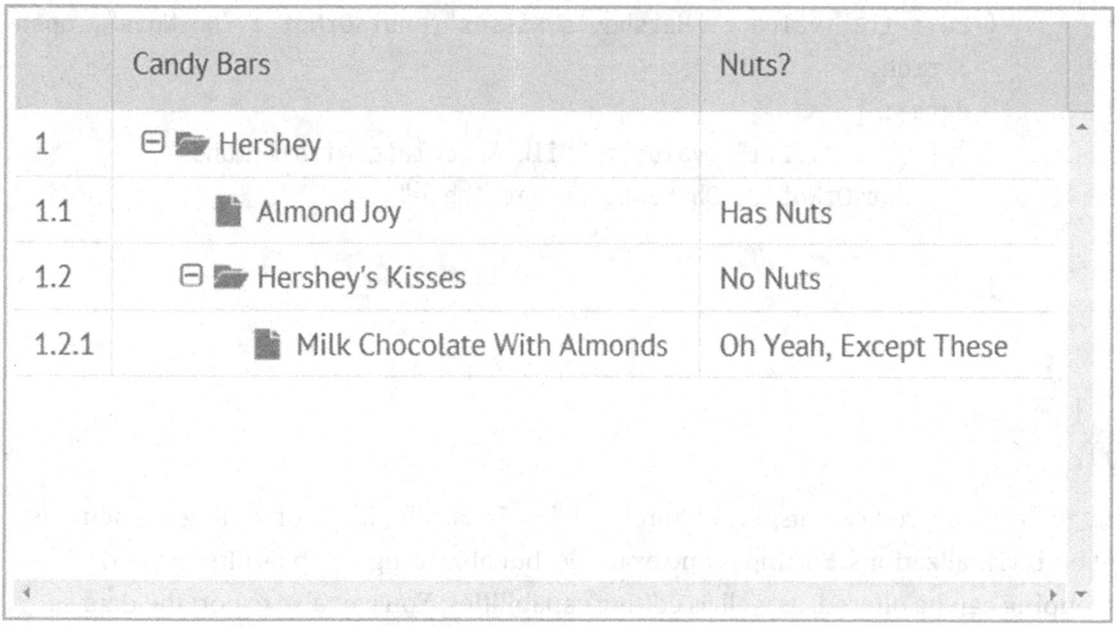

	Candy Bars	Nuts?
1	⊟ 📂 Hershey	
1.1	📄 Almond Joy	Has Nuts
1.2	⊟ 📂 Hershey's Kisses	No Nuts
1.2.1	📄 Milk Chocolate With Almonds	Oh Yeah, Except These

Figure 3-17. *What trees get turned into: the treetable*

One of the advantages of this combination is that things such as column sorting can then be provided just by setting a config option, as Listing 3-12 demonstrates.

Listing 3-12. The treetable Example Code

```
webix.ui({
  view : "treetable", width : 550, height : 300, borderless : true, css : {
  margin : "10px" },
  columns : [
```

```
  { id : "id", header : "", width : 50, sort : "string" },
  { id : "value", header : "Candy Bars", width : 300,
    template : "{common.treetable()} #value#", sort : "string"
  },
  { id : "nutsOrNot", header : "Nuts?", width : 180, sort : "string" }
],
data : [
  { id : "1", value : "Hershey", open : true,
    data : [
      { id : 1.1, value : "Almond Joy", nutsOrNot : "Has Nuts" },
      { id : 1.2, value : "Hershey's Kisses", nutsOrNot : "No Nuts", open
        : true,
      data : [
        { id : "1.2.1", value : "Milk Chocolate With Almonds",
          nutsOrNot : "Oh Yeah, Except These" }
      ]
    }
  ]
}
]
});
```

In this way, you can display hierarchical data in tabular form, providing the benefits of both visualizations. Sorting is one example, but also things such as filtering and grouping can be offered, as well as editing capabilities. You can also export the data as you can with a datatable.

Given that this is essentially just two components combined, the API for treetable is likewise basically just a combination of the tree and datatable APIs. With no exceptions that I can identify, you can do everything you can with each individual component. It's just a question of how it's visualized that makes this a unique component.

Before moving on, let's talk a little about the value of template there. With a tree or by extension treetable, you can present almost any kind of content on each node. It doesn't have to be just text, and if it is text, you can define it however you want. But, by default, each node will show an icon for expanding/collapsing the node, a folder or file icon depending on whether it has children, and some text string (the data value from the data source). The default template value is therefore "{common.icon()} {common.

folder()}<span>#value#<span>". You can, of course, change this however you like, and further, you are allowed to reuse those {common.xxx()} tokens to get values that Webix provides. In this example, I've used {common.treetable()}, which is specific to the treetable component and is essentially a combination of {common.icon()} and {common.folder()}. There is also {common.checkbox()} to render a checkbox for the node. The Webix documentation has more information on defining node templates, and there's quite a bit of flexibility there, but this gives you the basics.

treemap

There is one other hybridized form of the tree component, and that's treemap, but this one is only available with a Webix Pro license. Figure 3-18 shows what this looks like. Fair warning: it *doesn't* look much like a tree at all!

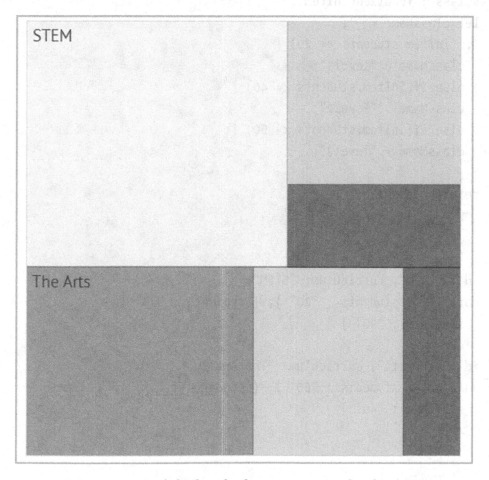

Figure 3-18. *A tree that won't be lost for long: an example of a treemap*

I have to be honest and say that I had never heard of a `treemap` before I began using Webix! The attraction of it, as stated in the Webix documentation, is that it's a way to display hierarchical data in a compact way. It also shows the relative size of a number of data sets in an interesting way. Let's take a look at the code for this thing; see Listing 3-13.

Listing 3-13. The treemap Example Code

```
webix.ui({
  view : "treemap", template : function(inItem)
  { return inItem.curriculum || ""; },
  value : "#students#", width : 400, height : 400, borderless : false,
  css : { margin : "10px" },
  type : {
    cssClass : function(inItem){
      let className = "";
      if (inItem.students <= 20) {
        className = "level1";
      } else if(inItem.students <= 40) {
        className = "level2";
      } else if(inItem.students <= 60) {
        className = "level3";
      }
      return className;
    }
  },
  data: [
    { id : "stem", curriculum: "STEM",
      data : [ { students : "20" }, { students : "40" },
      { students : "90" } ]
    },
    { id : "theArts", curriculum: "The Arts",
      data : [ { students : "60" }, { students : "15" },
      { students : "40" } ]
    }
  ]
});
```

This example shows the number of students in a series of (unnamed) school classes, where each class is part of a specific curriculum, either STEM (Science, Technology, Engineering, and Math) or The Arts (that's how it's a hierarchy: curriculum ➤ class ➤ number of students). The color of each block, one per class, will change based on the number of students in the class. The CSS classes referenced, level1, level2, and level3, are simply the following:

```
.level1 { background-color : #ff0000; }
.level2 { background-color : #00ff00; }
.level3 { background-color : #a0a0ff; }
```

You'll notice that the type attribute, which defines how each data record should be presented, specifies a cssClass attribute. This is a function that performs the logic to determine which CSS class to apply. This ability to use a function to choose a CSS class to apply dynamically is something that many Webix components provide, so it's good to see in action here.

The other key thing is the template attribute, which as usual informs Webix what data item to use for each record and how to display it. Here, it's simply the value of the students property. However, here's something else new: the value of template is a function. Webix will call this function for every record, and it will return either the curriculum value to display or an empty string. This way, only the block for the curriculum as a whole will have any text in them. The individual classes will not (because the objects in the data for them don't have a curriculum property).

One interesting config option is subRender. By default, this is true, which means that the subitems of the top-level records will be rendered. Here, that means whether the classes will have blocks rendered or not. If you set this to false, then you'll wind up with just two blocks rendered, one for each curriculum, with the STEM block being a little bigger than the block for The Arts because the total number of students is greater in STEM by a little bit.

Assuming your data records have IDs, you can call showBranch(), passing it an ID, to display just the records from a particular branch. For example, calling showBranch("theArts") on this example treemap instance will show you just the three blocks under The Arts.

gage

A gage is a component that is available only with a Webix Pro license and that allows for visualizing data in a format similar to the speedometer in your car. In fact, the example of this shown in Figure 3-19 is this very thing, from the perspective of the police!

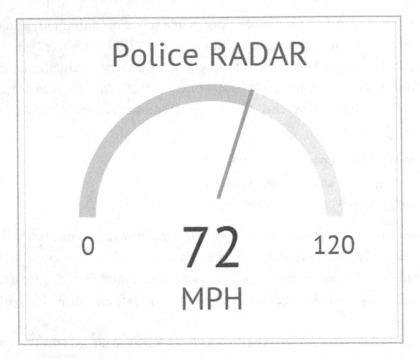

Figure 3-19. *A gage component*

The thing you can't see from a screenshot is that when the gage is initially loaded, the value animates. In other words, the pointer line starts at 0 and, like a speedometer, moves up to 72, while the color of the line changes from green to yellow. The code for a gage is straightforward, as Listing 3-14 demonstrates.

Listing 3-14. The Code for a Gage

```
webix.ui({
  view : "gage", width : 400, height : 340, borderless : false, css :
  { margin : "10px" },
  value : 72, minRange : 0, maxRange : 120, label : "Police RADAR",
  placeholder : "MPH",
  animation : true, stroke : 6
});
```

You can see that the animation can be enabled or disabled by setting the Boolean animation config option. The width of the line, the stroke of it, can be controlled as well. You can set minRange and maxRange to define the range of values visualized, and you can put a `label` above the gage and a `placeholder`, which is essentially a secondary label, below it. This component also offers basic methods such as `setValue()` to dynamically control the displayed value, as well as all the basics such as `enable()`, `disable()`, `hide()`, and `show()`.

Note   Just to save a little typing, I'll tell you here that for most of these examples you'll see the `borderless` option set to `false` and the `css` option specifying a margin of 10. This is done just so that when I show you individual components in a screenshot, they have a clear border and are also moved down and to the right from the upper-left corner of the page. It really is just to make the screenshots better! But, I think it's good to see because `borderless` is an option all components have, and knowing how to adjust basic CSS properties via the `css` attribute is good basic knowledge that you can also apply to all components as necessary.

---

bullet

The `bullet` component, another Pro-only widget, is based on the `gage` component and is, in fact, the same thing but displayed differently and with a few more features. Figure 3-20 shows a `bullet` in action.

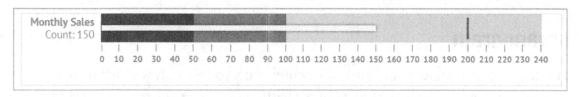

Figure 3-20. *A bullet! Take cover!*

If you picture the `bullet` bent in an upside-down U shape, you can begin to see how it's similar to a `gage`. However, the `bullet` component allows you the flexibility to define bands of color to give meaning to ranges of values, as well as to place a marker bar if you want. The code for all of this is not much more complex than that of the `gage`, as Listing 3-15 shows.

Listing 3-15. The Code for a bullet

```
webix.ui({ view : "bullet", minRange : 0, maxRange : 240, value : 150,
color : "#ffff00",
  label : "Monthly Sales", placeholder : "Count: #value#", marker : 200,
  borderless : false, css : { margin : "10px" }, width : 800, height : 100,
  bands : [
    { value : 240, color : "#00ff00"},
    { value : 100, color : "#ff0000"},
    { value : 50, color : "#0000ff"}
  ]
});
```

Since the bullet is based on the gage, the API for it is similar, so things such as minRange, maxRange, value, label, and placeholder are the same (although label and placeholder are now found on the left side). The marker option allows you to place a black line at a given value, perhaps to indicate a target that sales are supposed to reach in this example. The bands attribute allows you to define ranges of values and demarcate them with a specific color. The bands are listed in reverse order, and the value attribute defines the highest value the range covers, so the low value of the range is effectively the band defined below it (except for the final one, which assumes a lower range value of 0).

The methods available are the same as those for the gage, as are the remainder of the config options available.

organogram

The organogram component is one of the components you get only with a Pro Webix license and is used to generate hierarchical charts, most frequently seen in org charts for companies. Figure 3-21 shows what this looks like.

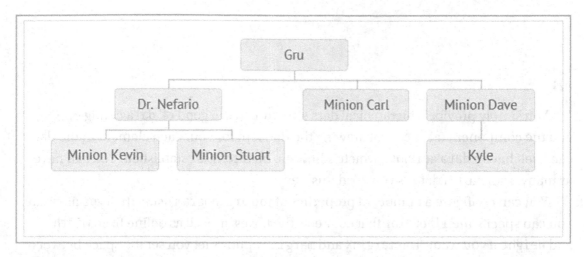

Figure 3-21. *Showing some organization with an organogram*

You might imagine that generating such a thing requires some complex coding, but in fact, it's as easy as any other Webix data widget, as Listing 3-16 demonstrates.

Listing 3-16. The organogram Example Code

```
new webix.ui({
  view : "organogram", borderless : false, css : { margin : "10px" },
  width : 600, height : 240,
  data : [
    { value : "Gru",
      data : [
        { value : "Dr. Nefario",
          data : [
            { value : "Minion Kevin", data : [] },
            { value : "Minion Stuart", data : [] }
          ]
        },
        { value : "Minion Carl", data : [] },
        { value : "Minion Dave",
          data : [
            { value : "Kyle", data : [] }
          ]
        }
```

```
        ]
    }
  ]
});
```

You simply provide a hierarchical data structure in the good ol' `data` config option, and the component takes care of drawing the diagram for you. Each element in the data can itself have a `data` attribute, which is how the hierarchy is established. You can have as many branches of data as you need this way.

You can configure a number of properties of the `organogram` using the `type` attribute. You can specify the `lineColor` that connects the boxes, as well as define fixed `width` and `height` if you want. The `marginX` and `marginY` options let you set the space between two items. Of course, `template` is how you specify what each item looks like if you want something other than just the `value` attribute of your data to be displayed.

You can get the ID of specific items based on relationships using the `getParentId()`, `getNextSiblingId()`, `getPrevSiblingId()`, and `getNextId()` methods (which allow you to get an item a specified number of steps from another item).

rangechart

The `rangechart`, another Pro-only component, is based on the `chart` component that you've already seen, but now with the added ability to view large sets of data based on frame limits. Figure 3-22 shows what this can look like.

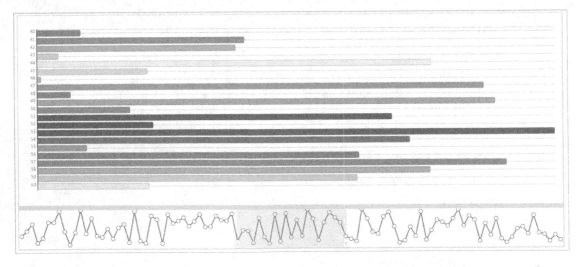

Figure 3-22. *Not Strider the ranger, or even ranger actually, but code for a rangechart*

To be precise, it's the bottom line chart that is the rangechart. What's above it is a plain old bar chart. However, a rangechart is frequently paired with another type of chart, and changing the range in the rangechart (by dragging that shaded section left or right or expanding or shrinking it by dragging its edges) will reflect in the paired chart. That's what this example does if you load it in your browser and play with it a bit, and that's why I said this is what it *can* look like. Actually, tying them together isn't hard, as Listing 3-17 shows.

Listing 3-17. The rangechart Example Code

```
let salesData = [];
for (let i = 0; i <= 100; i++) {
  salesData.push({ days : i, sales : Math.round(Math.random() * 3000) });
}

webix.ui({
  type : "wide", width : 1400, height : 600, borderless : false,
  css : { margin : "10px", border : "2px solid #00ff00" },
  rows : [
    { view : "chart", type : "barH", id : "myChart",
      value : "#sales#", yAxis : { template : "#days#" }
    },
    { view : "rangechart", height : 100, type : "line", value : "#sales#",
      padding : 0,
      frameId : "days", item : { radius : 4 }, data : salesData,
      range : { start : 40, end : 60 },
      line : { color : "#ff0000" },
      on : {
        onAfterRangeChange : function() {
          let mc = $$("myChart");
          mc.clearAll();
          mc.parse(this.getFrameData());
        }
      }
    }
  ]
});
```

First, some random sales data is generated. This is just the number of sales on each of the last 100 days. Next, you build a `chart`, which holds no surprises given your previous look at that widget.

The `rangechart` comes next, and here you have some configuring to do! Aside from the basics such as `view` and `height`, first you have to tell it what kind of chart to draw, a `line` chart in this case. Next, you tell it the name of the attribute in your data that defines your frame by specifying the `frameId` option, and I'm using days in this case. After that, you tell it the initial values for the range, 40 and 60 in this case, by specifying an object as the value of the `range` attribute that has two properties: `start` and `end`. You can do some styling-type stuff too if you like, such as defining the `radius` of the circles that are the data points in the `rangechart`, as well as tell the rangechart what color to make the `line`.

The next bit that's important is what to do when the range is adjusted. For that, you use the `on` attribute, which is generic to all components and allows you to define event handlers. Here, you want to handle the `onAfterRangeChange` event. When this event fires, what you do is get a reference to the plain `chart` and clear it by calling its `clearAll()` method. Then, you take the data that is now encapsulated in the new range, which you get via a call to `getFrameData()`, and pass it to the `parse()` method of the `chart`. That method is also one you'll see on many data-aware components and causes the component to parse the passed-in data and use it as its new data to display.

As I said, tying a `rangechart` to another type of chart is typical but by no means required. What you do in response to the `onAfterRangeChange` event is up to you. Maybe you'll just pass the data to a server or perhaps serialize it to JSON and copy it to the clipboard. Whatever your needs are, `rangechart` can address it if you need to deal with data ranges like this.

Summary

Whew, this was a biggie as far as chapters go! In this chapter, you learned about many more Webix facilities including forms, data entry controls, data handling, and data-aware components. You also saw a bit more of the general Webix API with which you work with the various components that comprise a Webix-built UI.

In the next chapter, I'll complete the overview of Webix and the key concepts you need to be successful building Webix applications.

Webix: The Final Frontier

In the previous two chapters, you saw a great deal of components and concepts that are keys to success with Webix. In this chapter, I'll introduce a few more concepts, and I'll complete the overview of the components Webix offers, including those that are "premium," meaning those you must pay for separately from Webix.

Note that for many of the examples shown in this chapter, they will need to be run from a web server of some sort. For example, the `excelviewer` and `pdfviewer` examples load data from a specified URL, which typically won't work if you simply load the examples in your browser off the local file system (although there are usually browser settings that allow you to do so). Whether you put them on a web server or want to mess with browser settings, this is left as an exercise for you.

Context Components

Let's begin with some more components, shall we?

context and contextmenu

`<sarcasm>`In an effort to be as confusing as possible, there is a context `context` component.`</sarcasm>` There is also a `contextmenu` component, and they are different despite their similar names (but in some ways, they are pretty similar too, which is why I've grouped them together). Check out Listing 4-1. (Note that unlike most of the examples, this one requires seeing the whole HTML document to understand what's going on—to get the *context*, you might say!)

© Frank Zammetti 2018
F. Zammetti, *Practical Webix*, https://doi.org/10.1007/978-1-4842-3384-9_4

Listing 4-1. The context and contextmenu Widgets

```
<!DOCTYPE html>

<html>

  <head>

    <title>context</title>

    <link rel="stylesheet" type="text/css" href="../webix/codebase/webix.css">
    <script type="text/javascript" src="../webix/codebase/webix_debug.js">
    </script>

    <script>

      webix.ready(function() {

        webix.ui({
          view : "context", master : "div1", width : 250, height : 150,
          body : { template : "Exterminate the Doctor! Exterminate!
          Exterminate!" }
        });

        webix.ui({
          view : "contextmenu", master : "div2",
          data : [
            { value : "Send To...", submenu : [ "Clara", "Billie", "Rose" ] },
            { value : "Add Companion" }
          ]
        });

      });

    </script>

  </head>

  <body>
    <div id="div1" style=" background-color:#ff0000;width:200px;
    height:200px;"></div>
    <br>
```

```
    <div id="div2" style=" background-color:#00ff00;width:200px;
    height:200px;"></div>
  </body>
</html>
```

You can see the difference between the two in Figure 4-1. Basically, the `context` component is a pop-up window triggered from the mouse right-click event into which you can put any arbitrary content you like. This is useful for things such as context-sensitive help for a control.

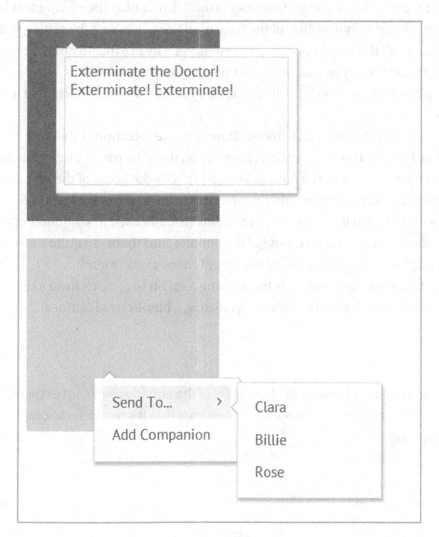

Figure 4-1. *The context and contextmenu widgets*

Notice the `master` attribute supplied when creating either the `context` or the `contextmenu`? This tells Webix what element should be the source of the right-click. In other words, you don't want the user to right-click anywhere on the page and trigger either of these; you want a right-click on `div1` to show the context, and you want a right-click on `div2` to show the `contextmenu`. That's where the `master` attribute comes into play.

As mentioned, the `contextmenu` component allows you to create nested lists of options if you want, which you do with the `submenu` option, and you can have submenus inside submenus inside submenus, as deeply as you need. (Keep in mind that too deep a hierarchy won't be especially usable for your users, so a little discipline goes a long way.)

You can make either of these components *modal*, meaning the component blocks the user from doing anything else on the page until they dismiss it, by setting `modal` to `true`. Of course, all the usual options are present, such as `width` and `height` to set the size and `left` and `top` if you want to force a position when shown. You can also have a header on by specifying the `head` attribute, and you can adjust the height of it with `headHeight`.

For the `contextmenu` widget, you can allow multiple selections by setting `multiselect` to `true`. If you set `navigation` to `true`, then the menu can be navigated with the keyboard as well as the mouse. You can specify the items of the menu with the `data` attribute as you've seen for other components, and you can set `scroll` to `true` to make the menu scroll if there are too many items (usually used in conjunction with the `height` attribute). These are just some of the options, and there are quite a few more, especially for the `contextmenu`, so the documentation is your friend!

The `contextmenu`, by contrast, is for showing a menu of options from a right-click. You can nest options as deeply as you like, creating a hierarchy of options.

menu

The `menu` component is actually the base class of the already seen `contextmenu` component, but its typical usage is different enough that it's worth seeing separately. Check out Listing 4-2.

Listing 4-2. The menu Widget

```
webix.ui({
  view : "menu", type : { subsign : true },
  data : [
    {value : "Man Tactical", submenu : [ "Worf", "Data", "Riker" ] },
    {value : "Fire Phasers" },
    {value : "Fire Torpedoes" }
  ]
});

webix.ui({ height : 20 });

webix.ui({
  view : "menu", layout : "y", width : 180, height : 300,
  select : true, type : { subsign : true },
  data : [
    {value : "Man Tactical", submenu : [ "Worf", "Data", "Riker" ] },
    {value : "Fire Phasers" },
    {value : "Fire Torpedoes" }
  ]
});
```

I've shown the code for the two forms the menu can take, horizontal and vertical, and Figure 4-2 shows both. By default, you'll get a horizontal layout, but the layout:"y" attribute changes that and provides the vertical layout (which most times will probably mean you'll also want to specify a size for your menu with width and height, but neither is required).

Figure 4-2. *The menu widget*

A menu is for allowing the user to select options; sometimes that will mean choosing from a single list, and other times it might mean you need to nest items. You can do both easy enough with submenu, when nesting is necessary, just as you saw with contextmenu.

The type attribute allows you to configure your menu a little more. In this case, the subsign:true option is responsible for showing the down or right arrow, depending on menu orientation, to indicate when there are submenu items to select.

Some other interesting options include the submenuConfig option, which takes an object as a value and allows you to define some characteristics of your submenus, including their width, a template to use to display them, and event handlers for the items in the submenu. There are also some neat methods, including move(), moveBottom(), moveTop(), moveUp(), and moveDown(), each of which lets you move a specified menu item around on the fly.

Note that when you specify a submenu, Webix will create an actual submenu component behind the scenes. This is another of those things that you don't usually have to know, but if you need do something with a submenu specifically, then it's good to know so you'll be able to find what you need in the documentation.

New Concept: Clipboard Support

Another interesting option is clipboard, which when true allows you to copy a selected menu item to the system clipboard. This is available on most data-aware components. The datatable, tree, and list components have it by default, but for others you'll need to extend the component to include the webix.CopyPaste mixin—but I'm getting ahead of things because extending components is something I'll talk about in the next chapter. For now, let's stick with this clipboard stuff!

When clipboard support is enabled via the clipboard option, you can optionally also provide a templateCopy attribute. This is a template that will be used to render the text copied to the clipboard. In this way, you can have a different format for your items when copied as when displayed on the screen. There is not an associated templatePaste option as you might guess; however, you can achieve the same basic thing by handling the onPaste event. The function that you write is called in response to this event and is sent the text from the clipboard as its argument, which you can then manipulate in any way you want and insert into the data of the component as needed.

If you want to see this in action, simply take the code in Listing 4-2 and add the following to the second menu configuration:

```
clipboard : true,
templateCopy : "You copied: #value#",
onPaste : function(inText) {
  this.data.push({ value : inText });
}
```

After doing that, you'll find that you can copy the items in the second menu, and what you'll get on the clipboard is a string in the form "You copied: XXX" where XXX is "Man Tactical," "Fire Phasers," "Fire Torpedoes," and so on. You'll also be able to select an item and paste in some text on the clipboard. (The text will actually replace the item you have selected, but that's just a result of whatever is written in the onPaste handler function, which could be anything you want.)

popup

The popup component is generally intended to show small pieces of temporary information that the user doesn't usually have to react to. They aren't usually intended to steal the user's focus, just to present some information quickly that may be helpful to them. They're simple components, as you can see in Listing 4-3.

Listing 4-3. The popup Widget

```
webix.ui({
  view : "popup", width : 375, height : 75, position : "center",
  body : { template : "I am the very model of a modern Major-General" }
}).show();
```

They're just as simple when rendered on the screen, as Figure 4-3 shows.

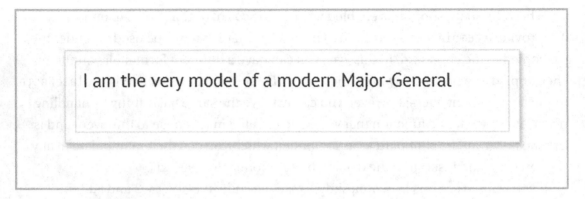

Figure 4-3. *The popup widget*

You can size them using `width` and `height`, along with `minWidth`, `minHeight`, `maxWidth`, and `maxHeight` if you are displaying dynamic content and want to ensure it never grows too big or gets too small. The `position` attribute allows you to place the pop-up either `center` on the screen or down from the `top`, horizontally centered. You can make a popup `modal` if you like, but that kind of defeats the usual intent. When the `move` attribute is set to `true`, then the user can drag the pop-up around, which can be handy if this is information they might need to fill out a form, for example.

As far as methods go, you can hide and show (with `hide()` and `show()`, of course) a pop-up like you can virtually any Webix component, and you can dynamically set the position (with `setPosition()`) if you want.

sidemenu

The `sidemenu` component is how you can easily implement a function tray in an application, which you've certainly seen before. It's the menu that slides in, usually from the left, when you click a menu button, containing a list of functions you can access. The code for this component in Listing 4-4 gives you one or two new things to look at.

Listing 4-4. The sidemenu and submenu Widgets

```
let sideMenu = webix.ui({
  view : "sidemenu", width : 200, position : "left",
  body : {
    view : "list", borderless : true, scroll : false,
    template : "<span class='webix_icon fa-#icon#'></span> #value#",
    data : [
      { value : "New", icon : "file" },
      { value : "Open", icon : "folder-open" },
      { value : "Close", icon : "window-close" }
    ]
  }
});

webix.ui({
  rows : [
    { cols : [
      { },
      { view : "button", type : "iconButton", width : 36, height : 50,
      icon : "bars",
        click : function() {
          sideMenu.isVisible() ? sideMenu.hide() : sideMenu.show();
        }
      }
    ] },
    { }
  ]
});
```

When you click the menu icon, you get what you see in Figure 4-4, after the sidemenu has slid smoothly in from the left.

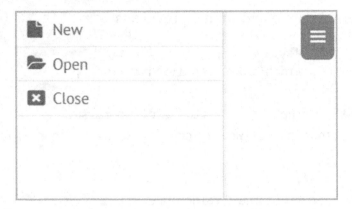

Figure 4-4. *The sidemenu and submenu widgets*

First, you build the `sidemenu` itself. The `position` attribute tells Webix where you want the menu to slide in from (you can also do `top`, `bottom`, or `right`). When sliding it from `left` or `right`, it usually makes sense to define a `width`, so I have here. The `body` of the `sidemenu` can be anything you want, which could be statically defined rows, buttons, or any combination you want. (It's just a view, in other words, a simple layout, so you can do all the usual Webix things with that.) However, a typical pattern is to use a `list` component, which I won't go into too much detail here as I'll cover it later, but I'll give you a little taste.

A `list` lets you use `data` to define the items you want to display, which is a nice way to do it in case you need to define the items dynamically. This again uses the data replacement tokens you saw earlier. In addition, the `borderless` attribute hides the border that is normally placed around the `list`, which makes the `sidemenu` look cleaner I think. The `scroll` attribute ensures that you will get scrollbars if there are too many items (which of course means you must make sure there never are too many items!).

Next, you create a layout and put the triggering button in it. Note that the `sidemenu` isn't part of this layout, which makes sense. It's going to slide in from off-screen, so it shouldn't be part of the layout. The layout that's created uses a spacer to push the button all the way to the right side of the page. If it was on the left, then it would be covered by the `sidemenu`, which means you couldn't close the `sidemenu`. Putting it on the right avoids that.

However, you do have to do some extra work to get the open/close toggling you want on that button since Webix doesn't offer that out of the box, and that's where the `click` handler comes in. As you can see, it's a simple toggle: call `hide()` on the `sidemenu` when it's visible, as reported by its `isVisible()` method, or call `show()` when it's not visible.

Most of the config options that you should be starting to be familiar with are available on a `sidemenu`. `width`, `height`, `minWidth`, `maxWidth`, `minHeight`, `maxHeight`, `modal`, and `left` all work as previously discussed. Similarly, the common methods such as `enable()`, `disable()`, `show()`, `hide()`, and `setPosition()` are available.

tooltip

A `tooltip` is nothing but some static text rendered into an absolutely positioned container. In general, you don't need to create tooltips yourself as many Webix components create them automatically as part of their normal functioning (usually as an option you can specify). However, you can create them yourself for any purpose you want, and it's easy to do, as Listing 4-5 shows.

Listing 4-5. The tooltip Widget

```
webix.ui({
  view : "tooltip", template : "Hello! I am a tooltip that says: '#value#'"
}).show({ value : "Webix rocks!"}, { x : 25, y : 25 });
```

The result is frankly kind of unremarkable, but it serves the purpose fine, as Figure 4-5 shows.

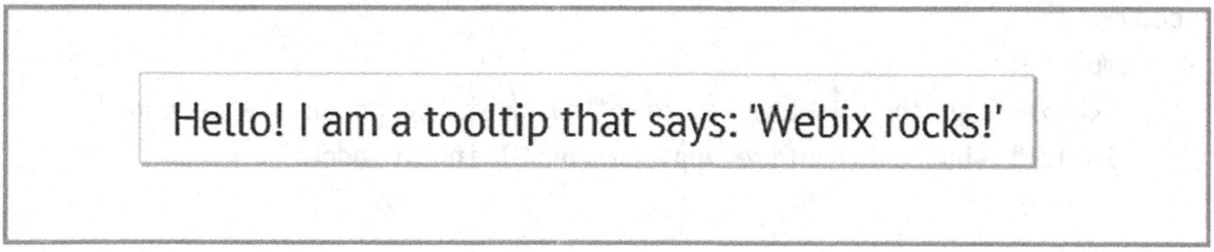

Hello! I am a tooltip that says: 'Webix rocks!'

Figure 4-5. *The tooltip widget*

You can supply static text when the tooltip is created, or you can use the same sort of data insertion that you've used elsewhere, whatever suits your needs. When you call the `show()` method, you can pass in the data to use and let the `tooltip` replace the tokens in the `template` with it. You also specify the x and y locations to show the tooltip at, and you're basically done.

If, instead, you'd like the `tooltip` to appear near the user's cursor, which is typical, you can specify the `dx` and `dy` attributes instead.

There really isn't much more to a `tooltip` than that for most use cases.

window

The final context component to look at is the window component, and in many ways, it's like the popup and even tooltip components to a certain degree, but it's generally the basis for richer desktop-like interfaces. Listing 4-6 shows the code for a window.

Listing 4-6. The window Widget

```
webix.ui({
  id : "myWindow", view : "window", width : 300, height : 200, left : 100,
  top : 100,
  move : true, resize : true,
  head : {
    view : "toolbar",
    cols : [
      { view : "label", label : "A window unto the world" },
      { view : "icon", icon : "times-circle",
        click : function() { $$("myWindow").close(); }
      }
    ]
  },
  body : {
    template :
      `<br>We can show HTML here, or other Webix components - we could,
      in fact, build an entire application UI in a window!`
  }
}).show();
```

Of course, code without a screenshot isn't all that helpful, so check out Figure 4-6.

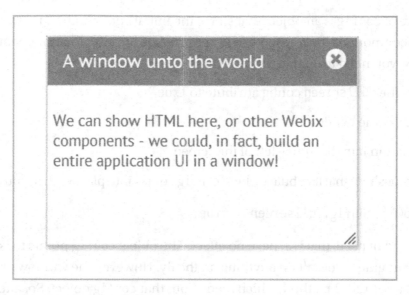

Figure 4-6. *The window widget*

By default, a window won't look very much different than a popup, but when you start playing with some options, you get something that looks more like a window that you know from your desktop OS. Specifically, setting move to true lets the user drag the window around, and setting resize to true gives them the little handle on the lower right to adjust the size of the window with.

Then, when you add a head and build a toolbar into it, you can add things like a close icon as I've done here. Since the window has an id, I can use $$() to get a reference to it (rather than having to stash that reference in a JavaScript variable) and then call close() on it when that icon is clicked. You could implement a minimize icon that just calls hide() on the window, and maximize can be implemented by adjusting the fullscreen attribute, which actually takes us into another new Webix concept!

New Concept: "Other"

You may think I just made that up or got lazy, but no, the Webix documentation actually *does* refer to them as Other. They are the properties that, mostly, begin with a $ symbol. They are for internal logic and aren't generally things you should touch directly. But, you can. More important for our purposes here, it's one of these Other properties that *doesn't* actually begin with a $ symbol (but is still an Other!) that we're interested in: config.

The value of `config` is an object that stores the initial configuration that you set when creating the component. The reason this is important is because to implement `maximize` for a window, you need to do these three things:

- Set the `fullscreen` config attribute to `true`

- Resize the window

- Position it in the upper-left of the screen

It's accomplishing that first bullet where `config` comes into play. With it, you can do this:

```
$$("myWindow").config.fullscreen = true;
```

Now, in and of itself, that will have no effect. The object `config` points to is effectively read-only; changing it doesn't do anything on the fly. However, the window component also exposes a `resize()` method, which reads from that `config` object. So, after you set `fullscreen` to `true`, you do the following:

```
$$("myWindow").resize();
```

Now, the window will be sized to fill the browser window. However, you've got a problem. Unless the window's upper-left corner is already in the upper-left corner of the page, then the window will be extending over the edges of the screen on the right and/or bottom. To fix that, you need to reposition it, and to do that, you'll use the `setPosition()` method.

```
$$("myWindow").setPosition(0, 0);
```

After executing those three lines, the window will fill the page and not be hanging off the edge of the browser window in any direction, just like you'd expect a maximized window to behave.

To finish up, I'll show another way to accomplish the same thing, by using the `define()` method. The `define()` method lets you set `config` attributes without directly accessing the `config` object, and `resize()` brings the changes into force. So, the previous sequence could be accomplished this way:

```
$$("myWindow").define("fullscreen", true);
$$("myWindow").define("top", 0);
$$("myWindow").define("left", 0);
$$("myWindow").resize();
```

Interestingly, the setPosition() call is effectively done as part of the resizing with this pattern, so that's one less thing you have to do explicitly, which is nice. Aside from that, there's not really any reason to favor one approach over the other as far as I can see, though three lines versus four lines of code might be enough reason. (One could argue that using define() ensures that any logic the component encapsulates is fired as expected, and that's probably fair, though at least in this specific instance that doesn't come into play at all.)

HTML-Oriented Components

Let's move on to what Webix calls HTML-oriented components. HTML-oriented components are basically components that mimic some common HTML elements but are wrapped in Webix goodness. The first of these is iframe.

iframe

The iframe component is just like its HTML <iframe> (inline frame) counterpart in that it can show content from a remote system in a region of the page that can be independently interacted with. In fact, in most browser implementations, it is quite literally a browser window embedded inside the page. The code for creating an iframe component is extremely simple, as Listing 4-7 proves.

Listing 4-7. The iframe Widget

```
webix.ui({ view : "iframe", width : 1024, height : 600, src : "http://www.
zammetti.com" });
```

What this looks like obviously depends on what value you give the src attribute, which is the URL to load into the iframe. Giving it the value that is the address of my personal web site results in Figure 4-7.

Figure 4-7. *The iframe widget*

Now, you could always just have an `<iframe>` element included in the HTML you feed to the template attribute of a Webix view, which would work just as well. However, using the `iframe` component means you get all the usual Webix attributes: `width`, `height`, `minWidth`, `minHeight`, `maxWidth`, `maxHeight`, `css`, `disabled`, `config`, and so on. You also get all the helper methods that you've seen: `enable()`, `disable()`, `show()`, `hide()`, `isEnabled()`, `isVisible()`, and so on. Put simply, you get an `iframe` wrapped in all the things Webix components give you, which makes it more pleasant to work with, especially in a Webix app.

scrollview

Like the `iframe` component before, the `scrollview` component effectively wraps a common HTML element, this time the `<div>` element. It allows you to create a scrolling area of your UI independent of the rest. Listing 4-8 shows how this can be coded.

Listing 4-8. The scrollview Widget

```
webix.ui({
  view : "scrollview", scroll : "xy", height : 200, width: 200,
  css : { "border" : "2px solid #ff0000" },
  body : {
    rows : [
      { width : 500, height : 26, template : "2001: A Space Odyssey" },
      { width : 500, height : 26, template : "Rambo: First Blood Part II"
},
      { width : 500, height : 26,
        template : "Doctor Strangelove or: How I Learned To Stop Worrying
        And Love The Bomb"
      },
      { width : 500, height : 26, template : "The Godfather" },
      { width : 500, height : 26, template : "Thor: The Dark World" },
      { width : 500, height : 26, template : "Guardians Of The Galaxy" },
      { width : 500, height : 26, template : "Die Hard" },
      { width : 500, height : 26, template : "Star Wars" },
      { width : 500, height : 26, template : "Real Genius" }
    ]
  }
});
```

This code should look quite familiar to you by this point, but aside from the view attribute set to scrollview, of course, note the scroll attribute. This tells the component which direction, or directions, to allow scrolling in (values can be x, y, or true; xy; or false to disable scrolling—of course, then, why would you be using a scrollview?!). What I've done is coded one row in the layout to be much longer than the others so that horizontal scrolling will be necessary, and the height of the scrollview is defined such that vertical scrolling will be required too, as you can see in Figure 4-8.

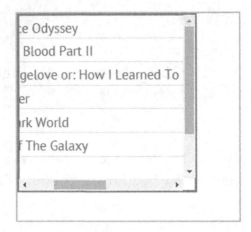

Figure 4-8. *The scrollview widget*

Here, I've scrolled to the right a little to show the far end of the long movie title just to show what that looks like, and you can see there is also a vertical scrollbar to scroll through the list.

As far as properties and methods go, this component doesn't really offer any config options that you haven't previously seen, and for the most part that's true of methods too. However, a few new ones are indeed present, including scrollTo(), which allows you to programmatically scroll the scrollview to a position of your choosing; showView(), which allows you specify the id of a view in the scrollview to scroll to (so, if the Die Hard row had an id of DieHard, then you could call showView("DieHard") to jump to it); and getBody(), a method available on not only scrollview but other components that have a body element to get a reference to.

template

The final HTML-oriented component to look at is template. This component is in most ways like scrollview in that it basically wraps a <div>, but the difference is that template isn't really expected to scroll (though you can accomplish that with the same scroll attribute as scrollview supports). Listing 4-9 shows this component in action, well, sort of—Figure 4-9 is really where it's shown in *action* I suppose!)

Listing 4-9. The template Widget

```
webix.ui({
  width : 400, height : 120, padding : 20, css : { "border" : "2px solid
  #000000" },
  rows : [
    { view : "template", type : "section", template : "Snarky Greeting" },
    { view : "template", type : "clean", template : "Hello there, ugly bag
    of mostly water!" }
  ]
});
```

——— SNARKY GREETING ———

Hello there, ugly bag of mostly water!

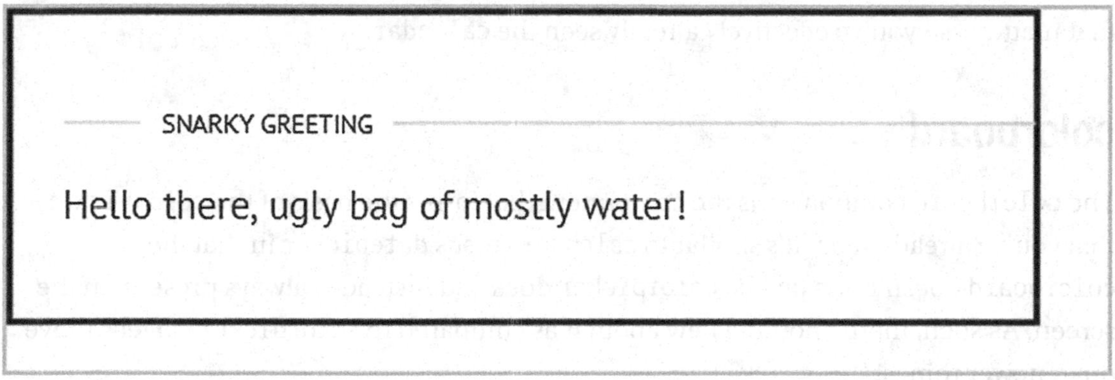

Figure 4-9. *The template widget*

Here I've in fact created two template components, and I've done this to show you that a template can have a type. Four types are available: the default (when you specify no type), which is just a box with a border; clean, which is the same as the default but with no border; header, which renders what looks like a header bar that you've seen before; and section, which is what I've used for the "Snarky Greeting" text. This shows a line on either side of the template content and is usually used to demarcate a section of content.

The content shown in a template can also be loaded from a remote address using the url attribute, but in that case, the expected result is JSON data that is the Webix configuration you want to display. Otherwise, most of the same config options, methods, and attributes that scrollview supports are also supported by template.

Specialized Widgets

Specialized widgets, or *specific* widgets as the Webix documentation refers to them as, are components that serve a specialized purpose of some sort. Either way, they're just another group of components for you to look at!

calendar

The `calendar` component is one I won't go into much detail on because it is basically nothing but the `datepicker` that you've already seen with one key difference: `datepicker` pops up its calendar when the user triggers it, but a `calendar` is always present on the screen. Aside from that difference, though, they are the same in every way that matters, so you've effectively already seen the `calendar`.

colorboard

The `colorboard` component is the component that forms the basis of the `colorpicker` that you've already seen. It's similar to `calendar` versus `datepicker` in that the `colorboard` doesn't pop up like `colorpicker` does and instead is always present on the screen. As such, there's nothing new about it as compared to `colorpicker`, so let's move on to newer things!

excelviewer

The `excelviewer` component (available only with a Pro license) is one such new thing. It's a component that allows you to view a Microsoft Excel file. This is essentially a giant grid, as you can see in Figure 4-10.

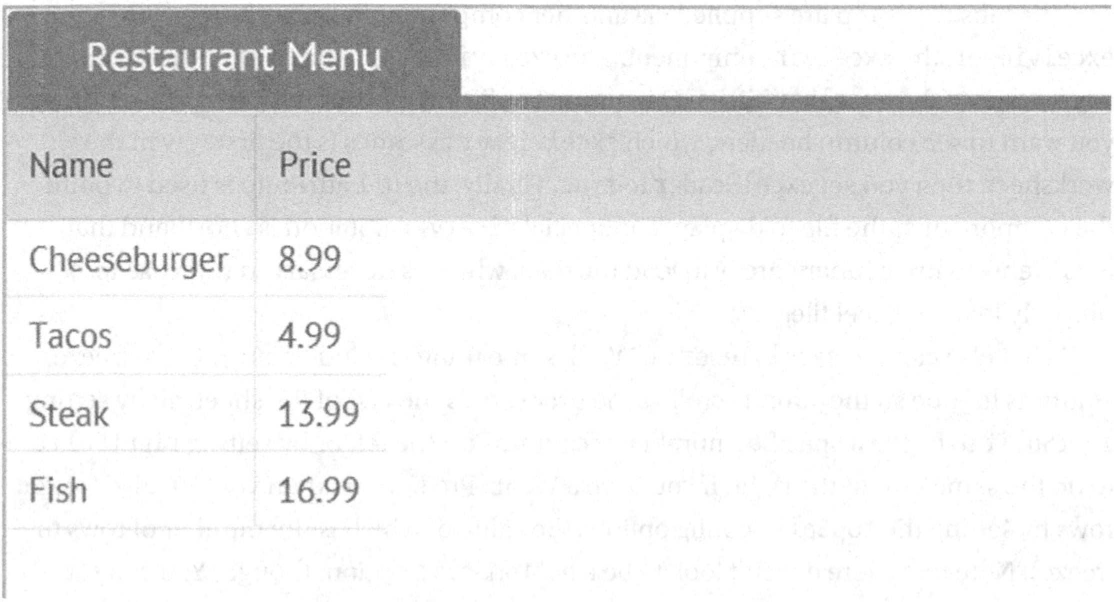

Restaurant Menu	
Name	Price
Cheeseburger	8.99
Tacos	4.99
Steak	13.99
Fish	16.99

Figure 4-10. *Who says spreadsheet are boring? The excelviewer component*

Each worksheet in the Excel workbook gets a tab at the top, with there being only one in this example. Then, the columns and rows displayed come from the spreadsheet.

You might guess that there is a lot of complicated code to make this happen, and maybe there is deep in the bowels of Webix, but as far as the API you interact with goes, it's exceedingly simple, as Listing 4-10 proves.

Listing 4-10. The excelviewer Example Code

```
webix.ui({ rows : [
  { view : "excelbar", id : "toolbar" },
  { view : "excelviewer", toolbar : "toolbar", excelHeader : true,
    url : "binary->excel.xlsx"
  }
] });
```

The tabs at the top are supplied via another component that goes along with excelviewer, the excelbar component. The excelviewer is defined after that, with a reference to the excelbar via its ID in the id config attribute of the excelviewer. If you want to see column headers, which excelviewer assumes is the first row in the worksheet, then you set excelHeader to true. Finally, the url attribute is used to point the component at the file to display. The special binary-> notation is shorthand that tells Webix to use a binary proxy to load the data, which is necessary in this case to properly load an Excel file.

What else can the excelviewer do? Well, some things include being able to freeze columns for one so they don't scroll as the user scrolls the rest of the sheet, all by setting leftSplit to freeze a specified number of columns on the left or by setting rightSplit to do the same but on the right. If you have a Webix Pro license, then you can also freeze rows by setting the topSplit config option (the value of which is the number of rows to freeze). Note that there doesn't look to be a bottomSplit option, though. You can set headermenu to true to enable a menu on column headers to allow for hiding columns.

You are supposed to be able to set editMath to true to be able to use formulas in cells, but to be honest, I can't seem to get this to work! I also wasn't able to find an example of it working, so my best guess is this feature may have some bugs. However, I wanted to at least point it out because it is, in theory, a neat feature, and I want you to be aware of it in case you need it and want to pursue it on your own.

google-map

The google-map component is an easy widget you can use to interface with Google's mapping service and display geographic data with it. Figure 4-11 shows this in action.

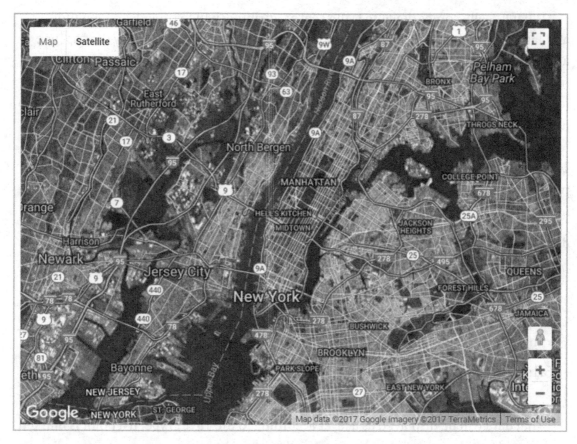

Figure 4-11. *Beautiful, beautiful maps, courtesy of google-map*

To use this component, you'll first need to obtain an API key for your application (at the time of this writing, the address for this is https://developers.google.com/maps/documentation/javascript/get-api-key). Once you have that, Webix makes it easy to display a map, which you can see for yourself in Listing 4-11.

Listing 4-11. The google-map Example Code

```
webix.ui({
  view : "google-map", width : 640, height : 480, borderless : false, css :
  { margin : "10px" },
  key : "AIzaSyAiOoVNVO-e6O3aUY8SILdD4v9bVBkmiTg", zoom : 11, mapType :
  "HYBRID",
  center : [ 40.758896, -73.985130 ]
});
```

What it really comes down to is the center attribute, which provides a longitude and latitude to serve as the center of your map. You can optionally specify the mapType attribute, as I've done here, specifying that I want to display a HYBRID map that shows roads and satellite imagery. (No, it's not real-time satellite imagery. Calm down there, Jason Bourne!) You can also specify values of ROADMAP to see only roads, SATELLITE to see just satellite imagery, and TERRAIN to see a terrain map.

You can also show layers as you can with Google Maps itself, though only a layerType value of marker (which is the default) or heatmap (which uses colors to show points) are supported. For either of these, you specify a collection of data, which might look like this:

```
data : [
  { id : 1, lat : 25.355,  lng : 2.324, label : "Point A", draggable :
  true },
  { id : 2, lat : 25.444,  lng : 5.43, label : "Point B", draggable :
  false },
  { id : 3, lat : 25.123, lng : 12.375, label : "Point C", draggable :
  false }
]
```

That data will be displayed as a layer according to the layerType. If a point is marked as draggable, then the user can drag it around to move it.

video

It seems like every web site I go to these days wants to show me its content in the form of a video, which is kind of annoying if you ask me (hey, you kids, get off my lawn!). But sometimes, a video is something you want to show for a good reason, and Webix makes it easy with the video component, shown in Figure 4-12.

Figure 4-12. *Poetry in motion with the video component*

In typical Webix fashion, the code behind this is trivial—just look at Listing 4-12 to be convinced of this!

Listing 4-12. The video Example Code

```
webix.ui({
  view : "video", width : 640, height : 360, borderless : false, css : {
  margin : "10px" },
  src : [ "video.mp4" ]
});
```

Really, all it takes is the `src` attribute. This can be a single URL, or it can be an array. When it's an array, each element is a different format of the video, perhaps MP4 and OGV, for example. That way, the browser will use whichever version it understands.

There isn't a whole lot to the API of the video component, but you can hide or show the playback controls on the bottom there with the `controls` Boolean config option, which is nice. Other than that, it's got all the usual `hide`, `show`, `borderless`, `width`, `height`, and the rest of the usual suspects—ditto methods and events as well.

barcode

A Webix Pro license–only component, the barcode widget generates those barcodes that are on virtually every consumer package in existence—you know, the ones like that shown in Figure 4-13.

Figure 4-13. *Hey 1980s kids, recognize the number? It's a barcode example*

I'm not entirely sure what purpose this serves in a web app, though certainly if you have a need for it, then you know that and will be happy that Webix provides it. The code is, as usual, very basic, as Listing 4-13 shows.

Listing 4-13. The barcode Example Code

```
webix.ui({ view : "barcode", type : "ean13", value : "867530911111" });
```

You just need to provide a type, which must be one of ean8, ean13, or upcA (and I'd be lying if I said I knew what those are!) and of course a value to be encoded in the barcode. You can set the value dynamically with setValue() as well, but beyond that, it's a simple component with just the basic Webix API that all components share beyond that.

daterange

Like the calendar/datepicker and colorboard/colorpicker relationships, daterange is just a daterangepicker that doesn't pop up and is instead "embedded" statically on the page. Unlike those other two, however, daterange requires a Webix Pro license. As with those other two combinations, I won't go into detail here because you've effectively already seen this when you looked at daterangepicker, so let's move on, shall we?

pdfviewer

The `pdfviewer` component is a lot like the `excelviewer` component except that now you're viewing Adobe Acrobat PDF files, of course, and also that `pdfviewer` requires a Webix Pro license. Figure 4-14 gives you an example of this.

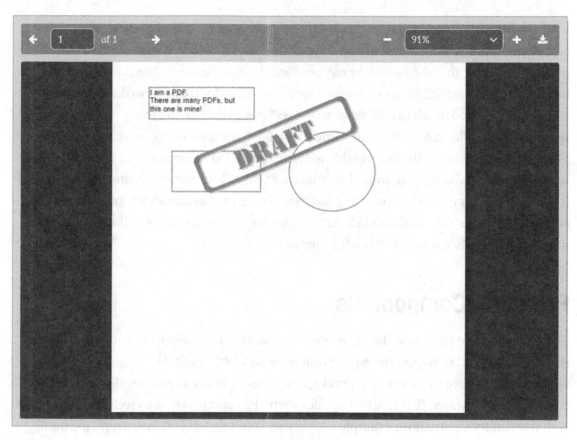

Figure 4-14. *Viewing PDFs couldn't be easier with pdfviewer*

This is just displaying a quick PDF I threw together to show that it can display text and also handles shapes and embedded content just fine. Also, like `excelviewer`, there is a partner component involved here, `pdfbar`, and the API looks familiar too, as you can see in Listing 4-14.

Listing 4-14. The pdfviewer Example Code

```
webix.ui({ type : "space", rows : [
  { view : "pdfbar", id : "pdftoolbar" },
  { view : "pdfviewer", toolbar : "pdftoolbar", url : "binary->pdf.pdf" }
] });
```

Like `excelbar`, the `pdfbar` component generally goes on top of a `pdfviewer` component, though that's entirely up to you. You want it below or to the side? No problem! Simply alter the layout. In any position, it provides some basic functionality including page navigation, zoom control, and the ability for the user to download the file.

There's not too much to add as far as the API goes, though one thing you can do is specify `downloadName` to define the name of the file if the user chooses to download it. There are also some methods available to navigate the PDF documented, which should be pretty obvious based just on their names: `nextPage()`, `prevPage()`, and `renderPage()` (that last one essentially jumps to any page you specify). You can also programmatically set the view scale with a call to `setScale()`, and you can trigger a download via a call to the unsurprisingly named `download()` method.

Premium Components

The following five components are premium widgets, which means they need to be downloaded (and even purchased) separately from Webix itself. This means providing a working example of these wouldn't make a lot of sense because you wouldn't be able to try them out for yourself. While this applies to the Pro components as well, the difference is that if you try to run those examples, Webix will politely tell you they aren't available to you, while these premium components will just error out on you. Therefore, I'm going to describe them and show them to you briefly, but I'm going to skip any example code for these, and I'm not going to go into any detail about their APIs. If you are interested in these, then by all means throw your money at Webix and grab 'em because they are indeed quite nice, as you're about to see!

filemanager

The Webix `filemanager` component provides a UI for navigating through a file system containing files and folders and performing basic operations on them such as copying, pasting, renaming, and so on.

In fact, this component, which you can see in Figure 4-15, can work with any type of hierarchical data. There's nothing that says it must represent a file system.

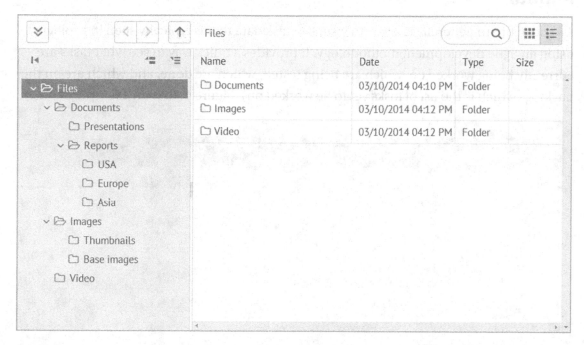

Figure 4-15. *Managing files with filemanager (what did you expect?)*

It should be understood that this component doesn't actually *do* anything on its own. In other words, deleting a "file" in a `filemanager` instance doesn't actually delete a file at all. You would need to hook up event handlers for various operations and tie them back to some (likely) server-side code to perform the specified function if you wanted to do anything like that. Instead, `filemanager` will simply modify the data that you load into it (which is data just like any other data components would use) just like an editable list does. What you do as a result of those changes is up to you (it won't by default even persist the changes to the data).

The `filemanager` offers more "advanced" functionality too, such as searching and drag-and-drop interactions. It can even support uploading and downloading files, but again, this requires you to write some server-side code.

It's a powerful, full-featured "file" manager component to be sure, saving you a lot of time and effort building such an interface if you need such an interface.

kanban

A kanban board generally is a way to visualize task data that is typically seen in projects using an agile development methodology. It provides a quick way to see what tasks are currently being worked on, which are being tested, which are done, and which are on the backlog (which is the list of tasks yet to be worked on). Figure 4-16 is an example of this.

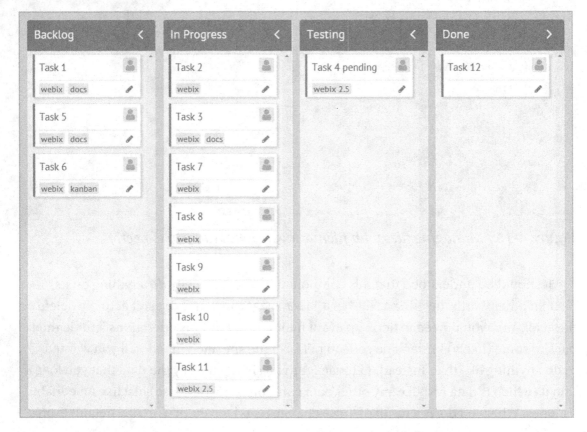

Figure 4-16. *Who makes all the kids happy? The kanban man can!*

The kanban component allows you to create whatever high-level groups you want, those being Backlog, In Progress, Testing, and Done in this example, so it's a highly flexible display that can be tuned to fit your needs.

With kanban, you can build any arbitrarily complex workflow. For example, you can hook a context menu to the tasks listed and provide features such as re-assigning tasks or of course changing their status, which is then reflected in the item moving to the appropriate group. The groups themselves can be collapsed and expanded as needed and can even be moved around. So if workflows are something you need to deal with in your application, then consider kanban for your needs.

pivot

The pivot component allows you to visualize and work with huge sets of data and create reports from it. It generally looks like a grid, but with a lot of added functionality. Figure 4-17 is an example of a pivot.

[Click to configure]	2005		2006		2007
	oil (min)	oil (sum)	oil (min)	oil (sum)	oil (min)
⊟ 📂 Republic	0	541.746	0	679.657	0
📄 Argentina	1.545	1.545	1.732	1.732	2.845
📄 Austria	7.600	7.600	9.344	9.344	9.864
📄 Belarus	4.375	4.375	6.093	6.093	7.721
📄 Brazil	11.779	11.779	15.365	15.365	20.408
📄 Central African Republic	0.034	0.034	0.050	0.050	0.068
📄 Chad	0.253	0.253	0.594	0.594	0.298
📄 China	59.615	59.615	84.061	84.061	98.845
📄 Colombia	0.518	0.518	0.651	0.651	0.875

Figure 4-17.   *Pivot left, pivot right, pivot however you like with the pivot component*

The thing that makes a pivot so powerful is what you get when you click the "[Click to configure]" text, which is shown in Figure 4-18.

163

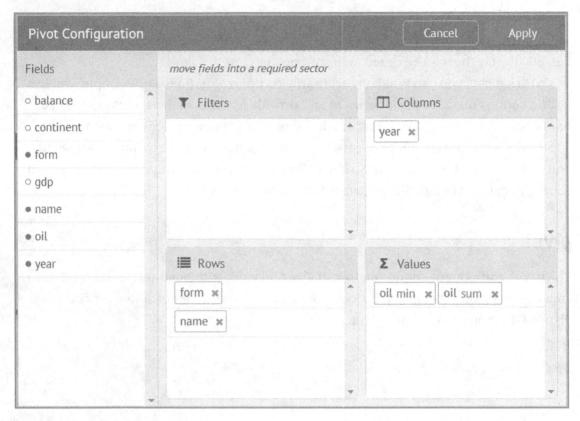

Figure 4-18. *Configuring a pivot*

Here, you have the ability to hide and show fields (column), and you can filter the data, select values, and otherwise slice and dice the data in myriad ways that other components don't allow for.

One of the best features of `pivot` is its built-in support for WebWorkers, which allows you to load data into the `pivot` without blocking the main JavaScript thread, which keeps the UI responsive while enabling you to load a huge amount of data into the pivot for the user to work with.

The `pivot` component is an excellent way to deal with a lot of information in a highly flexible way so if that's a capability you need, then be sure to explore this widget further.

scheduler

The scheduler component, shown in Figure 4-19, provides what most of us know as an agenda and provides a way to maintain the appointments on your agenda.

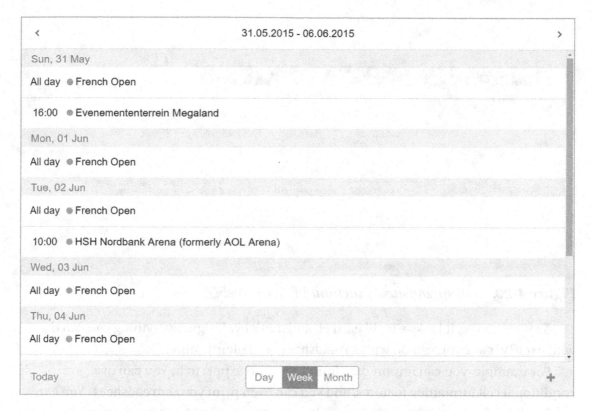

Figure 4-19. *Scheduling made fun (kinda?) with the scheduler component*

The scheduler provides all the user interface you need for something like this including pop-ups to add events and to edit existing events. Of course, being Webix, you can style and modify those elements as you see fit, and the same is certainly true of the agenda list. The scheduler can handle recurring events as well as events that span multiple days.

I'm not sure too many people should go off and build Outlook themselves from the ground up, but if you ever decided to do something like that, then the scheduler can get you a decent head start on at least part it!

spreadsheet

The final component to look at takes the previously seen excelviewer and pushes it to its logical conclusion, that being a (more or less) full-featured spreadsheet. Take a look at Figure 4-20 to see it.

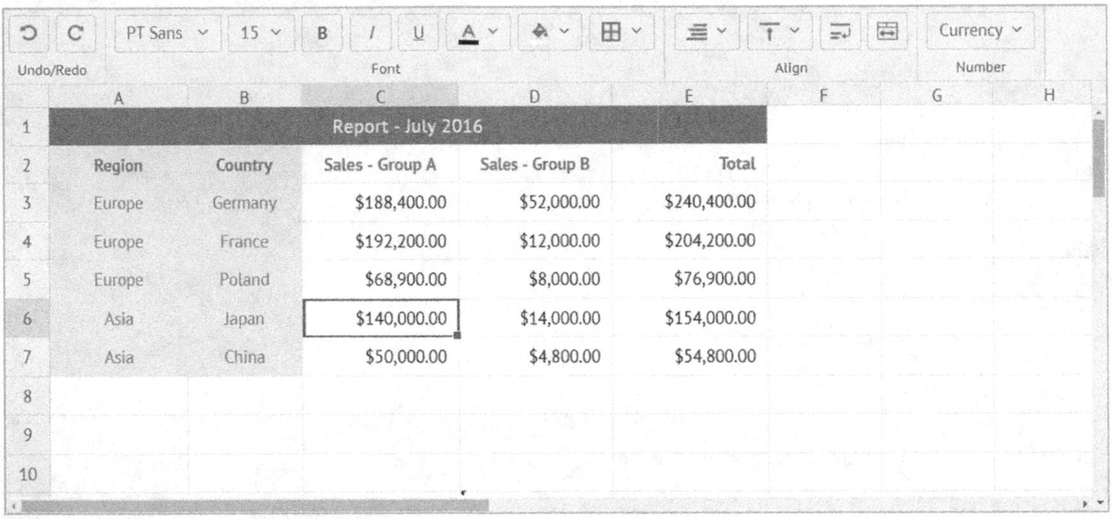

Figure 4-20. *Full spreadsheet functionality with Webix!*

As you can see, it looks a lot like Excel, and that's by design. Everything you can do with `excelviewer` you can do with `spreadsheet`, and plenty more!

For example, you can import data from Excel and export to it. You can use conditional cell formatting features, and you can even print your `spreadsheet`. You can use formulas, and you can manipulate columns in terms of hiding/showing, moving, deleting, and inserting. This widget provides a rich API to do all of this programmatically as well as providing a ready interface for a lot of it as you can see.

Feel like competing with Google Docs? Well, grab the Webix `spreadsheet` component, and you'll be well on your way!

Strutting with Style

Styling is, of course, an important aspect of web development, and this is no less true when using Webix. Although much of the styling is in a sense automatic when using Webix, there's plenty of flexibility available to you as a developer.

You have of course seen the usage of the `css` property and the `cssClass` property for a few components. You've also seen that when you import Webix onto a page, you include the `webix.css` file. This provides the basic styles Webix needs to draw its components properly. As with any CSS file, you can modify this, although that's generally not encouraged, certainly not by me. Instead, you should include your own CSS file after the `webix.css` file and override any Webix styles you might want to.

All of the style classes defined in webix.css begin with .webix_ or .webixtype_, and what follows is usually pretty obvious. For example, you'll see a .webix_tree_item class, and even without looking at the documentation, you can be pretty sure that gets applied to items in a tree. This class is defined in webix.css as follows:

```
.webix_tree_item {
  clear : both;
  height : 28px;
  line-height : 28px;
  white-space : nowrap;
}
```

So, if you wanted, you could include a custom.css file after webix.css is imported (or just add a <style> section to the <head> of the page after the import of webix.css and define your styles there, whichever makes the most sense for your development) and do the following:

```
.webix_tree_item {
  background-color : #ff0000;
  clear : both;
  height : 28px;
  line-height : 28px;
  white-space : nowrap;
}
```

Granted, that makes a tree look pretty ugly, but you can add that background-color if you want to anyway, overriding the Webix style, which surely is nice and is the point here.

One of the best things about Webix and its documentation is that for each component you'll find a CSS map to refer to. An example of this is shown in Figure 4-21, this one for the button widget. Note that the maps can be a little difficult to find, but at the time of this writing they are in the "Guides" section of the Webix documentation, under the "Styling and Animation" section's Component Styling item (or, to save you time: https://docs.webix.com/desktop__css_image_maps.html).

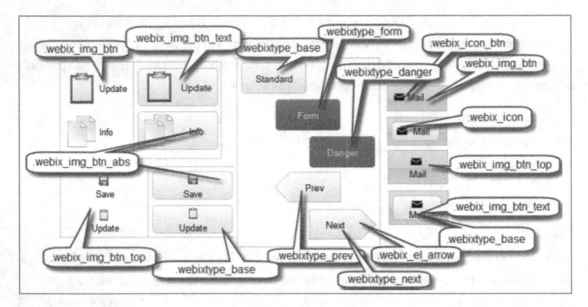

Figure 4-21. *CSS map for the button widget*

This map tells you what classes are applied to what parts of the button. Want to change the text color on that last Mail button on the right? Just override the .webix_img_ btn_text class.

Note   Don't be surprised if you sometimes have to use !important to get your styles to apply. You usually want to try to avoid that, but sometimes it's the only way to get Webix to cooperate!

You can also, for components that use data, apply inline styles to specific data elements. For this, you include a $css property. For example, looking back at the tree example from earlier, if you wanted to make Metallica's "Enter Sandman" red, and only that item, you would do the following:

```
data : [
  { open : true, value : "Metallica",
    data : [
      { value : "Enter Sandman", $css : { color : "#ff0000" } },
      { value : "Ride the Lightning" },
      { value : "Hero of the Day" }
    ]
```

```
  },
  { value : "Billy Joel",
    data : [
      { value : "Movin' Out" },
      { value : "Piano Man" }
    ]
  }
]
```

In this way, you have a great deal of control over individual data items and how they're displayed.

Finally, you can dynamically add and remove styles from components using the addCss() and removeCss() functions, respectively. This allows you to do things like the following:

```
webix.html.addCss( $$("myDataview").getNode(), "myCSS");
webix.html.addCss( $$("myDataview").getNode(), "myCSS");
```

Assuming you have a dataview with an ID of myDataview, and assuming you have a CSS class named myCSS defined, the first line will apply that style to the component, and the second will remove it. You can do this for any Webix component that you have or can get a reference to.

Skins

While Webix has a pretty nice look to it by default, in my opinion anyway, you saw in Chapter 1 that Webix also offers so-called skins, which change the entire look and feel of your UI. You saw that you can build them with the Skin Builder tool yourself. Before you go through the effort of creating a skin, though, Webix offers a number of skins right of the box, including Air, Air Compact, Clouds, Compact, Contrast, Flat (which is the default), Glamour, Light, Material Design, Metro, Terrace, Touch, and Web. Note that all of these are included with Webix except the Material Design skin, which must be downloaded separately (at the time of this writing, you can get it at https://github.com/webix-hub/material-design-skin). It's worth looking at each of these skins to see if they suit your needs, and remember, you can always tweak them if they aren't perfect (either by using Skin Builder or by just overriding things as necessary via CSS as previously described).

Whether it's included with Webix or not, actually using a skin is simple. You import it in place of `webix.css`. As an alternative, if you define a `webix_skin` variable *before* importing `webix.js` and as its value you name a skin, then Webix will take care of loading the skin CSS file for you (which must be located in the `webix/codebase/skins` directory). My advice is to *not* use this approach since keeping things out of global scope is a good guideline, but as with most guidelines, you don't have to follow this one if you have a reason not to.

One other thing you can do with a skin applied is to adjust the sizes of some UI elements via JavaScript in a global way. To do this, Webix offers a `webix.skin.xx` object where xx is the name of the skin you want to alter. Within it, you'll find a number of attributes including things such as `sliderHandlerWidth`, which defines the width of the handle on a slider widget; `calendarHeight`, which is the default height of a calendar widget; and `menuHeight`, which is the height of a `menubar`. It's not just sizes here either. You'll also see things like `customCheckbox`. So, if you want to use plain old HTML check boxes by default across your entire UI, then you can set `webix.skin.flat.customCheckboxes` to `false` (assuming you're using the flat skin).

In addition, you can alter things about the currently active skin using `webix.skin.$active`. For example, if you wanted all your input component to be 75 pixels wide, then you could do `webix.skin.$active.inputWidth=75`.

Skins give you a great starting point and can change the entire look of your UI, but even with a skin you still have multiple ways to alter things to suit your needs at the global level, the specific component level, or even the data element level. That's the flexibility of styling with Webix. You get lots of choices and lots of options but all while being rather simple to deal with!

Drag and Drop

A number of components you've seen to this point have allowed for drag-and-drop interaction with the user, but did you know you can arbitrarily apply this functionality to virtually anything in the DOM with Webix? Well, now you do! Take a look at the example in Listing 4-15.

Listing 4-15. A Simple Drag-and-Drop Example

```
<!DOCTYPE html>

<html>

  <head>

    <title>Drag-And-Drop</title>

    <link rel="stylesheet" type="text/css" href="../webix/codebase/webix.css">
    <script type="text/javascript" src="../webix/codebase/webix_debug.js">
    </script>

    <script>

      webix.ready(function() {

        webix.DragControl.addDrag("src", {
          $dragCreate:function(inSource, inEvent) {
            return inSource;
          },
          $dragDestroy : function(inDrag) { }
        });
        webix.DragControl.addDrop("dest", {
          $drop : function(inSource, inTarget, inEvent) {
            console.log("You dropped:", inSource);
          }
        });

      });

    </script>

  </head>

  <body>

    <div style="width:100px;height:100px;">
      <div id="src" title="I am the source"
        style="width:100px;height:100px;background-color:#ff0000;">
      </div>
```

```
    </div>

    <div style="height:100px;"></div>

    <div id="dest" title="I am the destination"
      style="width:200px;height:200px;background-color:#00ff00;">
    </div>

  </body>

</html>
```

Skip down to the <body>, and you'll see you have a couple of <div>s. The two that matter the most are the src and dest elements. The src <div> will become draggable, and the dest <div> will become a drop target, and they will become these things by virtue of the code executed in the webix.ready() function (the other two <div>s consist of the one that contains the src <div>, which I'll return to later, and the empty <div>, which is just for spacing purposes). To do so, the webix.DragControl.addDrag() function is called, passing it the ID of the draggable <div>. Webix adds the plumbing to this element that allows it to be dragged.

But, since I'm talking drag *and* drop, not just drag, you also need a drop target, and that's where the call to webix.DragControl.addDrop() comes in, to make the dest <div> a drop target.

That's all you need to do to make things draggable and to be drop targets, but you'll notice each of those calls has a second argument that supplies some optional callback functions. These are necessary for this example because without them you would see that the src <div> is actually "ghosted," meaning a copy of it gets dragged around and the original stays where it is. You would also see that when you drop it on the dest <div>, nothing actually happens. Webix leaves all of this to you because what should occur in these situations is dependent on your application. For this example, all I want to happen is that you drag the *real* src <div> around without that ghosting, and then I just want to display information about the object that was dropped when that event occurs.

So, when the drag event begins, I want to redefine the $dragCreate() method, which is a control method related to drag-and-drop functionality that is executed when the user begins dragging the <div> around. Note that Webix has default implementations for this and the other control methods: $drag(), $dragCreate(), and $dragDestroy(), so this really is redefining that. The return value from $dragCreate() is the object to be dragged around, so obviously it should be the source of the event, which is the object that the

user dragged. Then, providing an empty $dragDestroy() function results in the src
<div> from being removed from the DOM, from its original location more accurately,
so it can be the thing being dragged around. This is the reason for the container <div>.
Without that, the area the src <div> was in would collapse as the page reflowed, and
everything would shift up as a result. Putting it in the container <div> means that the
space doesn't collapse and everything stays where it is, which is almost certainly what
you would want to happen in such a situation.

Then, on the drop side, the only override necessary is on the $drop() method
(there's also $dragIn() and $dragOut() available) where you do a simple console.
log() on the source object.

With this simple API, you can enable drag-and-drop functionality on virtually
any element you like and can provide any functionality you like for the various events
associated with it whether you're dealing with Webix components or not.

Extensibility and Integration Points

Webix on its own is pretty great, but sometimes you need just a little more from it, and
that's where extensibility comes into play. You already saw one component of that,
namely, the ability to extend components. You actually saw another: integration with
services, by way of the google-map component. But, it doesn't end there! Webix offers
integration with other third-party libraries via extension points, all of which combined
means that Webix can be greater than the sum of its parts!

Integration with jQuery

jQuery is one of the most popular JavaScript libraries of all time. In fact, an argument can
be made that it is *the* most popular of all time. There's a lot of jQuery knowledge in the
JavaScript development community, and while JavaScript itself has evolved to the point
where you can do most things without the need for jQuery any longer, jQuery still has its
place, and you may want to use it in addition to Webix. Rest assured, you most definitely can!

To do so, you need to add what Webix calls the *jQuery adapter* to the mix. This isn't
included with Webix any longer, so you need to go grab it here: https://github.com/
webix-hub/webix-jquery. Specifically, download the index.js file in the sources directory.
Then, you'll need to include both jQuery (obviously!) and that index.js file. I prefer to
rename index.js to adapter.js; you can see the resulting example in Listing 4-16.

Listing 4-16. jQuery Integration Example

```
<!DOCTYPE html>

<html>

  <head>

    <title>jQuery Integration</title>

    <link rel="stylesheet" type="text/css" href="../webix/codebase/webix.css">

    <script type="text/javascript" src="../jQuery/jquery-3.2.1.min.js">
    </script>
    <script type="text/javascript" src="../webix/codebase/webix_debug.js">
    </script>
    <script type="text/javascript" src="../jQuery/adapter.js"></script>

    <script>

      webix.ready(function() {

        $(".caldiv").webix_calendar();

      });

    </script>

  </head>

  <body>

    <div class="caldiv"></div>
    <div class="caldiv"></div>

  </body>

</html>
```

The order of the `.js` imports is important. jQuery must come first, then Webix, and then the adapter. Once that's done, you can begin using the integration. This example shows one of the benefits of this integration: being able to create multiple instances of a Webix component based on the CSS class. The jQuery `$(".caldiv")` call returns an array of DOM nodes (wrapped in some jQuery magic), and then because of the adapter extending Webix to be jQuery-aware (and vice versa), the `webix_calendar()` function is available, and a calendar is created in each matching `<div>`.

Another benefit is that you can reference container `<div>` elements on the page using class names and not just IDs, as is the case with the Webix `$$()` function because you can use the jQuery `$()` function instead, which has more flexibility in getting references to DOM nodes.

Another benefit is that HTML `<table>` elements can be a data source for data-aware Webix components. Each column in the table becomes a `template` item for the component. For example, if you have the following:

```
<tr>
        <td>Frank</td>
        <td>Zammetti</td>
        <td>U.S.A.</td>
</tr>
```

then you can do the following:

```
template : "#data1#, #data0# (#data2#)"
```

The columns are named `data0-data2` here; it's a simple incrementing number scheme. You can specify this template in a list, for example, and you would see `Zammetti, Frank (U.S.A.)` as one item in that list.

Finally, remember that you now have access to the vast world of jQuery components. So, if Webix doesn't have what you're looking for, then the huge jQuery ecosystem probably does.

Integration with Third-Party Libraries

In addition to jQuery, Webix integrates with a number of other popular JavaScript libraries and frameworks. At the time of this writing, integration is available for the following:

- Angular

- Angular 2

- Backbone

- Firebase

- Meteor

- React

- TypeScript

- Vue JS

- dHTMLx

As with jQuery, an adapter is required for many of these. Once you have the adapter added to your page, with Webix and of course whatever imports are required for the library you're integrating with, you can use them together easily.

Of course, each of these libraries is different, *vastly* different in some cases, so showing examples of each could easily take a whole chapter by itself, and possibly one for each library! However, I'll give you one or two examples just so you have an idea what it might look like, depending on which library you're working with. Let's start with React since that's one of the more popular ones at the time of this writing. Once you have all the necessary code imported on the page, you'll be able to do things like this:

```
const ui = { view:"slider" };
const value = 123;
 const SliderView = () => (
  <Webix ui={ui} data={value} />
)
```

This creates a React component with a Webix `slider` widget inside of it. If you're familiar with React, then this should look pretty straightforward to you.

What about Angular 2? In that case, you will create a normal Angular 2 component and nest a `webix.ui()` call inside of it, like so:

```
import { Component, ElementRef, OnDestroy, OnInit } from '@angular/core';

@Component({ selector : "datatable", template : "" })
export class DataTableComponent implements OnDestroy, OnInit {

  private ui : webix.ui.datatable;

  constructor(root : ElementRef) {
    this.ui = <webix.ui.datatable> webix.ui({
```

```
      container : root.nativeElement
      view : "datatable", autoConfig : true, url : "data.php"
    })
  }

  ngOnInit(){
    this.ui.resize();
  }
  ngOnDestroy(){
    this.ui.destructor();
  }

}
```

For TypeScript, Webix defines its widgets and mixin interfaces in an `index.d.ts` file. Once that's done, the types will be available in your TypeScript code, and you'll have the benefit of static typing of Webix types.

Another bit of integration to mention is with a host of third-party text editors. Webix offers components for the popular editors Ace, Mercury, NicEdit, TinyMCE, CodeMirror, and CKEditor. All you need to do for these is add the appropriate JavaScript important for the editor you want, and then you can do the following:

```
webix.ui({ id : "editor", view : "tinymce-editor" });
```

That's it! You'll now have a TinyMCE editor available, which provides rich text editing including HTML styling and all those sorts of goodies.

Finally, what do you do if you want Webix to integrate with a library that isn't explicitly supported? Are you dead in the water? Nope! You can implement this integration yourself because Webix provides extension points for doing exactly that, which is the basis of all the integration described earlier.

The first step is to define a Webix component that will "host" the UI of the thing you're integrating with. All that takes is this:

```
webix.protoUI({
  name : "myCustomComponent",
  $init : function(config){
```

```
      // Do initialization here
    },
    .. // Add other methods as necessary
  }, webix.ui.view);
```

The name is what you'll specify as the view attribute value when you make a webix. ui() call later to instantiate this component, and the second argument to webix. protoUI() is the base class to build your component from, which will almost always be webix.ui.view. Exactly what initialization code or other method you may need to implement depends entirely on what you're integrating with. You may need to do nothing at all in fact.

Once that's done, you can instantiate this component with a plain old webix.UI({ view : "myCustomComponent" }); call and you're off to the races! Remember that because this component extends from webix.ui.view, it means that all the basic Webix config options, methods, and events that you've learned about thus far are available despite this being a third-party component in essence.

The sky is the limit given this mechanism and the other integration opportunities. Webix will often be all you need, but if not, you aren't boxed in either. Pretty sweet, right?

Summary

This chapter is the last of the "overview" chapters wherein you learned about some new things such as context components, HTML-oriented components, "specialized" widgets, skinning, and extensibility.

With that, you should now have a pretty clear picture of what Webix has to offer and have a solid foundation for building some real applications with Webix.

In the next chapter, you'll begin building one such application, wxPIM. You'll take the basics that you've learned and start to apply them for real to create an application that you can actually use, and in the process, you'll gain a deeper familiarity with Webix and see how to use it for real.

Get ready; it's going to be a ride!

CHAPTER 5

Getting Practical: Building wxPIM

Over the previous four chapters, you have surveyed the Webix landscape and gotten familiar with many of its concepts. You've gained a familiarity with what the library has to offer and seen how to put most of its widgets to use, at least in very simplistic examples.

With that knowledge in hand, it's time to take the next step, which is to build an application with Webix to learn how it all fits together. I'll break this exercise down into a couple of steps spread across a couple of chapters, but this chapter will be key in that you'll actually build the application in its basic form. You'll then expand on it in subsequent chapters, but you need to build the foundation first.

Of course, as with building a house, it's hard to build something if you don't have an idea of what it's supposed to look like in the end, so let's begin by discussing what this wxPIM application is all about.

First Things First: What's a PIM, and What's wxPIM?

The term *PIM* was made popular back in the days of the original PalmPilot devices, though it existed before then. PIM stands for "personal information manager" (or "management," depending on who you ask) and is basically a fancy way to say an application (or device, in the case of the PalmPilot) that stores some basic information that most busy, modern people need to know and allows it to be consumed easily. Before the electronics age, you might have a little notepad with tabs for various bits of information, but it all amounts to about the same thing either way. What data constitutes a PIM can vary, but for most people, there are four basic pieces of information: appointments, contacts, notes, and tasks. There can be others, and there can even be some overlap between those four, but those are generally considered to be the basics, and they are exactly what wxPIM will contain.

179

© Frank Zammetti 2018
F. Zammetti, *Practical Webix*, https://doi.org/10.1007/978-1-4842-3384-9_5

This application will present four modules, each covering one of those pieces of information. You'll provide a way for the user to enter items of each and store them and then present a way for them to be viewed, edited, and deleted. Also, you'll build a "day-at-a-glance" screen that presents items that are time-sensitive, namely, appointments and tasks for the current day, in a unified view.

As you build the app, you'll do so in a modular way so that later, if you want, you can add other modules to deal with other types of data. Maybe bookmarks are something you'd like in your PIM, or maybe recipes if you're a chef. The point is, you'll be able to add them without much difficulty because you'll design the code to be reasonably modular.

In Figure 5-1 you can see this day-at-a-glance screen, and this is what will serve as the starting point for the application, the first thing the user sees when it is launched.

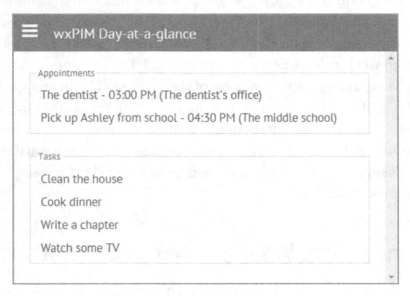

Figure 5-1. *wxPIM day-at-a-glance*

As you can see, I've got two appointments today (although arguably only one is really an appointment; that's the overlap I mentioned before) and four tasks to accomplish today. There may be many more appointments and tasks that I've created, but these are just the ones for today.

Sitting above the day-at-a-glance content is a header that will tell the user what module they're in. Whatever module they're in will appear below the header in what we'll call the *module content area*.

You'll also notice the "hamburger" menu icon in the upper left. This is how the user navigates the application. Clicking it reveals a `sidemenu`, a component you've seen before and which is shown in Figure 5-2.

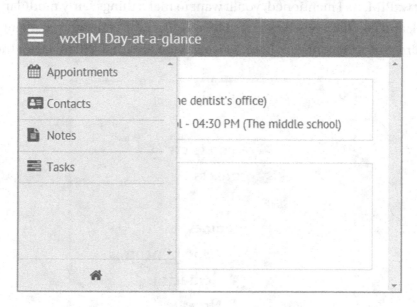

Figure 5-2. *Navigating wxPIM with the sidemenu menu*

In addition to links for the four modules previously described, you'll notice there's a home icon at the bottom. That allows the user to return to the day-at-a-glance screen.

I'll show the four modules in turn as you explore the code for each, but for now, let's discuss how the data will be stored. In the first iteration of wxPIM, the data will be stored locally in the browser using local storage. While this limits how much data a user can store, the average across all browsers is right around 2.5MB, so it's a decent chunk of space available, and most browsers actually allow for more, so in terms of whether this is useful or not for this application, it actually is. More important, however, is that local storage is exceedingly simple to use, and since we're more interested in using Webix than worrying about what the most robust data storage mechanism in a browser is, local storage does the trick. Of course, as an exercise, you should feel perfectly free to change the code to deal with something like IndexedDB if you want.

High-Level Code Structure

Speaking of code, let's jump right into that now by first talking about how you'll organize the code for wxPIM. As I mentioned, you'll want to make things fairly modular so it can be extended, and you'll want to reflect that in how the code is structured. Figure 5-3 shows the directory structure you'll use, as well as the files that will make up the app.

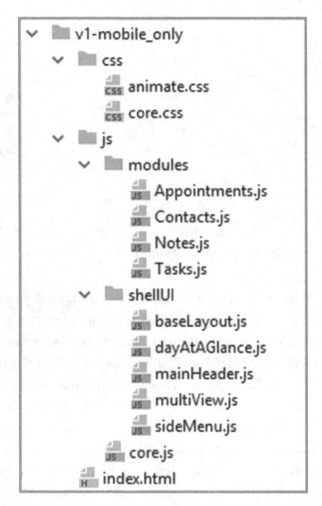

Figure 5-3. *Directory/application code structure*

The top-level directory could be named anything, so that's not important, other than the fact that there's an index.html file in it, which is the launching point for the app. Under the root directory there are two subfolders, css and js, to hold stylesheets and the application code, respectively. The css directory contains two files, animate.css and core.css. I'll skip animate.css for now since that's something I'll touch on later, but core.css is where you'll find the styles for WxPIM, what few there are in this iteration. You'll look at that file in detail later.

The js directory is further broken into a modules directory, which will store the code for the four modules (one .js file for each), and a shellUI directory, which will store the code for the application shell.

Speaking of the application shell, this is a common pattern used by mobile apps, and really any web app, mobile or otherwise, that is intended to be in some way modular, often even when modularity isn't a concern. The idea here is that you have a core application, or a core user interface, that you put pieces of functionality into, rather than trying to build a single, monolithic application. The files in the shellUI directory comprise that core application, that shell, so to speak. You'll look at each of these, in turn, to give them meaning, but at a high level, the baseLayout.js file provides the high-level layout of the app, which includes the header found in mainHeader.js and the multiView.js file, which is essentially that module content area I mentioned. The dayAtAGlance.js file contains the day-at-a-glance screen, which is, in essence, another module, though a somewhat different one in terms of code structure, as you'll see. Finally, the sideMenu.js file contains, naturally, the sidemenu. Breaking the UI up into files like this provides an organization to it, rather than having one big chunk of JSON to deal with, though it's entirely optional to do this (and in fact, as you'll see, the modules themselves *do not* do this).

You can also see there is a core.js file in the js directory, and this is, as the name implies, the core code of the application. This is where you'll find the logic that switches between modules, as well as helper functions that the modules can use to do their work. This is where execution begins once index.html is loaded and processed, and index. html is the first stop in our code exploration.

index.html

To kick off wxPIM, index.html is loaded by the browser. It's a simple HTML page and probably holds little surprise, but check out Listing 5-1 to be the judge of that!

Listing 5-1. The index.html File

```
<!DOCTYPE html>

<html>

  <head>

    <meta charset="UTF-8">
    <meta name="viewport" content="width=device-width,height=device-
    height,initial-scale=1.0,minimum-scale=1.0,user-scalable=yes">

    <link rel="stylesheet" href="../webix/codebase/webix.css" type="text/css"
      media="screen" charset="utf-8">
    <link rel="stylesheet" href="css/animate.css" type="text/css"
      media="screen" charset="utf-8">
    <link rel="stylesheet" href="css/core.css" type="text/css"
    media="screen" charset="utf-8">

    <script src="../webix/codebase/webix.js" type="text/javascript"
    charset="utf-8"></script>

    <script>
      // Webix debug flags.
      //webix.debug = true;
      //webix.debug_size = true;
      //webix.debug_render = true;
      //webix.debug_proto = true;
      //webix.debug_time = true;
    </script>

    <script src="js/core.js" type="text/javascript" charset="utf-8"></script>
    <script src="js/shellUI/baseLayout.js" type="text/javascript"
    charset="utf-8"></script>
    <script src="js/shellUI/dayAtAGlance.js" type="text/javascript"
    charset="utf-8"></script>
    <script src="js/shellUI/mainHeader.js" type="text/javascript"
    charset="utf-8"></script>
```

```
<script src="js/shellUI/multiView.js" type="text/javascript"
charset="utf-8"></script>
<script src="js/shellUI/sideMenu.js" type="text/javascript"
charset="utf-8"></script>
<script src="js/modules/Appointments.js" type="text/javascript"
charset="utf-8"></script>
<script src="js/modules/Contacts.js" type="text/javascript"
charset="utf-8"></script>
<script src="js/modules/Notes.js" type="text/javascript"
charset="utf-8"></script>
<script src="js/modules/Tasks.js" type="text/javascript"
charset="utf-8"></script>

<title>wxPIM</title>

</head>

<body></body>

</html>
```

As I said, this should all look familiar to you by now. Of note, though, is the second meta tag, which sets up the UI so that it's scaled 1:1 on the screen to begin with. It also allows the user to scale it thanks to the user-scalable=yes setting. This is a little unusual in a mobile app because usually they can't be scaled (by the using pinching and zooming, for example). I prefer this be allowed, though, since my eyes are getting older and being able to zoom is more useful than I'd like to admit these days!

The Webix stylesheet is imported, along with the animate.css file (which, again, I'll talk about later) and the core.css file that I previously described. After that comes the importing of the main Webix script.

After that you'll notice a <script> block with some Webix stuff that you haven't seen before. Webix offers some debugging help in the form of these debug flags, but this is true only if you use the debug version of Webix by loading webix_debug.js instead of webix.js. If you do, then these flags become available. They are as follows:

- webix.debug: Enables event logging, which allows you to see what events are available and what events fire

- webix.debug_size: Enables logging of component sizes

- `webix.debug_render`: Enables logging about components that are rendered

- `webix.debug_proto`: Enables logging of information about how components are created

- `webix.debug_time`: Enables logging of component render-time data

Enabling these will generate *a lot* of log messages in your browser's console, but this can be beneficial to figure out issues you're having when needed. They're commented out for that reason, but they're present and ready to be used if needed.

After that comes the imports of the various script files that make up the application code. Note that the `core.js` file *must* be imported first because all the others refer to it and extend the object that's constructed in it. The order of the others shouldn't matter, though.

That is, as they say, all there is to that! You'll note that there isn't even a JavaScript call to kick off the application, which may seem odd, but it's easily explainable and is part of the interesting stuff that begins in `core.js`, which is our next stop.

core.js

The `core.js` file is where most of the real action is. It defines an object named wxPIM, the only object in global scope other than its class definition in fact (always a good thing!), and all the other code files plug into it or make use of it. Rather than just showing a big listing, I'm instead going to break this file up into chunks to explain it, mostly broken down to functions, which should make it easier to digest (and I'll do this with the other source files as applicable too).

Note   I've taken some liberties with spacing and have removed all comments in the interest of condensing things as much as possible. That's why the actual code in the code bundle looks a bit different from what you see here. But rest assured that the actual code hasn't been changed at all; what you see here is what it actually is.

Preamble

To begin with, being good ECMAScript 6 (ES6) citizens, here you'll write your code in strict mode (which in fact became available with ES5). This has the consequence that this app won't work in Internet Explorer before v10, Firefox before v4, Chrome before v13, Safari before v5.1, and Opera before v12. Writing for modern browsers is always more pleasant when feasible, and for this app it definitely is (where "modern" means a wide swath of browsers). Note that this is going to be true of all the source files from here on out, so in the interest of not repeating myself, I'll leave this bit out going forward:

```
"use strict";

class WXPIM {
...
}
const wxPIM = new WXPIM();
```

After that, you create a class called WXPIM. The rest of this section will be looking at the members of this class, so I've shortened that all to the ellipses so that I can show you that after the class is declared, an instance named wxPIM is created. That's when the app execution actually begins because the constructor function for the class is executed at this point.

Constructor

The constructor performs a few key tasks.

```
constructor() {

  webix.rules.isNumberOrBlank = function(inValue) {
    if (inValue == "") { return true; }
    return webix.rules.isNumber(inValue);
  };

  webix.rules.isEmailOrBlank = function(inValue) {
    if (inValue == "") { return true; }
    return webix.rules.isEmail(inValue);
  };
```

```
  this.isEditingExisting = false;
  this.editingID = null;

  this.moduleClasses = { };
  this.modules = { };
  this.activeModule = null;

  webix.ready(this.start.bind(this));

}
```

First, two new Webix validation rules are needed. The reason for this is that the two predefined functions, `isNumber` and `isEmail`, consider a blank field as being invalid. But, in some cases, that's not really what you want because if the field is optional, then a blank is, in fact, a valid value. So, I've created these custom validation functions and added them to the `webix.rules` collection so that they can be used when needed. All that needs to happen is to add the initial check for a blank, after which the existing functions can be used, which is nice since it avoids duplicating code.

After that, there are two related members, `isEditingExisting` and `editingID`. These are for when you're editing an existing data item, be it an appointment, contact, note, or task. When the user selects the item they want to edit, `isEditingExisting` gets set to `true`, and the unique ID of the item, which each item has, is stored in `editingID`. That way, when the code that saves the item (which you'll see soon) is executed, it can look at the flag and know whether it's being called in response to adding a new item or editing an existing one. This way, you can have one common save function that handles both cases.

After that you have three members that are related to each other. The `moduleClasses` object is where the classes for each of the four modules is stored. The `modules` member is where the instances of those classes are stored. This is done primarily to keep those classes and instances within the `wxPIM` object, not in global scope. Finally, the `activeModule` member stores the name of the currently active module, meaning which one the user is currently working in. You'll see why that's needed before long.

The last line in the constructor is our friendly neighborhood `webix.ready()` call, specifying the `start()` method of the `wxPIM` object as the callback. Note that you want the `this` reference within `start()` to reference the `wxPIM` object, which it wouldn't without the `bind()` call, which is why that's done.

Lifecycle Event Function: start()

As you just saw, the `start()` method gets called thanks to the `webix.ready()` call in the constructor. This function is responsible for building the UI.

```
start() {

  this.modules.Appointments = new this.moduleClasses.Appointments();
  this.modules.Contacts = new this.moduleClasses.Contacts();
  this.modules.Notes = new this.moduleClasses.Notes();
  this.modules.Tasks = new this.moduleClasses.Tasks();

  webix.ui(this.getBaseLayoutConfig());

  webix.ui(this.getSideMenuConfig());

  wxPIM.dayAtAGlance();

}
```

First, each of the four modules is instantiated, and the reference to them is stored in the modules' members. Next, you use the `webix.ui()` function with which you're quite familiar to build the base layout. Don't worry about what `getBaseLayoutConfig()` does (or `getSideMenuConfig()` for that matter) because I'll get to those, but it's enough right now to know that they return an object that defines Webix components.

With the base layout and `sidemenu` built, all that's left is to display the data on the day-at-a-glance screen, which is what the call to `dayAtAGlance()` obviously does, but I'll cover that when you get to the `dayAtAGlance.js` file. Before that, let's continue with the `core.js` code.

Lifecycle Event Function: launchModule()

Whenever the user clicks one of the module names in the `sidemenu`, the `launchModule()` method is called. This is responsible for showing that module and making sure it's ready for use.

```
launchModule(inModuleName) {

  if (wxPIM.activeModule) {
    wxPIM.modules[wxPIM.activeModule].deactivate();
  }
```

```
    wxPIM.activeModule = inModuleName;

    $$("sidemenu").hide();

    $$("headerLabel").setValue(inModuleName);

    wxPIM.editingID = null;
    wxPIM.isEditingExisting = false;

    $$(`module${inModuleName}-itemsCell`).show();
    $$(`module${inModuleName}-container`).show();

    wxPIM.modules[inModuleName].refreshData();

    wxPIM.modules[inModuleName].activate();

}
```

The first step is to give whatever module is currently active, if any, a change to deactivate itself. What this means for a given module varies, and it could mean nothing in fact, as in there's nothing for a module to do. But, you give them a chance anyway by calling the deactivate() method (which I'll describe a little more when I cover the modules themselves).

Next, you record the name of the module being switched to. The argument passed into launchModule() will be one of Appointments, Contacts, Notes, or Tasks. After that, the sidemenu is hidden because if this isn't done, then it'll still be visible when the new module is switched to, and it's just not a great user experience then.

Now, the header text is updated to reflect the new module name. You'll be looking at the mainHeader.js code shortly where this header is found.

After that, the two editing-related members I previously explained are set so that the module initially won't think it's editing an existing item.

After that comes three lines that will make more sense once you examine the first module's code, but in short, they ensure that the module is showing its summary view (for example, the list of contacts in the Contacts module) and that the data displayed is fresh.

I know that it may be a little disconcerting to see all of this without having the context of the module's code yet, but I think this gives you the basic idea. Once you look at the code for the first module, I suggest coming back to examine this function because I think you'll understand what's happening once you do, if you don't right now. Until then, let's continue with the core.js code.

Utility Function: sortArray()

The next two functions are what I call *utility functions* in that they aren't Webix-specific; they are general-purpose JavaScript functions. The first of these is the sortArray() function. It's really nothing more than a typical JavaScript sorting function but one that includes a little extra logic so that it sorts objects in an array based on a specified property of those objects and in a specified direction.

```
sortArray(inArray, inProperty, inDirection) {

  inArray.sort(function compare(inA, inB) {

    inA = (inA[inProperty] + "").toLowerCase();
    inB = (inB[inProperty] + "").toLowerCase();

    if (inA > inB) {
      if (inDirection === "D") {
        return -1;
      } else {
        return 1;
      }
    } else if (inA < inB) {
      if (inDirection === "D") {
        return 1;
      } else {
        return -1;
      }
    } else {
      return 0;
    }

  });

}
```

As you can see, the inArray parameter is sorted based on the inProperty property of the objects in the array, and in the direction specified by inDirection. Note the first two lines in the sort() function; this function converts the property value to a string and lowercases it. This is so that a case-insensitive sort is done. Of course, the direction

191

specified is used to determine the correct return value from the sort() function, but ultimately this isn't anything Webix-specific at all; it's just plain JavaScript. You could use this in any other application whether it uses Webix or not. You'll see where this method is used when you look at some module code.

Utility Function: objectAsArray()

The objectAsArray() method is another general-purpose utility function that isn't Webix-specific at all.

```
objectAsArray(inObject) {

  const array = [ ];

  for (const key in inObject) {
    if (inObject.hasOwnProperty(key)) {
      array.push(inObject[key]);
    }
  }

  return array;

};
```

Its job is simply to take in an object and return an array where each element is one property of the object (the value of the property to be more accurate). So, given an object { a : "foo", b : "bar" }, you would get back an array ["foo", "bar"]. Alternatively, you might get back ["bar", "foo"] because the order of object key iteration is nondeterministic. But, if you're guessing that might be why the sortArray() method exists, then pat yourself on the back!

Module Helper Function: getModuleData()

The next three methods are what I call *module helper functions*. They are functions that encapsulate some common functions that all the modules need, so rather than duplicate them in each module, I pulled them out and made them common as part of the core code.

The first of these is getModuleData(), which is used to pull the data for a specified module out of local storage.

```
getModuleData(inModuleName) {

  let items = localStorage.getItem(`${inModuleName}DB`);

  if (!items) {
    items = { };
    localStorage.setItem(`${inModuleName}DB`, webix.stringify(items));
  } else {
    items = JSON.parse(items);
  }

  return items;

};
```

That's pretty simple, right? In addition to retrieving the data, which is stored
in local storage under a key formed by concatenating the module name with DB (so
AppointmentsDB or ContactsDB or NotesDB or TasksDB), it also includes logic that creates
an empty object in local storage if one isn't found. This way, assuming this function is
the only place that tries to retrieve the data for a module (hint: it is!), then you can be
assured that you'll never have null for a data collection fed to a module. That's a good
way to avoid errors!

Of course, local storage only stores strings, so you need to use JSON.parse() to
get a proper JavaScript object to return to the caller in the case where you already had
something stored for the specified module.

Notice the use of webix.stringify() rather than JSON.stringify() like you might
expect. The webix.stringify() function is one of a number of *common helpers*, as
they're called in the Webix documentation, that Webix supplies. There are quite a few
such functions, including things like this:

- animate(): Animates some HTML element

- clone(): Makes a shallow copy of an object

- copy(): Makes a deep copy of an object

- delay(): Waits a specified number of milliseconds and then executes
  specified code

- editStop(): Closes active editors in all Webix components

- `extend()`: Merges the contents of two objects together into the first object

- `isArray()`: Checks whether a passed value is an array

- `isDate()`: Checks whether a passed value is a `Date` object

- `jsonp`: Issues a JSON-P request

- `once()`: Allows you to call some code at most one time

- `print()`: Prints a view according to a specified string

- `send()`: Sends an HTTP request to a server, emulating form submission

- `toCSV()`: Exports the data to a data component as a comma-separated value file

- `uid()`: Returns a unique ID

As you can see, I've just pulled a few to show you, but there are quite a few more, some of which you'll see used throughout the rest of this book, but you should explore what's available as time allows in the Webix documentation.

For now, why use `webix.stringify()` rather than `JSON.stringify()` you ask? Well, the truth is that in this instance, it wouldn't have made any difference; I used it just to serve as an introduction to these helper functions. But, what `webix.stringify()` does that `JSON.stringify()` doesn't is convert `Date` objects into strings according to the current `webix.i18n.parseFormat`, which is a format specifier (`%Y-%m-%d %H:%i"` for the default `"en-US"` locale, for example) that tells Webix how to format a `Date` object when converting to a string. This means you can change how dates are converted throughout the UI globally by altering the format for a given locale, and then `webix.stringify()` will use it too, giving you an important part of internationalization in your Webix apps.

Module Helper Function: saveHandler()

The next method you'll encounter in `code.js` is `saveHandler()`, which is called by a module when the user clicks the Save button, whether while creating a new item or editing an existing one.

```
saveHandler(inModuleName, inFormIDs) {

  const itemData = { };
  for (let i = 0; i < inFormIDs.length; i++) {
    const formData = $$(inFormIDs[i]).getValues();
    webix.proto(itemData, formData);
  }
  itemData.id = wxPIM.editingID;

  delete itemData.$init;

  const moduleData = wxPIM.getModuleData(inModuleName);
  moduleData[itemData.id] = itemData;
  localStorage.setItem(`${inModuleName}DB`, webix.stringify(moduleData));

  wxPIM.modules[inModuleName].refreshData();
  $$(`module${inModuleName}-itemsCell`).show();

  webix.message({ type : "error", text : "Item saved" });

}
```

Most modules have a single form, but the Contacts module, as you'll see later, has two. Because of this, the inFormIDs argument is present. This is an array of Webix IDs of any forms a module needs to save, as many as it needs. So, the first step is to take each form, call getValues() on it to get the data the user entered, and then use the webix. proto() helper function to merge them. The webix.proto() function is one of those helper functions that takes one or more objects and merges them into the first one specified. So here, for each form, you merge it into the itemData object, which starts out empty. This is done for each form named in the inFormIDs array.

Once that's done, an id property is added using the value stored in wxPIM. editingID. This will be set when the user selects an item for editing, and it will also be set to a new value when they go to add an item.

Next, you have to take care of something: the $init member. The webix.proto() function adds this member to the target object, but you don't want to save that to local storage, so you can delete it here.

After that, a call to wxPIM.getModuleData() retrieves the data for the named module (named by the inModuleName argument, of course) from local storage. It's just a plain JavaScript object at this point, so the next line adds a new member, keyed by the item ID, to store the item in. Then, a call to localStorage.setItem() saves the data for the module back into local storage, overwriting what's there.

The next step is to return the user to the summary view for the module and ensure the data is refreshed. This means that after adding a contact, you want the user to see the contact list, including their new data, of course. Every module has a refreshData() method, as you'll see shortly, so that method is called through the wxPIM.modules object, which you'll recall stores a reference to the object instantiated for each module. After that, you have to switch from the detail view of the module to the summary view, which uses a common Webix ID format for each module (Appointments-itemsCell, for example).

Finally, a slide-down message is shown in the upper-right corner of the screen to indicate the item has been saved using the webix.message() helper function. You may find it odd that I've specified a type of error here, but the reason is that an error message is a red box, whereas a nonerror message is a plain white box. Frankly, the nonerror version is hard to see and can be missed by the user, but the error type stands out more. The message will go away on its own after a second, or the user can click it to dismiss it entirely. You may know this type of message as a *toast message*, by the way; it's essentially the same thing.

Module Helper Function: deleteHandler()

The final bit of code in core.js is another module helper function, deleteHandler(), which, like saveHandler(), provides a common bit of functionality to modules, this time to delete items. In Figure 5-4, you can see an example of what it looks like when the user wants to delete an item, an appointment, in this case, courtesy of this deleteHandler() method.

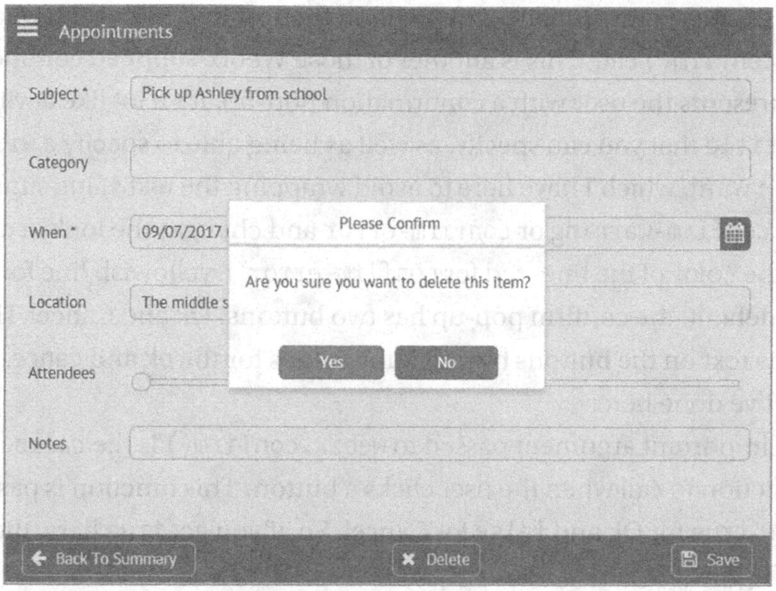

Figure 5-4. *An example of the delete dialog*

The code for this is pretty simple, although there's something new for you to see too.

```
deleteHandler(inModuleName) {

  webix.html.addCss(webix.confirm({
    title : `Please Confirm`, ok : "Yes", cancel : "No", type : "confirm-
    warning",
    text : `Are you sure you want to delete this item?`, width : 300,
    callback : function(inResult) {
      if (inResult) {
        const dataItems = wxPIM.getModuleData(inModuleName);
        delete dataItems[wxPIM.editingID];
        localStorage.setItem(`${inModuleName}DB`, webix.
        stringify(dataItems));
        wxPIM.modules[inModuleName].refreshData();
        $$(`module${inModuleName}-itemsCell`).show();
        webix.message({ type : "error", text : "Item deleted" });
      }
    }
  }), "animated bounceIn");

};
```

Let's skip the `webix.html.addCss()` function for now and talk about what's inside it, the `webix.confirm()` call. This is another of those Webix-supplied common helper functions. It presents the user with a confirmation pop-up. It's a lot like a window in that it's got a `title` that you can specify, as well as being able to specify a `width` and/or a `height` if you want, which I have here to avoid wrapping the text value supplied. The `type` is either `confirm-warning` or `confirm-error` and changes the look of the pop-up by changing the color of the line (red for `confirm-error`, a yellowish line for `confirm-warning`). By default, the confirm pop-up has two buttons: Ok and Cancel. However, you can set the text on the buttons by providing values for the `ok` and `cancel` config attributes, as I've done here.

The most important argument passed to `webix.confirm()` is the `callback` option. This is the function to call when the user clicks a button. This function is passed a Boolean value, `true` for Ok and `false` for Cancel. So, if you get `true` here, then you do the work of deleting.

Really, that code should look kind of familiar because it's not vastly different from the code in `saveHandler()`! You get the data for the module just like in that case, and then the property from the resulting data object is deleted based on the ID of the selected item, which is the key of the properties in the object. Then, the object is written back to local storage. Finally, as with `saveHandler()`, you show the user the module's summary view again, being sure to refresh the data, and then show a deleted message.

Now, let's go back to the `webix.html.addCss()` function that wraps the call to `webix.confirm()`. The `webix.html.addCss()` function is another kind of helper function Webix provides as part of the `webix.html` namespace. These are functions for dealing generically with HTML and the DOM. The `webix.html.addCss()` function adds a CSS class to a DOM node. In this case, it's the DOM node produced by the call to `webix.confirm()`. The class that's added, `"animated bounceIn"` (two classes in fact!), is provided by another library, one of which I'll quickly discuss now.

More helpers!   In addition to `webix.html.addCss()`, you'll also find in the `webix.html` namespace `addStyle()`, which adds a style definition to the page; `insertBefore()`, which inserts a new DOM node into the specified position; `pos()`, which returns the current mouse position relative to the upper-left corner of the page; and `remove()`, which removes an HTML element from the page, among others. Also note that there are other "helper" namespaces, namely, `webix.ajax`, which includes functions for making remote calls; `webix.clipbuffer`, which includes functions for working with the clipboard; `webix.color`, which includes color transformation functions; `webix.env`, which includes flags that describe the current runtime environment; `webix.history`, which includes functions for dealing with history tracking; `webix.i18n` (which you've seen some of already), which contains internationalization/number/date format functions; `webix.markup`, which contains functions for loading from HTML; `webix.promise`, which contains functions for working with promises; and `webix.rules` (which you've also seen) that contains validation rules. As I've been doing, I'll continue to introduce functions from these namespaces as needed, but there's far too much there to cover everything, so please do examine the Webix documentation to get a fuller picture.

animate.css

As I've mentioned, as powerful as Webix is, sometimes you need to hit up a third party to provide some extra oomph. One of those third parties you might use is the `animate.css` library, which is nothing more than a CSS file that provides additional CSS classes for you to use. The `animate.css` library's motto is "Just-add-water CSS animations," and that about sums it up: you just add classes to elements, and you'll get some wicked-cool animations with no more effort!

Because Webix is generally very lightweight, it's easy to get a reference to a top-level DOM node for any given component. With that, you can apply these animations trivially, as with the delete pop-up. The `"animated bounceIn"` classes being added results in the pop-up bouncing into view, growing and shrinking and gradually stopping. It's a nice little effect that gets the user's attention more than the pop-up just appearing would.

I highly recommend exploring the animate.css site at http://daneden.me/animate to see all that it offers because it's a nice complement to Webix (and you can of course use it without Webix too).

core.css

The next thing to look at is the core.css file, which contains the main stylesheet for wxPIM. There isn't much here, but I'll go through it anyway, starting with this class definition:

```
.cssSideMenu .webix_view {
  background-color : #eceff1;
}
```

This rule gives you a grayish color as the background of the sidemenu. The next class also deals with the sidemenu.

```
.cssSideMenu .webix_list_item {
  line-height : 35px;
  border-bottom-color : #d0d0d0;
}
```

This one is responsible for two things: making the items in the sidemenu a little thicker height-wise than they would be by default (to make them better touch targets) and adding a subtle divider line beneath each to give some visual separation to the items.

The final rule is a simple one.

```
.webix_window {
  box-shadow : 0 0 40px #202020;
}
```

This adds a deeper shadow to any Webix window, which includes the window seen in the Appointments module when the user clicks a date to see appointments for it. I just feel like the deeper shadow makes the window stand out better, which to me is more visually pleasing.

That's about all there is for styling in wxPIM, aside from some styling done inline for specific things later, which you'll see as you go through the module code. But, before you do that, let's talk about the code that builds the core shell UI.

baseLayout.js

The next file you'll look at is baseLayout.js, which, as the name implies, provides the base layout for the entire wxPIM application.

```
wxPIM.getBaseLayoutConfig = function() {

  return {
    rows : [
      wxPIM.getMainHeaderConfig(),
      wxPIM.getMultiviewConfig()
    ]
  };

};
```

Yes, that's all there is to it! All you have is the header up top and a multiview component beneath. The configurations for both are present in the mainHeader.js and multiView.js files, respectively, and each provides a function to call to get that configuration, so this is really all you need for the base layout.

mainHeader.js

The wxPIM.getMainHeaderConfig() function that you saw reference to in baseLayout.js is of course found in the mainHeader.js file, and its only job is to return an object that defines a Webix toolbar, which is what the header is built out of.

```
wxPIM.getMainHeaderConfig = function() {

  return {
    view : "toolbar", id : "toolbar",
    elements : [
      { view: "icon", icon: "bars",
        click : function() {
```

```
          if ($$("sidemenu").isVisible()) {
            $$("sidemenu").hide();
          } else {
            $$("sidemenu").show();
          }
        }
      },
      { id : "headerLabel", view: "label",
        label : "", defaultLabel : "wxPIM Day-at-a-glance"
      }
    ]
  };

};
```

The toolbar, which has an id because you'll need to be able to get a reference to it later in the sideMenu.js code, consists of just two elements: the hamburger menu icon that triggers display of the sidemenu and a simple text label (which again needs an id defined) where you'll show what module the user is currently in. Note that the label also has a non-Webix attribute, defaultLabel, that I use to store the text for the day-at-a-glance screen. It's interesting to know that you can add these sorts of arbitrary attributes, which you can then access via the config attribute of the component. It's a good way to convey extra information as part of a component, keeping it encapsulated within the component.

The click handler of the menu icon takes care of toggling the sidemenu. You can always tell if a Webix component is currently visible by calling the isVisible() method. Interestingly, you can also get this information by examining the config. hidden properly, which also gets updated as the visibility is changed. But, doing it that way feels weird to me because the config property is meant to convey what the initial configuration options are, so in my mind, they shouldn't change (and in practice, they mostly don't), but visibility is an exception. I suggest always using the method approach to avoid any potential problems, but I wanted to make you aware of the option.

multiView.js

Next up is the `multiView.js` file, which, like `mainHeader.js`, just contains a single function that returns the Webix configuration for a `multiview` component, one of the two main components of the base layout of wxPIM as you know.

```
wxPIM.getMultiviewConfig = function() {

  return {
    view : "multiview", id : "moduleArea",
    animate : { type : "flip", subtype : "horizontal" },
    cells : [
      wxPIM.getDayAtAGlanceConfig(),
      wxPIM.modules.Appointments.getUIConfig(),
      wxPIM.modules.Contacts.getUIConfig(),
      wxPIM.modules.Notes.getUIConfig(),
      wxPIM.modules.Tasks.getUIConfig()
    ]
  };

};
```

Each module gets a cell in the `multiview`, as does the day-at-a-glance screen, and since you'll be switching between these views programmatically, as you saw in `core.js`, the component needs an `id` so you can get a reference to it. In addition, I've specifically defined the animation type here to be a 3D flip animation horizontally. This to my eyes just looks cooler than the default slide animation that flipping between the cells of a `multiview` does.

sideMenu.js

The `sideMenu.js` file is next, which houses the code for the navigation `sidemenu`, and while it's got a little more meat on its bones, it's still not an especially complicated bit of code.

```
wxPIM.getSideMenuConfig = function() {

  return {
    view : "sidemenu", id : "sidemenu", width : 200,
    position : "left", css : "cssSideMenu",
```

```
      state : (inState) => {
        const toolbarHeight = $$("toolbar").$height;
        inState.top = toolbarHeight;
        inState.height -= toolbarHeight;
      },
      body : {
        rows : [
          { view : "list",scroll : true,
            select : false, type : { height : 40 }, id : "sidemenu_list",
            template : `<span class="webix_icon fa-#icon#"></span> #value#`,
            data : [
              { id : "Appointments", value : "Appointments", icon : "calendar" },
              { id : "Contacts", value : "Contacts", icon : "address-card" },
              { id : "Notes", value : "Notes", icon : "file-text" },
              { id : "Tasks", value : "Tasks", icon : "tasks" }
            ],
            click : wxPIM.launchModule
          },
          { height : 2, template : "<hr>" },
          { cols : [
            { },
            { view : "button", type : "icon", label : "", icon : "home",
              align : "right", width : 32,
              click : () => {
                wxPIM.dayAtAGlance();
                $$("sidemenu").hide();
                $$("dayAtAGlance").show();
              }
            },
            { }
          ] }
        ]
      }
  };

};
```

The sidemenu itself is specified to be on the left side of the screen with a width of 200 pixels, and it uses the cssSideMenu style rule that you saw previously to give it a grayish background color. The state option provides a function that defines the position and size of the sidemenu. The reason this is necessary is because by default, the sidemenu would overlap the header. That's not ideal because then the hamburger icon would be covered, and the user wouldn't be able to close the sidemenu, not without selecting a new module anyway (or the home icon). So, the code in the anonymous state function grabs the height of the toolbar and makes the height of the sidemenu the height of the screen minus the height of the toolbar; then it pushes the sidemenu down the same number of pixels as the height of the toolbar. That way, the sidemenu fills the entire left of the screen *except* for the height of the toolbar.

Within the sidemenu you have a list component that uses some inline data to show each of the modules. Each data item contains a FontAwesome icon reference, which is used as part of the template for the list to render each module's name and a suitable icon next to it. I've also made the height of each element 40 pixels using the type attribute that is used to further define the list items so that they are easier touch targets. Clicking any item in the list simply calls the wxPIM.launchModule() method you've already looked at.

Below the list is a plain old HTML <hr> element. Since the list by default will fill the sidemenu, this means the line will be down near the bottom because right after the line is another row where the home icon is. So, to visualize this, there are three rows in the layout that makes up the sidemenu: the list, which fills all available space; the row with the <hr>; and the row with the home icon. Since the latter two either have a height defined (in the case of the <hr> container row) or have a height by virtue of the content (in the case of the home icon row), the list won't fill all the space of the sidemenu, only the space available after Webix accounts for the other two rows. That's also why I've set scroll to true on the list. Without that, if you had a lot more modules, then on a nontouchscreen you wouldn't be able to scroll the list, and that would be obviously bad.

When the home icon is clicked, there are three steps to get the day-at-a-glance screen showing. First, the screen must be populated with data, which is what the wxPIM.dayAtAGlance() call does, which you'll be looking at next. Then, the sidemenu needs to be hidden, and finally, the day-at-a-glance cell of the multiview needs to be shown, so that's what's done in the click handler for the icon.

dayAtAGlance.js

The dayAtAGlance.js file contains all the code for the day-at-a-glance screen and is broken down into two functions that you need to look at.

getDayAtAGlanceConfig()

The first function is the one to get the configuration for the UI components, and it's very straightforward.

```
wxPIM.getDayAtAGlanceConfig = function() {

  return {
    id : "dayAtAGlance", view : "scrollview", borderless : true, body : {
      paddingX : 20, paddingY : 20, rows : [
        { view : "fieldset", label : "Appointments",
          body : { id : "dayAtAGlanceScreen_Appointments",  rows : [ ] }
        },
        { height : 20 },
        { view : "fieldset", label : "Tasks",
          body : { id : "dayAtAGlanceScreen_Tasks", rows : [ ] }
        }
      ]
    }
  };

};
```

I'm housing everything is a scrollview component so that the user can scroll through the items on the screen easily. I've removed the border here with borderless : true to make it all look a bit more clean because within the scrollview are two rows with each being a fieldset. A fieldset is a border with a text label, so having a border outside just doesn't look as clean. Note that I've used paddingX and paddingY to give some space around the two fieldset components on all sides. This again is just an aesthetic choice on my part. This is the same reason for the row with the height of 20 between them: it just provides some separation between the two fieldset components. Each fieldset, of course, has a label to tell the user what it is, and since appointments and tasks are the only two things in wxPIM that has a date attached to it, that's all you have a section for.

Within each `fieldset`, you should note that the `rows` attribute is an empty array. That's very much by design because those arrays will be dynamically filled by the next function you'll look at now.

getAtAGlance()

The `dayAtAGlance()` function is responsible for populating those two row arrays in the `fieldset` components and hence populating the screen. The way I've written it attempts to avoid as much duplicate code as possible.

```
wxPIM.dayAtAGlance = function() {

  if (wxPIM.activeModule) {
    wxPIM.modules[wxPIM.activeModule].deactivate();
  }

  wxPIM.activeModule = null;

  const worker = function(inWhich) {
    let sortProperty = "when";
    let sortDirection = "A";
    let dateProperty = "when";
    let template = webix.template("#subject# - #when# #location#");
    if (inWhich == "Tasks") {
      sortProperty = "value";
      sortDirection = "A";
      dateProperty = "dueDate";
      template = webix.template("#subject#");
    }
    let dataItems = wxPIM.getModuleData(inWhich);
    dataItems = wxPIM.objectAsArray(dataItems);
    wxPIM.sortArray(dataItems, sortProperty, sortDirection);
    const currentDate = new Date().setHours(0, 0, 0, 0);
    const rows = [ ];
    for (let i = 0; i < dataItems.length; i++) {
      const item = dataItems[i];
      const itemDate = new Date(item[dateProperty]).setHours(0, 0, 0, 0);
```

```
      if (itemDate == currentDate) {
        if (item.location) {
          item.location = "(" + item.location + ")";
        } else {
          item.location = "";
        }
        if (item.status == 1) {
          item.status = "Ongoing";
        } else {
          item.status = "Completed";
        }
        item[dateProperty] = webix.i18n.timeFormatStr(new
        Date(item[dateProperty]));
        rows.push({ borderless : true, template : template(item), height :
        30 });
      }
    }
    webix.ui(rows, $$(`dayAtAGlanceScreen_${inWhich}`));
  };

  worker("Tasks");
  worker("Appointments");

  $$("headerLabel").setValue($$("headerLabel").config.defaultLabel);

};
```

The first step is to give whatever module is current, if any, a chance to de-activate itself with a call to its deactivate() method. Remember that dayAtAGlance() will be called only when the app starts up or when the user clicks the home icon, and it's this latter case where deactivate() comes into play, but only for the Appointments module. The problem here is that, as you'll see, there is a window that can be displayed in that module, and a window sits above the z-order of the main layout of the app. This means that if you're in the Appointments Module and that window is showing and you click the home icon, without doing anything special that window will remain and obscure the day-at-a-glance screen. As you'll see, the deactivate() method of that module deals with hiding that window, but to keep things consistent, every module provides such a function in case they too need to do anything when they are switched away from.

208

Anyway, once that's done, you also must ensure that no module is registered as current, so that's where wxPIM.activeModule gets set to null.

After that comes the definition of the worker() function, but I want to skip looking at that code for just a second and go to the part after that where it's actually called, once for each module that you want to display data for. The two calls to the worker() function pass in the name of the module, and with that, it has all the information it needs to populate the data in a (mostly) generic way. This is where I was talking about avoiding duplicate code earlier. Having this one function means not having to largely duplicate the code, once for appointments and once for tasks.

Now, going back to the worker() code now, you see four variables defined first: sortProperty, sortDirection, dateProperty, and template. The first two define what property of an object a sort is done on and in what direction. The dateProperty variable tells you which property of the object contains the date. The template variable provides the template that will be used to render each row in the fieldset for the appropriate module within the scrollview of the day-at-a-glance screen that you saw in the previous section. Here, the webix.template() function is used, which converts a string to a Webix templating function. This isn't something you would typically do because simply passing the string to the data-aware component via its template config option is usually enough. However, I wanted to demonstrate it, and since the template must be defined dynamically here based on what type of data is being rendered, it made sense to show it in this case.

Note that you declare these variables assuming you're populating appointments but then override them for tasks.

Once that's done, a call to wxPIM.getModuleData() is done to get the data for the module named by inWhich. Then, since what you get from that is an object, a call is made to wxPIM.objectAsArray() to get an array of objects. See, those utility functions you looked at early are coming into play now! Once you have an array, it's time to sort it, and this is where those first two variables that deal with sort direction and what property to sort on are used.

After that, since this is day-at-a-glance, you care only about appointments or tasks that are due today, so you need to get the current date. Since you don't want to take time into account here, the setHours() method is called, which is a plain old JavaScript Date object method, and passing it all zeros results in the time being set to midnight. If you do the same for the date associated with the appointment or task, then you can match the dates based on the date only, and without having to pull out the individual month, day, and year values and comparing them individually.

Once you have a sorted array and the current date, then it's time to render configuration objects for the rows in the target `fieldset`, one for each data item, into the `rows` variable. But, you only want items for the current date, so the first step is to grab the date value for the data item, based on the `dateProperty` variable, since the object might (and in fact do) store their dates in different property names. The date is again "normalized" in terms of time, and then you can do a simple comparison on the `Date` objects. If the data item is for today, then it needs to be added to the array of rows.

But, first, there are some minor "fixups" to take care of to be sure everything displays how you want. For appointments, the `location` attribute you want to be surrounded with parentheses. That could have been done as part of the template, but then for appointments without a location, you'd see "()" on the screen, and that just looks kind of ugly, so this fixup avoids that. Then, for tasks, the `status` is a numeric code 1 or 2, but you want to display the status as Ongoing or Completed, so that is done as well. Finally, for tasks, while you couldn't consider time when comparing the `Date` objects, you *do* want to display the time of the appointment, so the `webix.i18n.timeFormatStr()` function is used, which formats the time component of the `Date` object only in a format according to the machine's current locale.

Finally, an object is added to the `rows` array for the data item, using the `template` determined earlier and the data item that is now all fixed up. After all the data items are processed, a call to `webix.ui()` specifying the `rows` array as well as the ID of the correct `fieldset` causes Webix to replace the current contents of that component with the new content, and you get your appointments and tasks on the screen!

And with that, you've looked at all the core code of wxPIM. All that's left is the code for each individual module, which you'll pick up in the next chapter.

Summary

In this chapter, I began to break down the wxPIM application and explore its code. You saw how a clearly defined structure allows for a clean, easy-to-understand application that is also modular and extensible if need be. You saw how you can use Webix to build a shell application that you can extend by plugging in more code to provide new functionality.

In the next chapter, you'll look at those modules in detail and see how each is built. You'll see a lot of Webix in action, taking all that you've learned so far and applying it as you continue to build this real application.

CHAPTER 6

Getting Practical: Building wxPIM Redux

In the previous chapter, you began dissecting the wxPIM application and looking at the core code that comprises it. In this chapter, you'll continue that exploration, ultimately finishing up the exploration of this code.

You'll pick up where you left off by examining the basic overall structure of modules. You should have an idea about this already given what you saw in the previous chapter, but let's make sure it's totally clear before you dive into the individual module's code.

Modules: Basic Structure

Each of the modules is housed completely in a single JavaScript source file, and each defines a class for the module. The class has a standard structure, as shown in Figure 6-1.

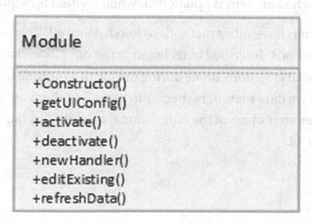

Figure 6-1. *Module class diagram*

© Frank Zammetti 2018
F. Zammetti, *Practical Webix*, https://doi.org/10.1007/978-1-4842-3384-9_6

In fact, the constructor isn't required, and as it happens, only one module provides a constructor. Still, I consider it part of the basic class structure since a JavaScript class will have a default constructor provided by JavaScript itself even if you don't specify one. However, the other methods you see here will be present in every module. You've already seen some of the methods a module provides, but now I'll get into what each is for and when they do it.

- getUIConfig(): Returns an object that defines the Webix component tree for the module's UI

- activate(): Called any time the user switches to the module. What it does, if anything, is dependent on the needs of the module.

- deactivate(): Called any time the user switches away from the module, meaning selects another module or goes to the day-at-a-glance screen. As with activate(), what deactivate() does, which could be nothing, is module-dependent.

- newHandler(): Called when the user clicks the New button to create a new item in the module.

- editExisting(): Called when the user selects an existing item to edit.

- refreshData(): Called any time the data on the summary screen of the module, which is where existing items are shown, needs to be refreshed. This can be when the module is switched to, when an item is added, when an item is updated, or when an item is deleted.

Some modules may have other methods as needed as well. Two of them do, and two just have the methods described here, but only the ones listed here are required as they are the ones called at various times during the life of a module by that core code. Modules may also have data members specific to them, but there are none required by the core code, so they aren't part of the foundational module class structure. They're used as needed, if at all.

In addition to a standard form in terms of code, wxPIM modules also have a regular pattern in terms of their UI. There is a `multiview` that has a summary view and a details view. The summary view presents a list of the items for the module, in some form or other (meaning in a literal Webix `list` component or maybe a `tree` or maybe something else entirely, but it's still a listing of items; that's the basic idea). This summary view provides the user with a chance to select an existing item to edit or to create a new item via a New button in a `toolbar` on the bottom of the screen. Doing either brings them to the details view, where they see the data for the selected item or an empty form if creating a new one. This is also where you find a Delete `button` on the bottom `toolbar` to delete an existing item, as well as a `button` to return to the summary view. This pattern works for all modules, and as you saw earlier, the core code makes some assumptions about this being the layout and the IDs that one or two specific components use.

That gives you the bird's-eye view of what the structure of a module's code is. With that in mind, let's begin looking at the code for the first module, notes.

Notes.js

Wait, what? Why are we looking at notes first? Isn't alphabetical order good enough for you, Mr. Zammetti? Shouldn't we look at appointments first?

Well, there's a simple reason I've chosen to do notes first; it's probably the simplest module of them all while still covering all the bases. Rather than jump into appointments, which has some peculiarities and more code, let's start off with a simpler one and build from there, so notes it is.

It would help to know what the notes module looks like, wouldn't it? This also provides you a general idea what all modules look like because of the common UI structure described in the previous section. Figure 6-2 shows the summary view of the notes module.

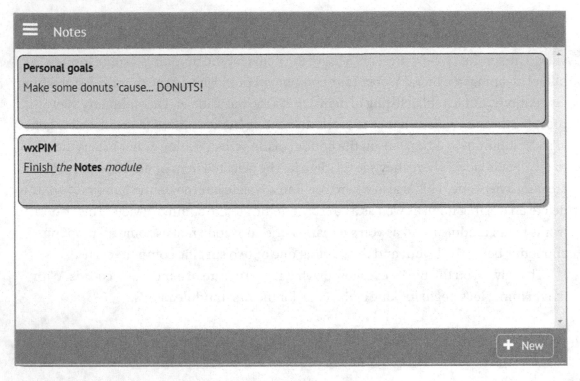

Figure 6-2. *The Notes module, in all it's note-y glory*

Each item can be clicked to edit it, or the New button can be clicked to create a new note. Doing either brings the user to the details view, as shown in Figure 6-3.

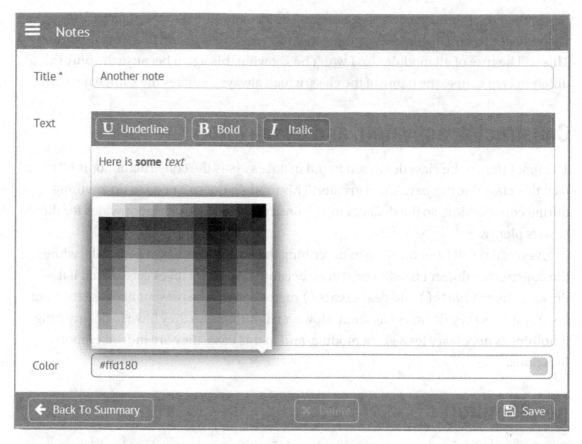

Figure 6-3. *The Note module's details view*

Here, I've clicked the `colorpicker` at the bottom to make the screenshot more interesting! I've also made some of the text for the note bold and some italic to remind you that the `richtext` component allows for this.

Neither of these views is very complicated, but then again, a note app doesn't need to be especially complicated, does it? Let's start looking at the code now, beginning with the opening of the `Notes.js` file.

```
wxPIM.moduleClasses.Notes = class {
...
}
```

Each of the module source files builds a class that is added to the `moduleClasses` property of the `wxPIM` object. Everything that follows here is inside this class definition. This will be true of all modules, so I won't be showing this again because the only thing different is of course the name of the class, which always matches the source file name.

Constructor, activate(), and deactivate()

The first thing in the class definition found in `notes.js` is the constructor...or is it? In fact, this class doesn't have a constructor! This module doesn't need to do anything during construction, so the default empty constructor that JavaScript provides for the class is plenty.

As you'll recall from the section describing the basic structure of a module, while the constructor doesn't need to exist at all because JavaScript takes care of that if it doesn't, the `activate()` and `deactivate()` methods must be present because the core code assumes they do and calls them. However, nothing says they have to do anything if nothing is necessary for a given module, and in this case, they are indeed empty functions.

getUIConfig()

The first real bit of code present in this class definition is `getUIConfig()`, which you know is responsible for providing the Webix component definition for this interface. Here is that method:

```
getUIConfig() {

  const cssListItem = `
    color : #000000;
    height : 66px;
    border : 1px solid #000000;
    border-radius : 8px;
    margin : 8px 10px 12px 4px;
    overflow : hidden;
    padding : 6px 6px 20px 6px;
    box-shadow : 4px 4px #aaaaaa;
    cursor : hand;
  `;
```

```
const cssListItemTitle = `
  font-weight : bold;
  padding-bottom : 6px;
`;

return {
  id : "moduleNotes-container",
  cells : [

    { id : "moduleNotes-itemsCell",
      rows : [
        { view : "list", id : "moduleNotes-items",
          type : {
            templateStart :
              `<div style="${cssListItem}background-color:#color#;"
              onClick="wxPIM.modules.Notes.editExisting('#id#');">`,
            template :
              `<div style="${cssListItemTitle}">#title#</div>#text#`,
            templateEnd : `</div>`
          }
        },
        { view : "toolbar",
          cols : [
            { },
            { view : "button", label : "New", width : "80",
              type : "iconButton", icon : "plus",
              click : this.newHandler.bind(this)
            },
            { width : 6 }
          ]
        }
      ]
    },

    { id : "moduleNotes-details",
      rows : [
        { view : "form", id : "moduleNotes-detailsForm", borderless : true,
```

```
    elements : [
      { view : "text", name : "title", label : "Title", required :
      true,
        bottomPadding : 20, invalidMessage : "Title is required",
        attributes : { maxlength : 50 },
        on : {
          onChange : function() {
            if (this.getParentView().validate()) {
              $$("moduleNotes-saveButton").enable();
            } else {
              $$("moduleNotes-saveButton").disable();
            }
          }
        }
      },
      { id : "moduleNotes-detailsForm-text", view : "richtext",
        name : "text", label : "Text", attributes : { maxlength :
        1000 }
      },
      { view : "colorpicker", name : "color", label : "Color",
        id : "moduleNotes-detailsForm-color"
      },
    ]
  },
  { view : "toolbar",
    cols : [
      { width : 6 },
      { view : "button", label : "Back To Summary", width : "170",
        type : "iconButton", icon : "arrow-left",
        click : () => {
          $$("moduleNotes-itemsCell").show();
        }
      },
      { },
      { id : "moduleNotes-deleteButton", view : "button",
        label : "Delete", width : "90", type : "iconButton",
```

```
          icon : "remove", click : () => { wxPIM.
          deleteHandler("Notes"); }
        },
        { },
        { view : "button", label : "Save", width : "80",
          type : "iconButton", icon : "floppy-o",
          id : "moduleNotes-saveButton", disabled : true,
          click : function() {
            wxPIM.saveHandler("Notes", [ "moduleNotes-detailsForm" ]);
          }
        },
        { width : 6 }
      ]
    }
  ]
}

];

}
```

Before the configuration object is built, two strings are defined that provide some
style information. The cssListItem string will provide the styling for the items in the
list (yes, a literal Webix list component in this case). I wanted a rounded-off box with
a little bit of a drop shadow, an attempt to look sort of like a sticky note (hey, work with
me here a little!). The cssListItemTitle string provides styling for the title in the note to
make it bold and to provide some space between it and the note text. I also set overflow
: hidden so that if you have a really long title or text for a note, it'll just cut off, which I
felt looked better than possibly getting scrollbars in individual notes.

Why not main.css?   You may quite reasonably wonder why I didn't put these styles in `main.css` instead of embedding them in strings here. That certainly would have been possible, but remember that one of the goals is to make each module as pluggable as possible, which means having styles for various modules in a single CSS file wouldn't be a good design. Sure, each module could have its own CSS file, but that's more to load. In the end, keeping everything encapsulated in a JavaScript file, given that there's not very much styling required anyway, felt like a cleaner approach. If these modules had a lot more CSS in them, I assuredly would have separated it all out.

After those two strings, the configuration object definition begins. Remember, at a high level, you've got two areas, one for the summary view and one for the details, and you need to be able to flip between them. That sounds like a `multiview`, no? But hey, where's the `view : "multiview"` like you see in `multiView.js`? Well, here's the thing: if you don't specify a view but you do specify the `cells` attribute, then Webix recognizes that and knows you want a `multiview` and implicitly creates one for you. That's what I've done here.

The first cell is the summary view, and it has an `id` of `moduleNotes-itemsCell`, since you'll need to be able to hide and show that later (with `hide()` and `show()`). This cell has two rows in it; the first is the `list` component, and the second is the `toolbar` component. The `list` has a `type` attribute that specifies `templateStart`, `template`, and `templateEnd`, and that's something you haven't seen before. The `templateStart` attribute provides Webix with the information needed to render the container element for a data item, wrapping the elements defined by `template`. It's the opening element, usually a `<div>`. The `templateEnd` is the opposite. It renders the closing element begun with `templateStart`. Using all three gives you more flexibility than just using `template` to render items in some components (`dataview`, `list`, `grouplist`, `unitlist`, `menu`, `tree`, `datatable`, and `treetable`), and flexibility is needed here to render the notes in the list like I wanted to.

The `toolbar` is a simple one with an empty element to push the button all the way to the right, with a small element to the right of the button just to keep it off the edge of the screen a bit.

After the summary cell is the details cell where you find an entry `form` and a `toolbar`. The `form` consists of three elements: a `text` component for entry of the note subject, a `richtext` component for entry of the note itself, and a `colorpicker` for selecting a background color for the note. The subject entry field is interesting because it has `required : true` on it, which results in a red asterisk being placed by its label to indicate it's a required field (and it's the only one that is required). I've also specified an `invalidMessage` attribute to define the message that will be shown below the field when nothing has been entered in it. However, this message will show up only if there is room for it, which by default there isn't, and that's where setting `bottomPadding` comes into play.

The `attributes` config option is new, and this gives us a way to feed attributes to the underlying HTML text field, which Webix renders (and then augments) under the covers. Here, I'm specifying the `maxlength` attribute to limit how many characters the user can enter to 50. Similarly, the note text entry area has a limit of 1000 characters defined in the same way.

The subject entry field also has an `onChange` event handler defined. Every time the field changes, which occurs when it loses focus, the `validate()` method on the form is called, which you can always get a reference to by calling `this.getParentView()` within the event handler since the `this` keyword here is a reference to the field itself, so Webix can look up the component hierarchy to find the parent form (although, be careful, because depending on how you create your layout, then the parent of the field might not actually be the form, in which case you'd likely need to reference its `id` directly). If `validate()` returns `true`, then the Save button is enabled; otherwise, it's disabled. The only thing that this form validates is whether the subject field is filled in since `required : true` is the only validation rule applied to any of the form's fields. That's why this logic works out.

The `toolbar` is just three buttons: the Back To Summary `button`, then a spacer, then the second Delete `button`, then another spacer, and then the final Save `button`. For the Back To Summary `button`, you just need to show the `moduleNotes-itemsCell` element of the implicit `multiview`. For Delete, it's simply a call to the common `wxPIM.deleteHandler()` function, passing the name of the module. For Save, it's the same sort of thing as Delete, but now it's `wxPIM.saveHandler()`, passing it the name of the module and the ID of the form to get the data to save from.

And that's all there is to this UI definition!

newHandler()

Whenever the New button on the summary screen is clicked, the uncreatively named `newHandler()` method is called, and it's a pretty simple bit of code.

```
newHandler() {

  wxPIM.isEditingExisting = false;
  wxPIM.editingID = new Date().getTime();

  $$("moduleNotes-details").show();
  $$("moduleNotes-detailsForm").clear();
  $$("moduleNotes-detailsForm-text").setValue("");
  $$("moduleNotes-detailsForm-color").setValue("#ffd180");
  $$("moduleNotes-deleteButton").disable();

}
```

First, the flag that tells you whether you're editing an existing item or not is set to false, and a new ID is created for this note. After that's done, it's just a matter of switching to the detail screen and clearing the form. Note that the richtext component seems to not be cleared by the call to clear() on the form, so that's cleared separately. Likewise, the colorpicker doesn't reset to a default color, or at least not the color I want to be the default, so a default is explicitly set. Finally, since you're creating a new item here, the Delete button doesn't come into play, so it's disabled.

editExisting()

When an existing note is clicked on the summary screen, editExisting() is called to kick off editing of the existing note. If this code looks a bit like newHandler(), that shouldn't be surprising. You're doing essentially the same thing with just a few differences.

```
editExisting(inID) {

  const notes = JSON.parse(localStorage.getItem("NotesDB"));
  const note = notes[inID];

  wxPIM.isEditingExisting = true;
  wxPIM.editingID = inID;

  $$("moduleNotes-detailsForm").clear();

  $$("moduleNotes-details").show();
```

```
  $$("moduleNotes-detailsForm").setValues(note);

  $$("moduleNotes-deleteButton").enable();

}
```

The first difference is that you need to get a reference to the note being edited, so you first get the data for this module, and then since the returned object is keyed by ID, a reference to the note is grabbed using the `inID` passed in by the click handler. After that, the `wxPIM.isEditingExisting` flag is set, to `true` this time, and the `inID` is stored in `wxPIM.editingID`.

Now, you clear the form so that you have a clean slate to start. After that, the details cell is shown. After that, `setValues()` is called on the details form, passing it the note object that was pulled out of the module's data collection. It's important to say that if you try to do the `setValues()` call before showing the form, then you'll see a JavaScript error and things will break. I'm not certain of the reason for this error, but it's related to the `richtext` component, and my guess is that Webix lazy-builds that component, and it might not be present until you actually show the form. In any case, just keep this in mind to avoid the problem in your own code.

Once the form is populated and shown, then the only thing left to do is to enable the Delete button, since you can of course delete an existing note.

See, that wasn't so bad, was it?

refreshData()

The final method in the `Notes` class is `refreshData()`, which as you know by now is called any time the summary view needs to be updated, either after an item is added, updated, or deleted or when the module is switched to.

```
refreshData() {

  const dataItems = wxPIM.getModuleData("Notes");

  const itemsAsArray = wxPIM.objectAsArray(dataItems);

  wxPIM.sortArray(itemsAsArray, "id", "D");

  $$("moduleNotes-items").clearAll();
  $$("moduleNotes-items").parse(itemsAsArray);

}
```

It doesn't take much for this module. You just fetch the data for this module from local storage, then convert the object to an array, then sort the array in descending order on the id property (so that newer notes are always shown at the top), call clearAll() on the list component to start fresh, and then finally call parse(), passing it the fetched data, for the list to render.

That's really all there is to it for this particular module!

Commonality makes things easier.   Note that for two of the three remaining modules, they are pretty similar overall in terms of the code, so I'm going to go over them pretty quickly. Therefore, make sure you understood all the code for the notes module because if you did, then you already, by and large, can understand the contacts and tasks modules without much explanation. Appointments, which you'll look at last, has some differences to it, but even it isn't very different from the others.

Tasks.js

Now you'll look at the tasks module, beginning with what it looks like. Figure 6-4 shows the summary view, which uses a tree to show the notes, broken down by category (those with no category are in the first "empty" group).

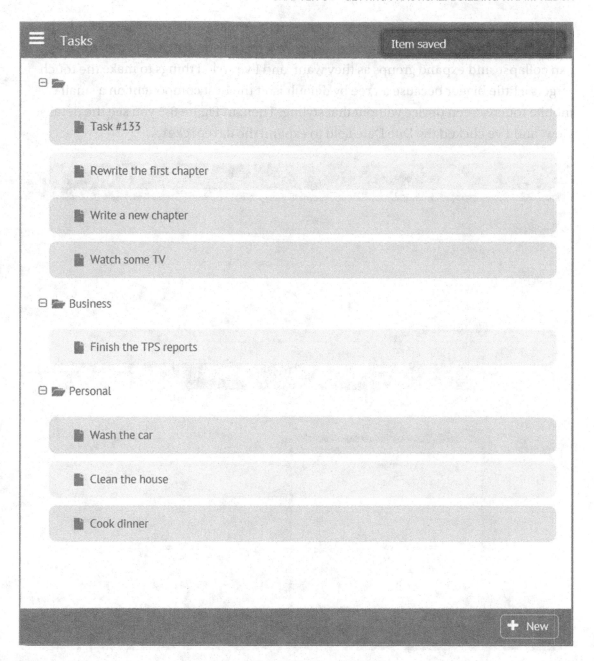

Figure 6-4. *The summary view of the tasks module*

Complete tasks are shown in green while ongoing tasks are shown in red. Only the task's title is shown since that's good enough for a basic listing. Being a `tree`, the user can collapse and expand groups as they want, and I've styled things to make the touch targets a little bigger because a `tree` by default isn't the best component on a small mobile touchscreen device without that styling. Then, in Figure 6-5 you see the details view, and I've clicked the Due Date field to expand the `datepicker`.

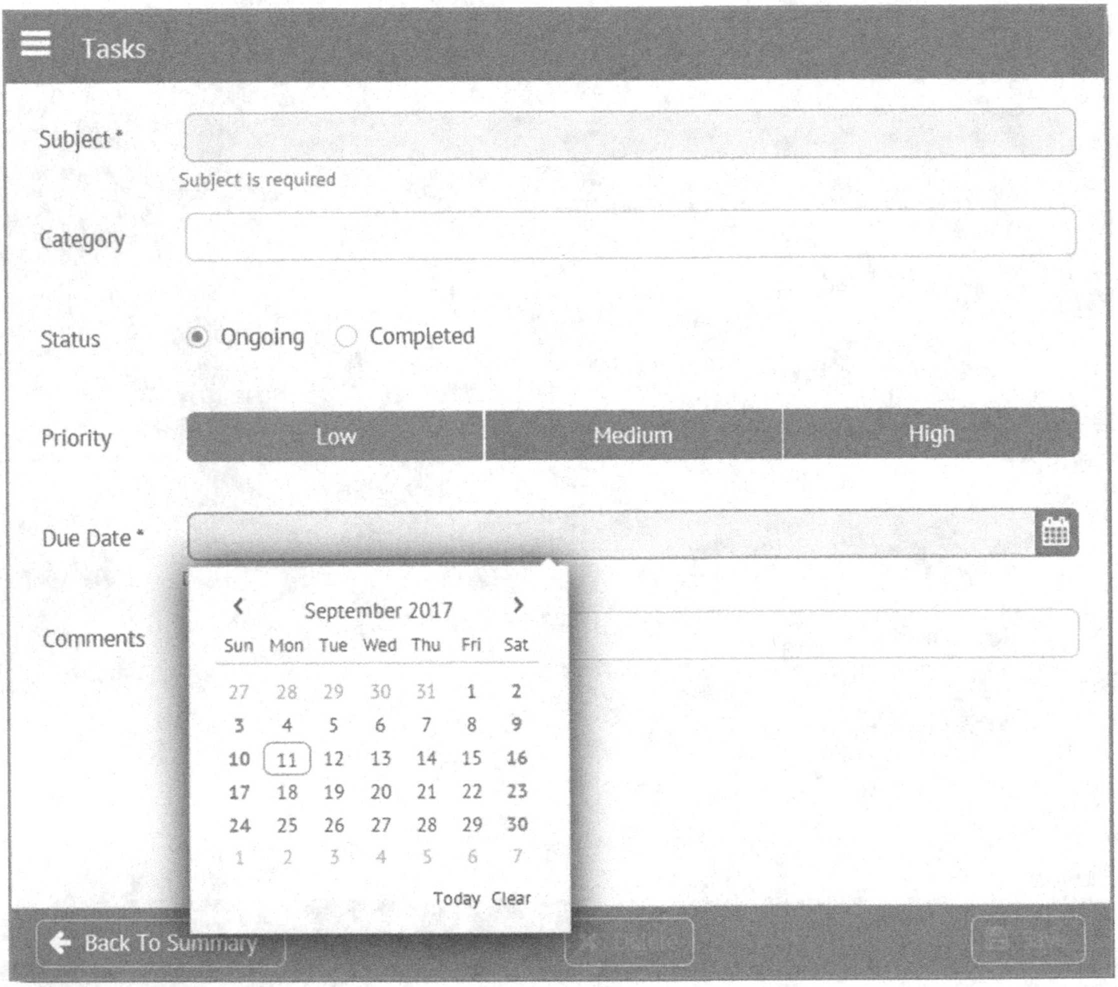

Figure 6-5. *The tasks module's details view*

I chose to use a segmented component for the priority since with a limited number of choices that provides a direct means to access the options. Of course, that would have been a fine choice for the Status field as well, but being a learning example, I tried to use a decent variety of components for you to see in action.

The Subject field is required (as is Due Date), and you can see that it's marked as such with the red asterisk, and you can also see the message when it's not filled out below the field.

Now, on to the code!

Constructor, activate(), and deactivate()

As with the notes module, the `constructor`, `activate()`, and `deactivate()` methods in the `Tasks` class definition in the `tasks.js` file are all empty since this module doesn't have any work done in those, so let's move on to the `getUIConfig()` method.

getUIConfig()

Although a bit more voluminous than the notes module, the code inside `getUIConfig()` is still pretty basic Webix config data, with just a few minor exceptions. Walk through this code to see:

```
getUIConfig() {

  return {
    id : "moduleTasks-container",
    cells : [

      { id : "moduleTasks-itemsCell",
        rows : [
          { view : "tree", id : "moduleTasks-items",
            on : { onItemClick : this.editExisting.bind(this) }
          },
          { view : "toolbar",
            cols : [
              { },
              { view : "button", label : "New", width : "80",
                type : "iconButton", icon : "plus",
                click : this.newHandler.bind(this)
              },
              { width : 6 }
            ]
```

```
          }
        ]
      },

      { id : "moduleTasks-details",
        rows : [

          { view : "form", id : "moduleTasks-detailsForm", borderless : true,
            elementsConfig : { view : "text", labelWidth : 100,
            bottomPadding : 20,
              on : { onChange : () => {
                $$("moduleTasks-saveButton")[$$("moduleTasks-detailsForm").
                validate() ?
                  "enable" : "disable"]();
              } }
            },
            elements : [
              { name : "subject", label : "Subject", required : true,
                invalidMessage : "Subject is required",
                attributes : { maxlength : 50 }
              },
              { view : "text", name : "category", label : "Category",
                suggest : [
                  { id : 1, value : "Personal" },
                  { id : 2, value : "Business" },
                  { id : 3, value : "Other" }
                ],
                on : {
                  onItemClick : function() {
                    $$(this.config.suggest).show(this.getInputNode());
                  }
                }
              },
              { view : "radio", name : "status", label : "Status", value : 1,
                id : "moduleTasks-category",
                options : [
```

```
          { id : 1, value : "Ongoing" }, { id : 2, value :
          "Completed" }
        ]
      },
      { view : "segmented", name : "priority", label : "Priority",
      value : 1,
        options : [
          { id : 1, value : "Low" },
          { id : 2, value : "Medium" },
          { id : 3, value : "High" }
        ]
      },
      { view : "datepicker", name : "dueDate", label : "Due Date",
        id : "moduleTasks-dueDate", required : true,
        invalidMessage : "Due Date is required"
      },
      { name : "comments", label : "Comments",
        attributes : { maxlength : 250 }
      }
    ]
  },

  { },

  { view : "toolbar",
    cols : [
      { width : 6 },
      { view : "button", label : "Back To Summary", width : "170",
        type : "iconButton", icon : "arrow-left",
        click : () => {
          $$("moduleTasks-itemsCell").show();
        }
      },
      { },
      { id : "moduleTasks-deleteButton", view : "button",
        label : "Delete", width : "90", type : "iconButton",
```

```
            icon : "remove", click : () => { wxPIM.
            deleteHandler("Tasks"); }
          },
          { },
          { view : "button", label : "Save", width : "80",
            type : "iconButton", icon : "floppy-o",
            id : "moduleTasks-saveButton", disabled : true,
            click : function() {
              wxPIM.saveHandler("Tasks", [ "moduleTasks-detailsForm" ]);
            }
          },
          { width : 6 }
        ]
      }
    ]
  }
];

}
```

As you look through that code, it should look quite familiar by now as it's the same overall basic structure as the notes module, and there's really nothing here that you haven't seen before. In fact, the only thing especially worth discussing is the onChange handler for the form. In contrast to the notes module, where there was an onChange handler attached to the Title field's onChange event, here I've attached it to the form. This is the better approach if you have more than one field that's required because that way you don't need to attach code to every required field. What this is doing is calling a method on the Save button using bracket notation. Remember that x[y]() can always be used to call a method y of object x in JavaScript, which is the "trick" used here. The name of the method that's being called is determined based on the result of the call to the form's validate() method. If it's true, then "enable," if false, then "disable." It's a simple, concise way to write this code rather than a larger if block of code.

Actually, one other thing warrants mention too, and that's the `onItemClick` handler of the Category `text` component. What that one line of code does is it finds the `suggest` component that Webix constructed under the covers as a result of supplying the `suggest` configuration attribute and shows it anchored to the `text` component. A `suggest` component doesn't do anything on its own; you have to actually show it, and that's all it takes to do so.

How do you write code? It's a matter of debate for sure in the programming world, but I almost always choose longer, clearer code over more terse code. I don't mind typing more if it makes the code easier to read. Unfortunately, the trend in JavaScript these days is to write more concise code, but whether it's truly clearer or not is sometimes questionable. This is an example of where I break my own rule essentially, but I do so because I think this form is no less clear ultimately than an expanded `if` block. Still, I'm not holding this up as the right or wrong approach; that's for you to decide. But seeing an alternate approach I think has value if for no other reason than making you stop and consider your own viewpoint on the matter. It's always good to question things, even if what you're questioning is considered a "best practice," in my opinion.

---

newHandler()

When the New button is clicked, the `newHandler()` function is called, just like in the notes module, and the code in it is just about the same.

```
newHandler() {

  wxPIM.isEditingExisting = false;
  wxPIM.editingID = new Date().getTime();

  $$("moduleTasks-details").show();
  $$("moduleTasks-detailsForm").clear();
  $$("moduleTasks-category").setValue(1);
  $$("moduleTasks-deleteButton").disable();

}
```

The Category field gets a default value of 1, which means Ongoing, which is the logical default for a new task. Otherwise, there's no real difference from what you say in the notes module.

editExisting()

The editExisting() method is called when an existing task is clicked, and it too is similar to its counterpart in the notes module, but this time there are a few differences.

```
editExisting(inID) {

  const tasks = JSON.parse(localStorage.getItem("TasksDB"));
  const task = tasks[inID];
  if (!task) {
    if ($$("moduleTasks-items").isBranchOpen(inID)) {
      $$("moduleTasks-items").close(inID);
    } else {
      $$("moduleTasks-items").open(inID);
    }
    return;
  }

  wxPIM.isEditingExisting = true;
  wxPIM.editingID = inID;

  $$("moduleTasks-detailsForm").clear();

  $$("moduleTasks-details").show();

  if (task.dueDate) {
    task.dueDate = new Date(task.dueDate);
  }

  $$("moduleTasks-detailsForm").setValues(task);

  $$("moduleTasks-deleteButton").enable();

}
```

The first big difference here is that because this is called in response to the onItemClick event in the tree, it will be called whether the user clicks a task or a category tree node. In the latter case, you obviously aren't editing anything, but being a tree, you want that click to expand or collapse that node. So, after getting the data for the module, you then attempt to get the data for the note with the specified inID. For a node that isn't a note, inID will be some internal Webix ID, not a valid note ID, which means you won't find a note in the data. That's where the if branch after that comes into play. When you don't find a node, then you use the isBranchOpen() method on the tree to see whether the specified branch is currently open or closed, and the state is toggled based on that. Of course, in this case, your work is done, so the code immediately returns.

If you *do* find a note, though, then the code continues, skipping the if block. Then, you do all the same sorts of things that you saw in the notes module. However, the Due Date field needs to be handled specially, because when it's pulled out of local storage, it's a string, but the form needs a Date object, so that conversion is done before passing the data to the form's setValues() method.

refreshData()

The final method in this module is refreshData(), and it's a bit different (though not all *that* different!) than the one in the notes module, as you can see for yourself.

```
refreshData() {

  const dataItems = wxPIM.getModuleData("Tasks");

  const tasksData = { };
  for (const taskID in dataItems) {
    if (dataItems.hasOwnProperty(taskID)) {
      const task = dataItems[taskID];
      if (!tasksData[task.category]) {
        tasksData[task.category] = {
          $css : { padding : "10px" }, value : task.category,
          open : true, data : [ ]
        };
      }
      tasksData[task.category].data.push(
        { $css : {
```

```
                padding : "10px", margin : "10px", "border-radius" : "10px",
                "background-color" : (task.status === 1 ? "#ffe0e0" : "#e0ffe0")
            },
            id : task.id, value : task.subject
        }
    );
  }
}

const itemsAsArray = wxPIM.objectAsArray(tasksData);

wxPIM.sortArray(itemsAsArray, "value", "A");

$$("moduleTasks-items").clearAll();
$$("moduleTasks-items").parse(itemsAsArray);

}
```

The tree needs data, of course, but after getting the data for the module, what you have is a plain old array of objects, not in any sort of hierarchy; there's no data items nested inside others. That won't work. Therefore, the job here is to create that hierarchical data in the tasksData object from this flat array. So, for each task, you pull out the category and add a member to the tasksData object for it; this is a member that is itself an object and that has a data member, which are the tasks that are children of that category. Then, each task gets added to the data array for the appropriate category. You wind up with an object that has properties, one for each category, and the data array for each of those contains the tasks within that category.

For each data object describing a node in the tree, be it a category or a task, the $css property is present to provide some styling to the tree node. For the category nodes, this is just some padding to make it a larger touch target and therefore make it easier to expand and collapse categories on a small mobile touchscreen. For the tasks themselves, there is again some padding to provide separation between them (and make it less likely for the user to tap the wrong thing) and a color choice based on the status of the task. The container for the task is rendered with some rounded corners, just to make it look a little nicer.

Next, the tasksData object that was just built is converted to an array, and the array is sorted based on the value property. Remember that the tasksData object will have properties now corresponding to your categories, and the category names are stored in that value property, so sorting it means the categories will be displayed alphabetically

234

(and with tasks with no specified category at the top). Finally, it's a simple matter of clearing the tree and passing the final day array to its `parse()` method, and you've got beautiful tasks displayed in a tree!

Contacts.js

Next up you have the contacts module. This uses a different component for its summary display, this time a `unitlist`, which you can see in Figure 6-6.

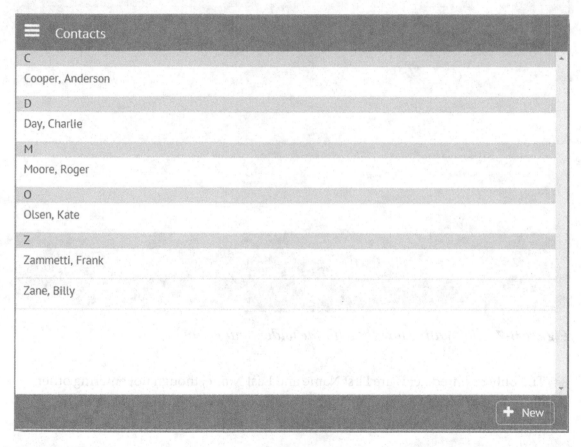

Figure 6-6. *The contacts summary display*

This makes sense for a list of contacts where, like a rolodex, it's typical to see it broken down alphabetically with headings to demarcate each section. I've chosen to sort by last name, though obviously that's a matter of choice.

235

When you create a new contact or edit an existing one, you're greeted by the detail display shown in Figure 6-7, where I've used an `accordion` to split between personal and business details, so you can use this contact list for either.

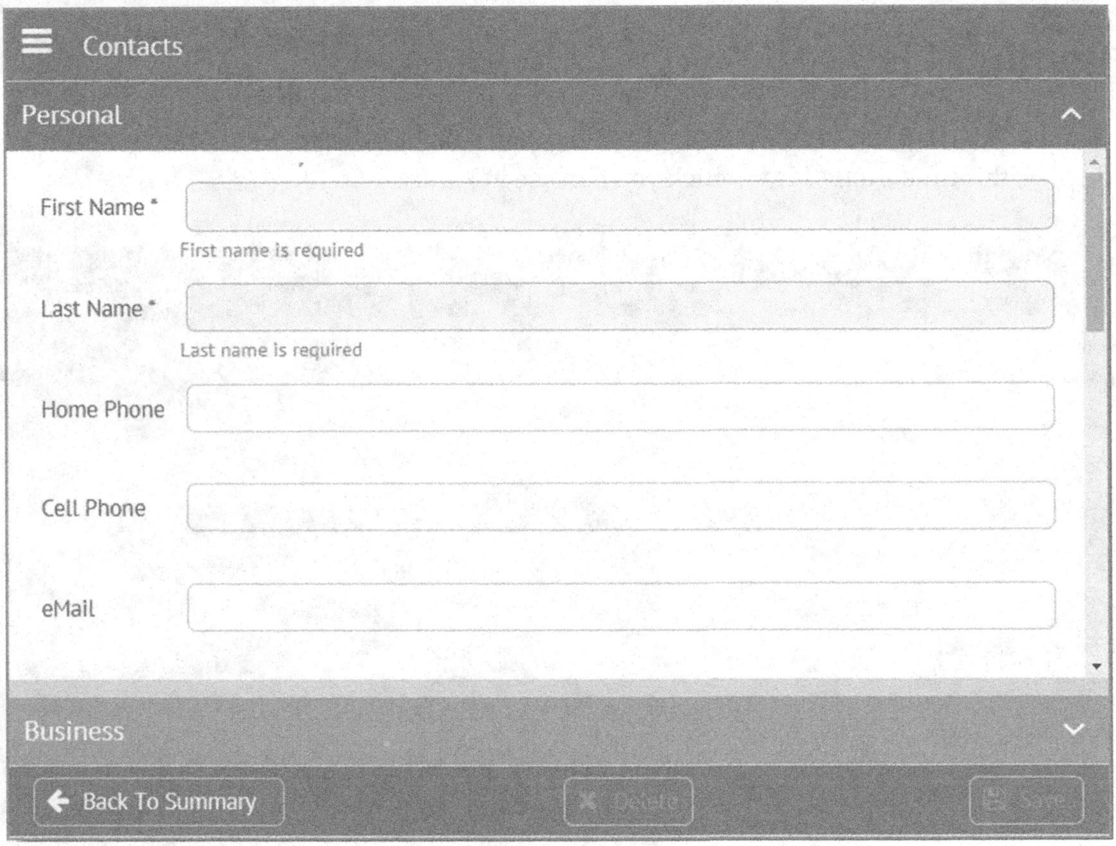

Figure 6-7. *Navigating wxPIM with the widemenu menu*

The only required fields are First Name and Last Name, though not entering other details probably isn't all that useful. When you flip over to the Business pane of the accordion, you have what you see in Figure 6-8.

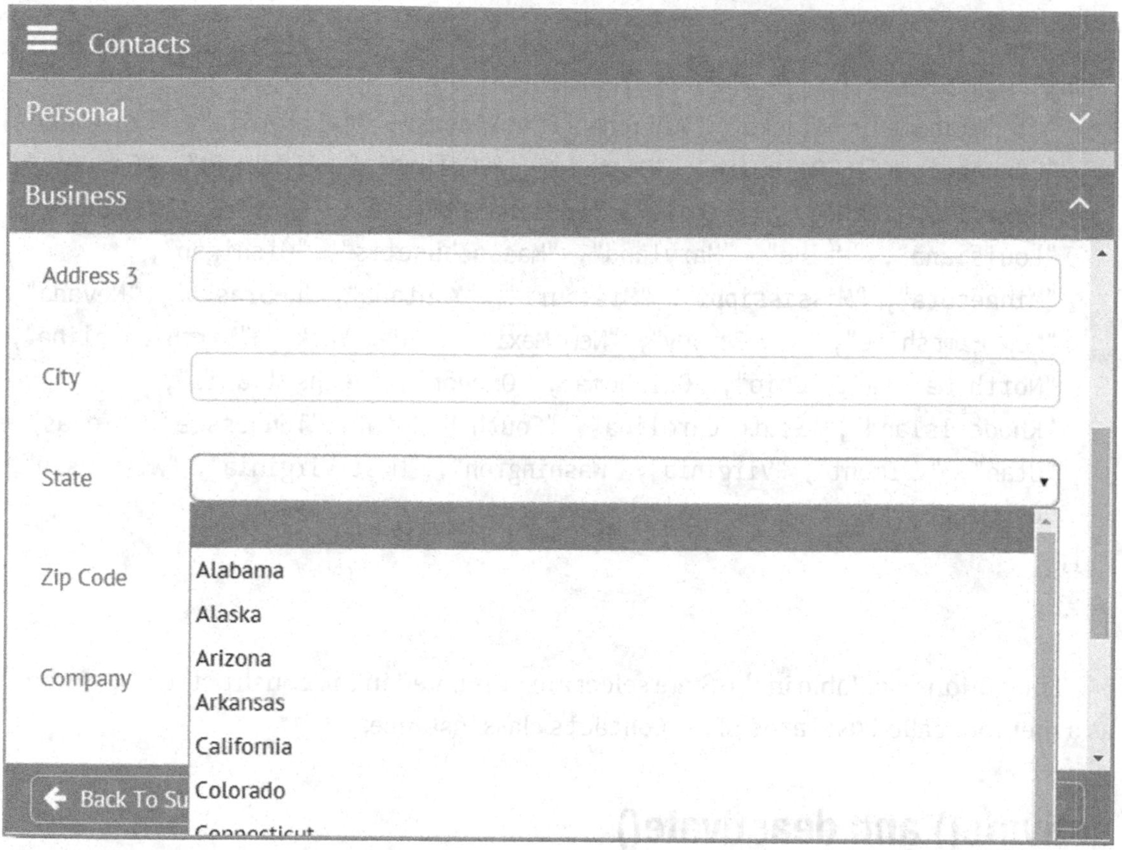

Figure 6-8. *The business pane of the contact's accordion*

The state is a select element, so the user doesn't have to type out the whole state, and you don't need to worry about whether they put in a full state name or just an abbreviation. Since contacts have quite a few more fields associated with them than do notes or tasks, scrolling may come into play depending on the screen size, as you can see in both of the previous screenshots.

Constructor

The code itself for this module, in the Contacts.js file, begins with the usual class definition, which has a constructor, where for a change you finally *do* have something to accomplish in it.

```
constructor() {

  this.usStates = [
    "", "Alabama", "Alaska", "Arizona", "Arkansas", "California", "Colorado",
    "Connecticut", "Delaware", "District of Columbia", "Florida", "Georgia",
    "Hawaii", "Idaho", "Illinois", "Indiana", "Iowa", "Kansas", "Kentucky",
    "Louisiana", "Maine", "Maryland", "Massachusetts", "Michigan",
    "Minnesota", "Mississippi", "Missouri", "Montana", "Nebraska", "Nevada",
    "New Hampshire", "New Jersey", "New Mexico", "New York", "North Carolina",
    "North Dakota", "Ohio", "Oklahoma", "Oregon", "Pennsylvania",
    "Rhode Island", "South Carolina", "South Dakota", "Tennessee", "Texas",
    "Utah", "Vermont", "Virginia", "Washington", "West Virginia", "Wisconsin",
    "Wyoming"
  ];

}
```

The options available in the State select are populated in the constructor and stored as a member called usStates of the Contacts class instance.

activate() and deactivate()

While the constructor has some content this time around, activate() and deactivate() again do not for this module, so there's no need to dwell; let's get right to getUIConfig().

getUIConfig()

The configuration object returned for this module is the longest of the bunch, but as you go through it, I think you'll find it to be quite straightforward. Let's meet up on the other side after you read through this, and I'll touch on one or two interesting points.

```
  getUIConfig() {

    return {
      id : "moduleContacts-container",
      cells : [

        { id : "moduleContacts-itemsCell",
          rows : [
```

```
{ view : "unitlist", id : "moduleContacts-items",
  type : { height : 40 }, template : "#lastName#, #firstName#",
  uniteBy : (inObj) => {
    return inObj.lastName.substr(0, 1);
  },
  click : this.editExisting.bind(this)
},
{ view : "toolbar",
  cols : [
    { },
    { view : "button", label : "New", width : "80",
      type : "iconButton", icon : "plus",
      click : this.newHandler.bind(this)
    },
    { width : 6 }
  ]
}
]
},

{ id : "moduleContacts-details",
  rows : [
    { view : "accordion", id : "moduleContacts-accordion",
      rows : [
        { header : "Personal",
          body : {
            view : "form", id : "moduleContacts-personalDetailsForm",
            scroll : true,
            elementsConfig : {
              view : "text", labelWidth : 100, bottomPadding : 20,
              on : {
                onChange : wxPIM.modules.Contacts.
                validateFormsOnChange.bind(this)
              }
            },
            elements : [
```

```
{ name : "firstName", label : "First Name", required
: true,
  invalidMessage : "First name is required",
  attributes : { maxlength : 20 }
},
{ name : "lastName", label : "Last Name", required :
true,
  invalidMessage : "Last name is required",
  attributes : { maxlength : 20 }
},
{ name : "homePhone", label : "Home Phone",
  attributes : { maxlength : 12 }
},
{ name : "cellPhone", label : "Cell Phone",
  attributes : { maxlength : 12 }
},
{ name : "personalEMail", label : "eMail",
  validate : webix.rules.isEmailOrBlank,
  invalidMessage : "Must be in the form xxx@yyy.zzz",
  attributes : { maxlength : 75 }
},
{ name : "personalAddress1", label : "Address 1",
  attributes : { maxlength : 50 }
},
{ name : "personalAddress2", label : "Address 2",
  attributes : { maxlength : 30 }
},
{ name : "personalAddress3", label : "Address 3",
  attributes : { maxlength : 30 }
},
{ name : "personalCity", label : "City",
  attributes : { maxlength : 30 }
},
{ view : "select", name : "personalState",
  label : "State", value : "", options : this.usStates
},
```

```
        { name : "personalZip", label : "Zip Code",
          validate : webix.rules.isNumberOrBlank,
          invalidMessage : "Must be numbers only",
          attributes : { maxlength : 5 }
        },
        { name : "im", label : "IM",
          attributes : { maxlength : 25 }
        },
        { view : "select", name : "imType", label : "IM Type",
          value : "",
          options : [
            { id : "", value : "" },
            { id : "aim", value : "AIM" },
            { id : "allo", value : "Allo" },
            { id : "facebook", value : "Facebook" },
            { id : "imessage", value : "iMessage" },
            { id : "kik", value : "Kik" },
            { id : "snapchat", value : "Snapchat" },
            { id : "skype", value : "Skype" },
            { id : "whatsapp", value : "WhatsApp" },
            { id : "yahoo", value : "Yahoo" }
          ]
        },
        { view : "datepicker", name : "birthday",
          label : "Birthday"
        },
        { name : "personalWebsite", label : "Website",
          attributes : { maxlength : 100 }
        },
        { name : "personalComments", label : "Comments",
          attributes : { maxlength : 250 }
        }
      ]
    }
  },
  { header : "Business", collapsed : true,
```

```
          body : {
            view : "form", id : "moduleContacts-businessDetailsForm",
            scroll : true,
            elementsConfig : {
              view : "text", labelWidth : 100, bottomPadding : 20,
              on : {
                onChange : wxPIM.modules.Contacts.
                validateFormsOnChange.bind(this)
              }
            },
            elements : [
              { name : "officePhone", label : "Office Phone",
                attributes : { maxlength : 12 }
              },
              { name : "businessEMail", label : "eMail",
                validate : webix.rules.isEmailOrBlank,
                invalidMessage : "Must be in the form xxx@yyy.zzz",
                attributes : { maxlength : 75 }
              },
              { name : "businessAddress1", label : "Address 1",
                attributes : { maxlength : 50 }
              },
              { name : "businessAddress2", label : "Address 2",
                attributes : { maxlength : 30 }
              },
              { name : "businessAddress3", label : "Address 3",
                attributes : { maxlength : 30 }
              },
              { name : "businessCity", label : "City",
                attributes : { maxlength : 30 }
              },
              { view : "select", name : "businessState",
                label : "State", value : "", options : this.usStates
              },
              { name : "businessZip", label : "Zip Code",
                validate : webix.rules.isNumberOrBlank,
```

```
              invalidMessage : "Must be numbers only",
              attributes : { maxlength : 5 }
            },
            { name : "company", label : "Company",
              attributes : { maxlength : 40 }
            },
            { name : "title", label : "Title",
              attributes : { maxlength : 25 }
            },
            { name : "businessWebsite", label : "Website",
              attributes : { maxlength : 100 }
            },
            { name : "businessComments", label : "Comments",
              attributes : { maxlength : 250 }
            }
          ]
        }
      },
    ]
  },
{ view : "toolbar",
  cols : [
    { width : 6 },
    { view : "button", label : "Back To Summary", width : "170",
      type : "iconButton", icon : "arrow-left",
      click : () => {
        $$("moduleContacts-itemsCell").show();
      }
    },
    { },
    { id : "moduleContacts-deleteButton", view : "button",
      label : "Delete", width : "90", type : "iconButton",
      icon : "remove",
      click : () => { wxPIM.deleteHandler("Contacts"); }
    },
```

```
          { },
          { view : "button", label : "Save", width : "80",
            type : "iconButton", icon : "floppy-o",
            id : "moduleContacts-saveButton", disabled : true,
            click : function() {
              wxPIM.saveHandler("Contacts", [
                "moduleContacts-personalDetailsForm",
                "moduleContacts-businessDetailsForm"
              ]);
            }
          },
          { width : 6 }
        ]
      }
    ]
  }
]
};
}
```

Like I said, most of it is stuff you've seen a few times before, but one or two things are new or interesting. First, the unitlist itself has a uniteBy function that uses the first letter of the last name to group the items by. If you prefer to see your list sorted by first name, then all you would need to do is change lastName to firstName in this function, and you'd be all set (and you would likely want to change the template as well, but then again, maybe not).

The next interesting thing to note is inside the two forms that you see, in its elementsConfig options more specifically. Notice how this time I've attached an onChange function here and it references a method of the Contacts class instance. This is yet another way you can handle enabling and disabling the Save button depending on the validity of the form (and you'll look at the validateFormsOnChange() method shortly). Which approach you take, if you need to handle changes at all, is entirely up to you, though I'd suggest either this or handling it at the form level is appropriate when you have more than one or maybe two fields that have some form of validation attached to them. On these forms, there's a couple, so it would make sense either how I've done it here or on the form itself as you saw in the tasks module.

244

Another thing of note is on the e-mail fields, namely, the usage of that custom `webix.rules.isEmailOrBlank` function that you saw when you looked at `core.js`. Remember, you want blank to be an allowed value, which the built-in `webix.rules.isEmail` doesn't do, which is why you have the custom function. This is also true of the Zip Code fields, though this time it's the `webix.rules.isNumberOfBlank` function being used.

The IM Type field has its `options` embedded in the component definition, while the State field uses that `usStates` member that you built in the constructor.

Finally, because there are two forms involved in defining a contact, the call to `wxPIM.saveHandler()` for the first (and only, as it happens) time is passed the ID of two forms.

As I said, it's a fair amount of code, more than notes or tasks, but it's code that doesn't hold too many surprises (at least I hope not at this point!)

newHandler()

The `newHandler()` for this module is nearly the same as the last two you've seen, though because there's two forms involved, plus an `accordion`, there are some small differences.

```
newHandler() {

  wxPIM.isEditingExisting = false;
  wxPIM.editingID = new Date().getTime();

  $$("moduleContacts-details").show();
  $$("moduleContacts-accordion").getChildViews()[0].expand();
  $$("moduleContacts-personalDetailsForm").clear();
  $$("moduleContacts-businessDetailsForm").clear();
  $$("moduleContacts-deleteButton").disable();

}
```

First, calling `getChildViews()` on the accordion component provides an array of the elements within it, the Personal and Business panes, so referencing the first element of the array means the Personal pane, which a call to `expand()` causes to be shown. (The Business pane is automatically collapsed as well, which is what an `accordion` does by default.) The `getChildViews()` method is available on all Webix components because it's a member of `ui.view`, which all Webix components extend from.

After that, *both* forms need to be cleared, and the delete button is disabled as always.

editExisting()

Editing as existing contact is much like the other two modules, but with one or two important differences.

```
editExisting(inID) {

  const contacts = JSON.parse(localStorage.getItem("ContactsDB"));
  const contact = contacts[inID];

  wxPIM.isEditingExisting = true;
  wxPIM.editingID = inID;

  $$("moduleContacts-personalDetailsForm").clear();
  $$("moduleContacts-businessDetailsForm").clear();

  $$("moduleContacts-details").show();
  $$("moduleContacts-accordion").getChildViews()[0].expand();

  if (contact.birthday) {
    contact.birthday = new Date(contact.birthday);
  }

  $$("moduleContacts-personalDetailsForm").setValues({
    firstName : contact.firstName,
    lastName : contact.lastName,
    homePhone : contact.homePhone,
    cellPhone : contact.cellPhone,
    personalEMail : contact.personalEMail,
    personalAddress1 : contact.personalAddress1,
    personalAddress2 : contact.personalAddress2,
    personalAddress3 : contact.personalAddress3,
    personalCity : contact.personalCity,
    personalState : contact.personalState,
    personalZip : contact.personalZip,
    im : contact.im,
    imType : contact.imType,
    birthday : contact.birthday,
    personalWebsite : contact.personalWebsite,
```

```
      personalComments : contact.personalComments
    });
    $$("moduleContacts-businessDetailsForm").setValues({
      officePhone : contact.officePhone,
      businessEMail : contact.businessEMail,
      businessAddress1 : contact.businessAddress1,
      businessAddress2 : contact.businessAddress2,
      businessAddress3 : contact.businessAddress3,
      businessCity : contact.businessCity,
      businessState : contact.businessState,
      businessZip : contact.businessZip,
      company : contact.company,
      title : contact.title,
      businessWebsite : contact.businessWebsite,
      businessComments : contact.businessComments
    });

    $$("moduleContacts-deleteButton").enable();


}
```

First, you're dealing with two forms of course, so both need to be cleared after the module's data and the data for the specific contact is fetched. Next, the birthday field needs to be a true JavaScript Date object rather than the string it comes out of local storage as, so that's done.

After that, you have to call setValues() on both forms, but here is where you run into an interesting little problem. In the previous two modules, you just passed a single object to setValues(), and here too you do have a single object in the contact object that has all the data for the contact. You might think that you can just pass that object to setValues() on both forms and Webix will just pull out the data it needs for each form and ignore the rest, but you would be mistaken! What really happens is that Webix stores *all* the data on *both* forms, even though there aren't fields for each in the forms (i.e., the Business data is stored on the Personal form even though there are only fields for the Personal data, and vice versa for the Business form). This becomes a problem when the wxPIM.saveHandler() function grabs the data from the forms. Recall that it will combine the data from the two forms into one. Well, walk through in your mind how this works:

- Start with an empty target object that will ultimately be saved.

- Into it, dump the data from the Personal form, which also includes the original Business data from when editExisting() populated the form. So far, that's not actually a problem.

- But now, dump in the data from the Business form, which also includes the original Personal data. To be clear, it's not the data from the Personal form; it's the Personal data that was retrieved from local storage when editExisting() executed.

- In other words, the Personal data will be overwritten in the target object with the Personal data stored on the Business form, which is what it was *before* the user edited anything. Translation: any changes the user makes to the Personal data is "reset" when saved to what it was *before* their edits. Their Personal changes are effectively lost.

- As a wise man named Homer Simpson once said, "D'oh!"

So, what's the solution? Well, it's pretty simple: instead of passing that single contact object, instead pass a new object to each setValues() call that contains only the data needed by each form. That avoids the overwrite situation entirely, and everything works as expected, though it means a bit more code required here, as you can see.

refreshData()

The refreshData() method is next, and it's entirely mundane at this point.

```
refreshData() {

  const dataItems = wxPIM.getModuleData("Contacts");

  const itemsAsArray = wxPIM.objectAsArray(dataItems);

  wxPIM.sortArray(itemsAsArray, "lastName", "A");

  $$("moduleContacts-items").clearAll();
  $$("moduleContacts-items").parse(itemsAsArray);

}
```

It's the same "grab the data, convert to an array, sort the array, clear the list, and populate it" sequence that you should be quite familiar with by now. The fact that it's a unitlist doesn't change anything; it's still basically a list at the end of the day, so there's nothing new to see here.

validateFormsOnChange()

What *is* new is that while refreshData() would usually be the last method in the class, there is, in fact, one extra new one for contacts; the validateFormsOnChange() method that you saw when you looked at getUIConfig() is called whenever the form changes.

```
validateFormsOnChange() {

  const areBothFormsValid =
    $$("moduleContacts-personalDetailsForm").validate() &&
    $$("moduleContacts-businessDetailsForm").validate();
    $$("moduleContacts-saveButton")[areBothFormsValid ? "enable" :
    "disable"]();

}
```

There's not much to it, but the trick is that you have to validate *both* forms and only enable the Save button if *both* are valid. So, validate() is called on both, and their return values and'd together into the areBothFormsValid variable. Then, the same sort of dynamic object method call using bracket notation as you saw in the tasks module is used to call either enable() or disable() on the Save button and you're good to go.

Appointments.js

The final module to look at is the appointments module, housed in the Appointments.js file. This module has a substantially different look to its summary view, as Figure 6-9 clearly shows.

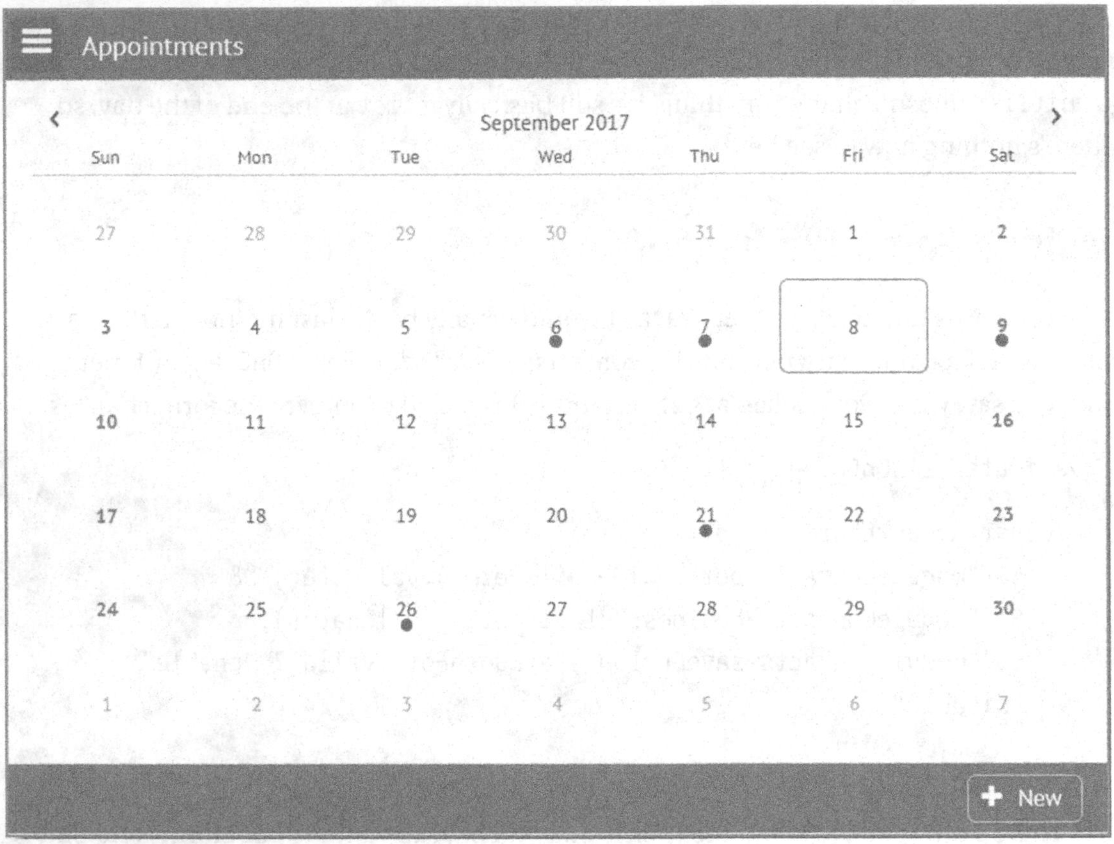

Figure 6-9. *Apppointments summary view*

This is a `calendar` component, stretched to fill its container. Dates that have appointments on them get the little red circle below them. I felt this display made more sense than some sort of list, and since you've seen two different types of list and a tree that in some ways looks like a list, I thought this would be more interesting.

When you click a date, you'll get a pop-up window, which I'll show in the section on the `selectDate()` method, which is what gets called when the user clicks a date. Assuming there is an appointment on the selected date, though, if the user clicks it, they'll find themselves in the details view shown in Figure 6-10.

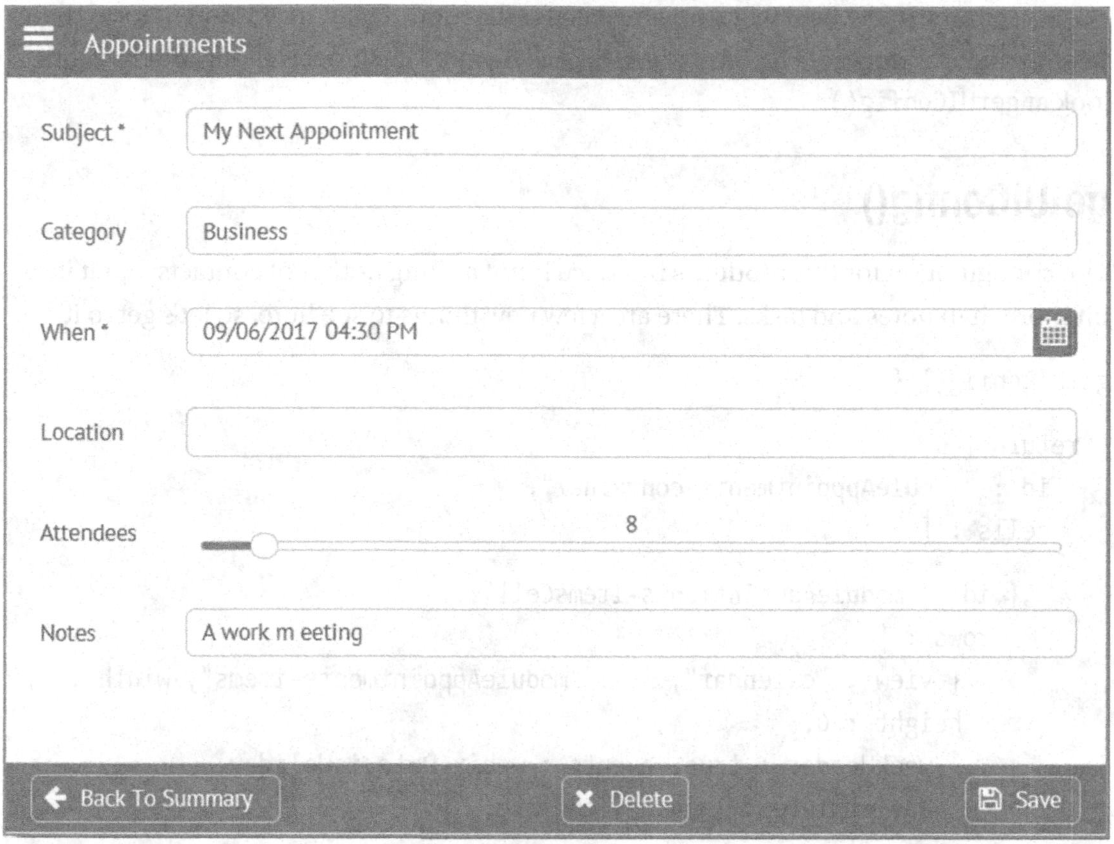

Figure 6-10. *Appointments entry screen*

Appointments always require a subject and a When value; otherwise, they wouldn't really be appointments. Everything else is optional.

Constructor

The constructor for this module, while not empty, does define a single property on the class instance that you'll need later.

```
constructor() {

  this.currentData = { };

}
```

The currentData field will store the data for the module but in a different form than its store in local storage. The reason for this will become clear before long, but first let's look at getUIConfig().

getUIConfig()

The configuration for this module's interface is not as long as that of contacts, but it is a bit more than notes and tasks. There are a few new things to see here, so let's get to it.

```
getUIConfig() {

  return {
    id : "moduleAppointments-container",
    cells : [

      { id : "moduleAppointments-itemsCell",
        rows : [
          { view : "calendar", id : "moduleAppointments-items", width : 0,
          height : 0,
            weekHeader : true, events : webix.Date.isHoliday,
            dayTemplate : this.dayTemplate,
            on : {
              onAfterDateSelect : this.selectDateHandler,
            }
          },
          { view : "toolbar",
            cols : [
              { },
              { view : "button", label : "New", width : "80", type :
              "iconButton",
                icon : "plus", click : this.newHandler.bind(this)
              },
              { width : 6 }
            ]
          }
        ]
      },
```

```
{ id : "moduleAppointments-details",
  rows : [
    { view : "form", id : "moduleAppointments-detailsForm",
    borderless : true,
      elementsConfig : { view : "text", labelWidth : 100,
      bottomPadding : 20,
        on : { onChange : () => {
          $$("moduleAppointments-saveButton")
            [$$("moduleAppointments-detailsForm").validate()?
            "enable" : "disable"]();
        } }
    },
      elements : [
        { name : "subject", label : "Subject", required : true,
          invalidMessage : "Subject is required", attributes : {
          maxlength : 100 }
        },
        { view : "text", name : "category", label : "Category",
          suggest : [
            { id : 1, value : "Personal" }, { id : 2, value :
            "Business" },
            { id : 3, value : "Other" }
          ],
          on : {
            onItemClick : () => {
              $$(this.config.suggest).show(this.getInputNode());
            }
          }
        },
        { view : "datepicker", name : "when", label : "When",
        required : true,
          invalidMessage : "When is required", timepicker : true
        },
        { name : "location", label : "Location", attributes : {
        maxlength : 200 } },
```

```
                { view : "slider", name : "attendees", label : "Attendees",
                  min : 1, max : 100, step : 1, title : "#value#",
                  id : "moduleAppointments-attendees"
                },
                { name : "notes", label : "Notes", attributes : { maxlength :
                250 } }
              ]
          },
          { },
          { view : "toolbar",
            cols : [
              { width : 6 },
              { view : "button", label : "Back To Summary", width : "170",
                type : "iconButton", icon : "arrow-left",
                click : () => {
                  $$("moduleAppointments-itemsCell").show();
                }
              },
              { },
              { id : "moduleAppointments-deleteButton", view : "button",
              label : "Delete",
                width : "90", type : "iconButton",
                icon : "remove", click : () => { wxPIM.
                deleteHandler("Appointments"); }
              },
              { },
              { view : "button", label : "Save", width : "80", type :
              "iconButton",
                icon : "floppy-o", id : "moduleAppointments-saveButton",
                disabled : true,
                click : function() {
                  wxPIM.saveHandler("Appointments", [ "moduleAppointments-
                  detailsForm" ]);
                }
              },
              { width : 6 }
```

```
        ]
      }
    ]
  }
]

};

}
```

The first thing of note is related to the calendar in the summary view. Note the width and height set to zero. This is a special case that tells Webix that you want the component to fill its parent container. If you don't do this, the calendar uses its default width and height, which is a few hundred pixels for both.

That same calendar has a weekHeader config attribute set to true, which results in seeing the days of the week along the top of the calendar. The events config option uses a built-in function, webix.Date.isHoliday, which by default returns true for Saturdays and Sundays. This results in the weekends being in different colors than weekdays, which is a helpful visual cue.

The dayTemplate is the biggest new item here, and it references the dayTemplate() method of the Appointments class instance, which tells the calendar how to render each date. Let's jump ahead and look at that right now:

```
dayTemplate(inDate) {

  const cssDayMarker = `
    background-color : #ff0000;
    border-radius : 50%;
    height : 8px;
    margin : 0 auto 8px;
    width : 8px;
    position : relative;
    top : -25px;
  `;

  const thisDate = new Date(inDate).setHours(0, 0, 0, 0);

  const appointment = wxPIM.modules.Appointments.currentData[thisDate];
```

```
let html = `<div class="day">${inDate.getDate()}</div>`;

if (appointment) {
  html += `<div style="${cssDayMarker}"></div>`;
}

return html;
```

```
}
```

The `calendar` calls this for each date, passing in the date, as a string. So, skipping over the `cssDayMarker` variable for a moment, the first step is to get a `Date` object from that string and use the same time normalization trick described earlier. Now, you do a lookup into the `currentData` object, which you saw defined in the constructor. This will be populated in `refreshData()`, as you'll see later, but the important thing about it is that the keys of it are dates. This is done so the lookup works, and if you get even one appointment for the date being processed by `dayTemplate()`, then you know the red dot has to be rendered. So, the HTML for it is constructed if you found an appointment. It's just a `<div>` that uses that `cssDayMarker` variable I mentioned earlier. This defines the style of the red dot and how to position it. It simply gets centered under the day's number, and I pull it up 25 pixels from where it would normally render so that it appears closer to the number, which I think looks better.

The rest of the UI config code here includes things you've seen before, save one thing: the `suggest` attached to the Category field. As you type in this field, you'll notice that a drop-down appears showing matching values from the list of options defined for the `suggest`. So, type a B, and the drop-down appears showing Business. Hit Delete and you'll see Personal, Business, and Other, because there's no match for an empty value.

A `suggest` is a component that you can attach to a Webix `text` field, a standard HTML input field, or a Webix text editor within a component item; it allows you to have a field that you can enter arbitrary text into but that also offers standard options that the user can choose from. The `suggest` won't automatically do anything, so you need to have code to show it. This is accomplished by the `onItemClick` handler for the Category `text` field. When the field is clicked and gains focus, the handler fires, retrieves a reference to the `suggest` component through the text component's `config` attribute, and calls `show()` on it, passing it a reference to the `text` field itself, more specifically, the underlying input component as provided by the `getInputNode()` method. This provides the tie-in to the suggest to be able to populate the field if and when the user selects a value from it. Interestingly, the suggest takes care of hiding itself when the field loses focus, so it's just showing it that you need to code for.

activate() and deactivate()

While the activate() method for this module is empty like the others, the deactivate() method has some work to do this time around.

```
deactivate() {

  if ($$("moduleAppointments-dateWindow")) {
    $$("moduleAppointments-dateWindow").close();
  }

}
```

Recall that deactivate() gets called any time the user switches away from the module, and although you haven't seen it yet, there's a potential problem here: when the user clicks a date, a window is shown to display any appointments for that date. However, if the user switches to another module or the day-at-a-glance screen, that window would still be present, floating over everything. That wouldn't be good! So, when this module is deactivated, if the window is showing, then it is closed, and that problem is avoided.

newHandler()

The newHandler() method for this module holds no surprises, except for one thing. See if you can pick it out!

```
newHandler() {

  wxPIM.isEditingExisting = false;
  wxPIM.editingID = new Date().getTime();

  if ($$("moduleAppointments-dateWindow")) {
    $$("moduleAppointments-dateWindow").close();
  }
```

```
$$("moduleAppointments-details").show();
$$("moduleAppointments-detailsForm").clear();
$$("moduleAppointments-attendees").setValue(1);
$$("moduleAppointments-deleteButton").disable();

}
```

Yep, you need to deal with that possible window again! Since for a new item you're switching between cells of a multiview, the window would still be present on the details screen, which again wouldn't be ideal, so you close it if it's open here as well.

editExisting()

The editExisting() method in this module is again just like the others, except for that pesky window once again!

```
editExisting(inID) {

  if ($$("moduleAppointments-dateWindow")) {
    $$("moduleAppointments-dateWindow").close();
  }

  const appointments = JSON.parse(localStorage.getItem("AppointmentsDB"));
  const appointment = appointments[inID];

  wxPIM.isEditingExisting = true;
  wxPIM.editingID = inID;

  $$("moduleAppointments-detailsForm").clear();

  $$("moduleAppointments-details").show();

  if (appointment.when) {
    appointment.when = new Date(appointment.when);
  }

  $$("moduleAppointments-detailsForm").setValues(appointment);

  $$("moduleAppointments-deleteButton").enable();

}
```

You have a date field to deal with here, but the rest is basically boilerplate at this point, aside from closing the `window` again because you're switching to the details screen once again, where the `window` isn't applicable.

refreshData()

Now you come to the anti-penultimate method of this class, `refreshData()`.

```
refreshData() {

  const dataItems = wxPIM.getModuleData("Appointments");
  wxPIM.modules.Appointments.currentData = { };
  for (const key in dataItems) {
   if (dataItems.hasOwnProperty(key)) {
     const item = dataItems[key];
     wxPIM.modules.Appointments.currentData[new Date(item.when).
     setHours(0, 0, 0, 0)] =
        item;
   }
  }

  $$("moduleAppointments-items").refresh();

}
```

This is a bit different than the others. First, after getting the data for the module, that `currentData` object needs to be built. As stated earlier, this is keyed by the date of the appointments, with the time component zeroed out since you don't care about that. Once that's done, the `refresh()` method is called on the `calendar` component. This method, which is available on some components, but not all, causes it to repaint itself. Because every date in the `calendar` will trigger a call to the `dayTemplate()` method, which uses the `currentData` object to determine how to render each date, the means that when you add, update, or delete items, the call to `refreshData()` will result in the call to `refresh()` being made, and you'll wind up with an updated `calendar` display on the summary screen.

selectDateHandler()

The final method to look at is one that is specific to this module and is the method called when the user clicks a date in the summary calendar, which is selectDateHandler(). But, before you look at the code, it would probably be helpful to know what the pop-up window that this method will construct looks like, and Figure 6-11 is exactly that.

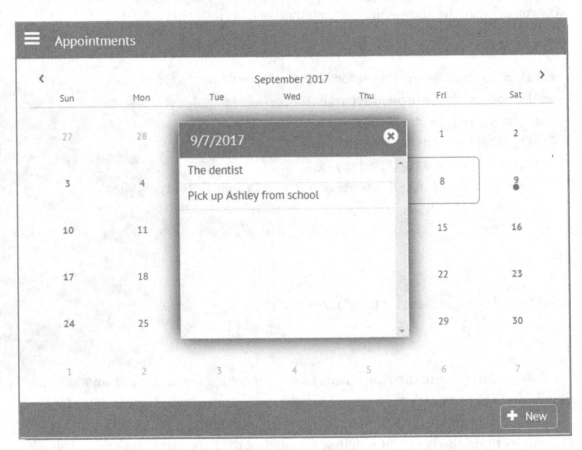

Figure 6-11. *Selecting a date on the summary view*

As you can see, it's a basic window that shows the selected date with any appointments for that date displayed in a scrolling list. If there are no appointments, then it will say that, and there is a close icon as well to dismiss the window. For simplicity, the window will always center itself on the screen.

```
selectDateHandler(inDate) {

  const appointments = wxPIM.getModuleData("Appointments");

  const selectedDate = new Date(inDate).setHours(0, 0, 0, 0);

  const listData = [ ];
  for (const key in appointments) {
    if (appointments.hasOwnProperty(key)) {
      const appointment = appointments[key];
      const appointmentDate = new Date(appointment.when).setHours(0, 0, 0, 0);
      if (appointmentDate == selectedDate) {
        listData.push(appointment);
      }
    }
  }

  if ($$("moduleAppointments-dateWindow")) {
    $$("moduleAppointments-dateWindow").close();
  }

  webix.ui({
    view : "window", id : "moduleAppointments-dateWindow", width : 300,
    height : 284,
    position : "center",
    head : {
      view : "toolbar",
      cols : [
        { view : "label", label : inDate.toLocaleDateString() },
        { view : "icon", icon : "times-circle",
          click : function() { $$("moduleAppointments-dateWindow").close();
}
        }
      ]
    },
    body : function() {
      if (listData.length == 0) {
        return { rows : [
```

```
          { },
          { borderless : true,
            template : `<div style="text-align: center;">Nothing on this
            day</span>`
          },
          { }
        ] };
      } else {
        return {
          view : "list", id : "appAppointments-itemsList", data : listData,
          template : "#subject#", click : wxPIM.modules.Appointments.
          editExisting,
        };
      }
    }()
  }).show();

}
```

Before the `window` is constructed, you have some setup work to do. First, of course, you get the data for the module from local storage. Then, the selected date is converted from a string to a `Date` object with the time zeroed out. Next, you need to go through all the appointments and pull out just those for the selected date. Remember that you have an array from local storage, so you can't do any sort of simple keyed lookup; you have to scan through the entire array. For each, if the appointment's when field has a date that equals the selected date, when time is taken out of the equation thanks to zeroing, then the appointment is added to the `listData` array.

With that data ready, now you can deal with the `window`. But first, you need to close any `window` that might be open now; otherwise, you'd just be building windows on top of windows. Once that's done, `window` construction can begin.

A `window` is conceptually a separate Webix UI context, meaning you can build a full UI in it independent of whatever is "beneath" it in the main UI. You can build any UI you want, of course, using all the same techniques as you've seen to this point, with no limitations. You do, however, need to take care to avoid ID collisions because a `window`, while it looks separate, is still part of the same DOM as everything else.

The `window` has `position` set to `center`, which tells Webix to center the `window` on the screen without you having to do anything else. The `window`'s UI is just a `toolbar` up top with a `label` for the date and the close `icon`, with its associated `click` handler function to close the window.

For the body of the window, you need to get a little fancy. An anonymous, immediately invoked function, allows you to have some logic based on whether there were any appointments for this day or not. If there weren't, then all you do is show the "Nothing on this day" text, centered horizontally (using a `<div>` with `text-align` set to `center`) and vertically, thanks to the spacer elements above and below the one with the text. If there are appointments, then you define a Webix `list` component with the `data` from `listData` that you populated earlier. The `template` just displays the subject of the appointment, and the `click` handler triggers the `editExisting()` method, as you'd expect.

And with that, you've now explored all the code of the wxPIM application, at least in its initial form!

Summary

In this chapter, you finished the journey through the code of wxPIM. Along the way, you saw some new components such as the suggest component, and you saw some real-world usage of many of the concepts that were discussed in the previous chapter.

In the next chapter, you'll take this application and expand on it in various ways, beginning with making it a little more desktop-centric, when applicable, to provide a more robust user experience when not used on a mobile device.

CHAPTER 7

Taking wxPIM to the Desktop

In Chapter 6, you built the first iteration of wxPIM. That version is quite mobile-centric, although it works completely on a nonmobile (and nontouchscreen) device. That's one of the big attractions of Webix: your code will, with few exceptions, work fine in both situations without doing a thing.

However, because it works doesn't necessarily mean it's ideal. A UI for a small screen will often need to be different than for a larger desktop monitor. Interactions will often need to be different between touchscreens and when users are using just a good ol' keyboard and mouse.

Fortunately, with just a bit of extra code, you can handle both situations pretty well with Webix while using the bulk of the same code, and that's exactly what you're going to do in this chapter! You'll take wxPIM and make it a little better suited to desktop use while maintaining the mobile experience you already have.

However, before you do that, something is bugging me...

First, Let's Fix a Few Things!

If you remember early on, I said that wxPIM is meant to be modular and that you should be able to easily add modules to it to get other functions you may want. For the most part, that goal has been achieved, but there are a few places where that model is broken because the core wxPIM knows about specific modules right now. So, let's take care of those cases before going any further.

Fortunately, the changes aren't necessarily drastic, mostly just some refactoring, but first, you have to add a few things that you'll need for this and the rest of the chapter, and it all kicks off in the wxPIM constructor.

© Frank Zammetti 2018
F. Zammetti, *Practical Webix*, https://doi.org/10.1007/978-1-4842-3384-9_7

```
this.registeredModules = [ ];

if (webix.env.mobile) {
  this.uiType = "mobile";
} else {
  this.uiType = "desktop";
}

webix.protoUI({
  name : "ani-window",
  $init : function() {
    this.$ready.push(function() {
      this.attachEvent("onShow", function() {
        let base = this.$view.className.split("animated")[0];
        this.$view.className = base + " animated bounceIn";
      });
      this.attachEvent("onHide", function() {
        this.$view.style.display = "block";
        this.$view.className = this.$view.className + " animated bounceOut";
      });
    });
  }
}, webix.ui.window);
```

First, notice what's missing: isEditingExisting and editingID. Those members become problematic when you make this a more desktop-centric app because it works fine, with them being members of the wxPIM object, when only a single module can be visible at any given time. But (spoiler alert!) that's not going to be the case by the end of this chapter. Instead, every module needs to track its own state with regard to whether it's editing something or not and the ID of that item. So, those two members are going to move to the constructors of each module (and you'll, of course, add a constructor if a given module doesn't have one already).

The next thing is this new registeredModules member. This is to meet the goal of not having the core wxPIM code knowing about modules. Instead, each module will "register" itself with wxPIM by a line in its source file before the class definition like so:

```
wxPIM.registeredModules.push("Appointments");
```

266

I'll come back to this shortly, but before I do, I should talk about the uiType member. Webix provides some interesting environment description flags in the webix.env namespace, one of which is mobile. This purports to tell you whether you're on a "mobile" device or not. I put mobile in quotes there because what that actually means is up for debate. There's no simple "are you a mobile device?" check that all computing devices or browsers support. If you look at the Webix source itself, you'll see that it's doing a simple check on whether the strings "Mobile" or "Windows Phone" appear in the navigator.userAgent string. Whether that's the right check or not is debatable, but I'd say it's a good starting point at least, and chances are it'll be right *most* of the time. But, rather than just use the flag's value directly, I instead pull it out into the uiType member. That way, if I want to enhance the logic that determines whether you're running in a "mobile" environment or not, I can do so without touching any other code in the app that depends on that determination.

This uiType string is going to be used a lot as you make the rest of the changes because branching based on whether you're on a mobile device or not is a key thing when rendering the UI or performing functions later. Don't worry; you'll see all of that shortly!

The next thing you see in the constructor is the creation of a new Webix component, which is something new! The webix.protoUI() method allows you to create a new view based on an existing view so that you can use it like any other view. In this case, I want to create a new type of webix.ui.window component that will have some animation when shown or hidden using the animate.css library that was previously discussed. Webix. protoUI() takes two objects as an argument. The first is the target object, the one you're creating. The second is the object it builds upon. Technically, you can also include one or more objects after that, which will be "mixed in" to the target object, but here that's not needed. The name attribute of the first object gives a name to the component that you can later use as the value of a view config option. An overridden $init() method is also required so the animation can be hooked into the window's lifecycle. Event handlers are pushed into the $ready collection for the component, one for handling the onShow event and one for the onHide event. The handler for each adds the appropriate animate.css class to the window, which triggers the animation.

That covers the constructor code, so now let's jump back to that registeredModules member. The first place you see that used is in the wxPIM.start() method.

```
for (let moduleName of wxPIM.registeredModules) {
  wxPIM.modules[moduleName] = new wxPIM.moduleClasses[moduleName]();
}
```

If you look back at the original code, you'll see that there were four explicit object instantiations there, one for each module. That of course meant that the wxPIM code had to be aware of every module, and that's what you're trying to avoid. By having each module add their name to the `registeredModules` array, you can just iterate the array in the `start()` method and instantiate the module's class for each module. wxPIM no longer knows what specific modules are present, at least to this point. There are some other places you have to deal with, though, and that's next.

Changing the Base Layout

The base layout also needs to be altered a bit. The change here is minimal but also consequential. The change is the addition of one config attribute, shown here:

```
id : "baseLayout"
```

This will come into play later, so let's continue for now. The base layout, you'll recall, calls the `wxPIM.getMultiviewConfig()` method to build the `multiview` that houses the UI for each of the modules. That call still occurs, but the method itself is now a bit different.

```
wxPIM.getMultiviewConfig = function() {

  const cellsConfig = [ wxPIM.getDayAtAGlanceConfig() ];
  if (wxPIM.uiType === "mobile") {
    for (let moduleName of wxPIM.registeredModules) {
      cellsConfig.push(wxPIM.modules[moduleName].getUIConfig());
    }
  }

  return {
    view : "multiview", id : "moduleArea", cells : cellsConfig,
    animate : { type : "flip", subtype : "horizontal" }
  };

};
```

The difference is that the original version was straightforward in that it had explicit cells for the day-at-a-glance screen and then the four modules, and that was it. But again, you want to be able to drop in new modules at will and not have to touch the core code, so this needs to change. First, the code makes a choice: are you on a mobile device or not based on the value of uiType? If not on mobile, then the only content that needs to be present in the multiview (which at this point wouldn't really be so much of a *multi*view) is the day-at-a-glance screen. That's because the UI of the modules will be displayed in a different way, not in the multiview, as you'll see shortly. If wxPIM *is* running in a mobile environment, then in addition to day-at-a-glance, you need a view for each of the modules registered with the core code. To accomplish that, the registeredModules array is iterated again, and a view is added to the cellsConfig array for each. Finally, what gets returned is the same as in the original version except that the value of the cells attribute is now the cellsConfig array rather than a hard-coded chunk of configuration and now contains *either* just day-at-a-glance when not on mobile *or* day-at-a-glance *plus* a view for every module when on mobile.

With the base layout out of the way, you can now address the one last place where the core code knows about modules, and that's the day-at-a-glance screen.

Now the Fun Stuff: Day-at-a-Glance Changes

The original wxPIM.dayAtAGlance() method, you'll recall, is that bit of code that has the worker function defined, and then a call is made to it for appointments and tasks, rendering their display on the screen. This was fairly nice in that it was common code shared between the two. But, the problem is that it's another place the core code knows about specific modules. It knows there is an appointments module, and there is a tasks module. Let's avoid that. The way you're going to do that is by using the registeredModules array again.

```
wxPIM.dayAtAGlance = function() {

  if (wxPIM.uiType === "mobile") {

    if (wxPIM.activeModule) {
      wxPIM.modules[wxPIM.activeModule].deactivate();
    }

    wxPIM.activeModule = null;

    $$("headerLabel").setValue($$("headerLabel").config.defaultLabel);

  }
```

```
for (let moduleName of wxPIM.registeredModules) {
  wxPIM.modules[moduleName].dayAtAGlance();
}
```

```
};
```

First, you need to take care of some mobile-only concerns, namely, that call to deactivate() of the currently active module, if any, and the setting of the header text. Remember that the header text reflects the module that is currently active, but as you'll see soon, that's no longer needed when in desktop mode.

One interesting thing here is that the header text is specified by the defaultLabel attribute of the config object of the label component where the header text resides, as you'll see a little later. If you go look up the configuration options for the label component in the Webix documentation, you won't find a defaultLabel option, and that may seem odd. But, here's the trick: you can specify anything you want in the configuration options for a component and Webix will just ignore anything it doesn't understand. Critically, though, Webix will *still* store those attributes in the component's config object. This is nice because it allows you to encapsulate extra information (or even functions if you want) with the component, and you can get at it later through config, as I've done here. That avoids having to have separate variables floating around your code. If it's related to the component, you can store it "in" the component, so to speak, which is a cleaner way to write code.

Once the mobile-only stuff is handled, then it's time to render the day-at-a-glance content. Now, though, it's yet another iteration of registeredModules (seeing a pattern yet?) and a call to the dayAtAGlance() method of each, which is new. Basically, you're now going to give each registered module a chance to render its own content for the day-at-a-glance screen. Of course, it's still only appointments and tasks that have anything to render (the contacts and notes modules still have a dayAtAGlance() method, but it's empty), but before they can, you need to have the baseline day-at-a-glance UI for them to render into. As it happens, this is simply the removal of the fieldsets (and separator views) that were hard-coded into the day-at-a-glance UI config. The config now is simply as follows:

```
wxPIM.getDayAtAGlanceConfig = function() {

  return {
    id : "dayAtAGlance", view : "scrollview", borderless : true, body : {
      id : "dayAtAGlanceBody", paddingX : 20, paddingY : 20, rows : [ ]
    }
```

```
  };

};
```

So, how does the content for each module get rendered? Glad you asked!

Letting a Module Provide Day-at-a-Glance

As I said, each module now provides a dayAtAGlance() method, and also as mentioned, only appointments and tasks have code in them. The code in them, which is almost identical between the two, should look pretty familiar to you.

```
dayAtAGlance() {

  if (!$$("dayAtAGlanceScreen_Appointments")) {
    $$("dayAtAGlanceBody").addView({
      view : "fieldset", label : "Appointments",
      body : { id : "dayAtAGlanceScreen_Appointments", rows : [ ] }
    });
    $$("dayAtAGlanceBody").addView({ height : 20 });
  }

  const template = webix.template("#subject# - #when# #location#");
  let dataItems = wxPIM.getModuleData("Appointments");
  dataItems = wxPIM.objectAsArray(dataItems);
  wxPIM.sortArray(dataItems, "when", "A");
  const currentDate = new Date().setHours(0, 0, 0, 0);
  const rows = [ ];
  for (let i = 0; i < dataItems.length; i++) {
    const item = dataItems[i];
    const itemDate = new Date(item.when).setHours(0, 0, 0, 0);
    if (itemDate == currentDate) {
      if (item.location) {
        item.location = "(" + item.location + ")";
      } else {
        item.location = "";
      }
      item["when"] = webix.i18n.timeFormatStr(new Date(item.when));
```

```
      rows.push({ borderless : true, template : template(item), height :
      30 });
    }
  }
  webix.ui(rows, $$("dayAtAGlanceScreen_Appointments"));

}
```

That's the code for appointments, of course, and yes, it's almost the same as the `worker` function code in the original version of wxPIM; it was just copied into the `Appointments.js` file and modified to not be general-purpose like it was before. Now it's specific to appointments. If you look at the `dayAtAGlance()` function in `Tasks.js`, you'll see that it's now almost identical to this as well. While duplicate code is usually something you want to avoid, it's tangential that the code is highly similar here. It could be vastly different, and the real point is you now want each module to have its own logic so each can render whatever is appropriate for it.

But, there are, of course, some differences here, beginning right at the top. Since the new version of the basic day-at-a-glance UI doesn't include views for any module, each module needs to add one using the `addView()` method of the `dayAtAGlanceBody` element. It also adds a spacer view below it so that the next module's contents don't run into this one. Once that view is added, though, then the code is not really any different from it was in the original version, minus all the branching that was necessary when this was shared code.

"Desktop-ization": A Window unto the World

So, we've (mostly!) assuaged my concerns about the modularity of wxPIM...I feel much better now, so let's at this point move on to making the app more desktop-friendly. What exactly does this mean? Well, there's certainly no one-size-fits-all answer to this; it means different things to different people. But, to me, and at a minimum, it means using the (typically) larger space that a desktop monitor affords more efficiently and making sure the interactions the user performs are optimized for keyboard and mouse.

But, it's important to remember that wxPIM, as it stands now, works perfectly fine on a desktop, sans any changes at all. That's one of the best things about Webix: the code you write will (generally) work fine on a mobile device or a desktop. However, that doesn't mean it's *optimized* for one or the other. So, let's see what you can do about that.

The first change that will be made is a minor thing on the `sidemenu`. Take a look at Figure 7-1. Do you see what's changed?

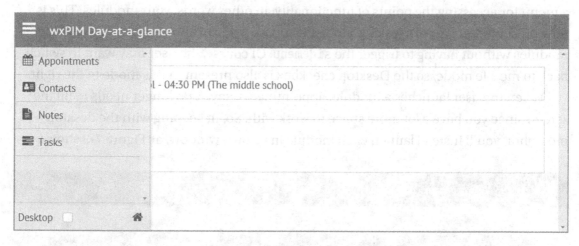

Figure 7-1.   Notice anything different and new?

There's that little Desktop check box down there, and the home icon has been shifted to the right. Although one of the more common approaches to dealing with the mobile/desktop dichotomy is to use responsive design (that is, using usually CSS to "reflow" the layout in various ways depending on the width of the screen), this isn't always the best approach. Especially when you're talking about an app built with a JavaScript-heavy framework (heavy in the sense that JavaScript is required for it to function, that is), then you might as well rely on JavaScript to do this, and at that point, you can do things other than simply reflowing the application. You can drastically change the presentation, as Figure 7-2 begins to show.

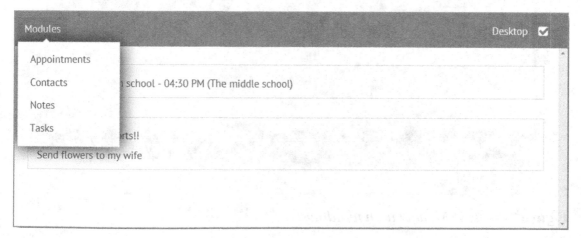

Figure 7-2.   Desktop mode means a different navigation scheme

273

When you switch to desktop mode by checking that box in the `sidemenu`, the UI changes to a layout that looks a lot like a typical operating system desktop, complete with a menu for accessing the points of functionality, in other words, your modules. This is now presented as part of a taskbar along the top, so you can always quickly access the modules without having to trigger the `sidemenu`. Of course, the user may want to switch back to mobile mode, so the Desktop `checkbox` is also present in this mode to the right.

When the user launches a module, appointments, say, it no longer needs to fill the screen since you have a lot more space to work with. So, in keeping with the desktop metaphor, you'll instead launch each module in its own window, as Figure 7-3 shows.

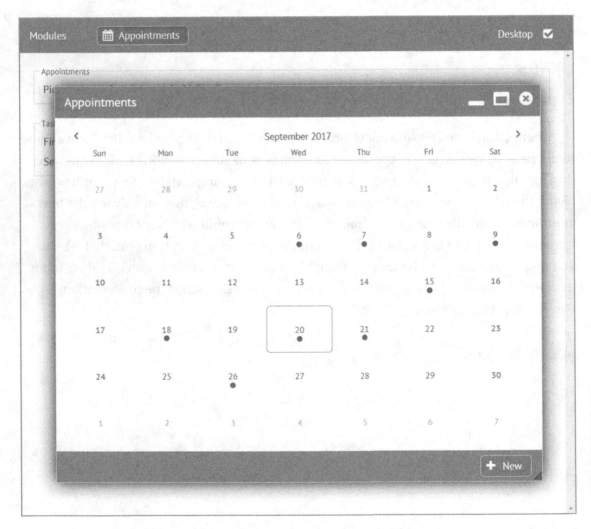

Figure 7-3. wxPIM, now with windows!

Each window can be dragged around, resized, maximized to fill the screen, or minimized, which just leaves its module icon up top, just like on the taskbar of any modern OS. They can be closed too, of course, or you can launch more than one, as Figure 7-4 shows.

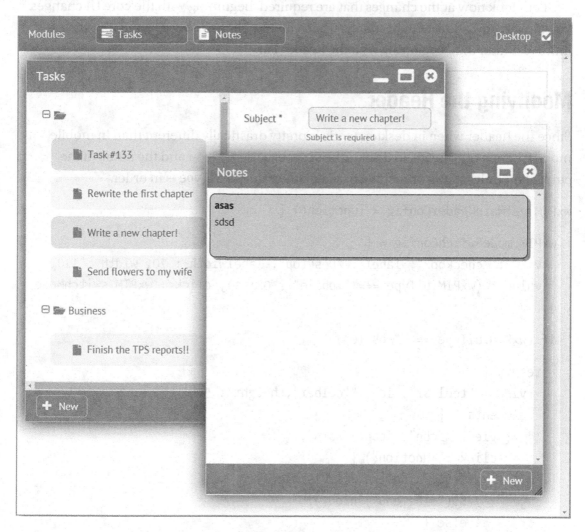

Figure 7-4. *No, really, it's like a desktop!*

Obviously, this is all pretty typical behavior, but it's also a pretty drastic departure from the user experience of the mobile version where you could see only one module at a time. You'll also notice that the tasks module, behind the notes module's window, looks a bit different. That's more of an attempt to better utilize space, but you'll get to that a little later.

The very best thing about this is that the changes required to make this happen are, all things considered, pretty minor! In fact, except for some branching in the module's UI configuration and a few minor points in their backing code, the only significant change is in the core code that launches the modules.

Let's look now at the changes that are required, beginning with the core UI changes. You already saw some of it, of course, when you modified the base layout, but there's more to it than that, beginning with the header bar.

Modifying the Header

Since the header when in desktop mode is pretty drastically different than in mobile mode where it only needs to display the sidemenu trigger icon and the name of the current module, a little branching based on the value of uiType is in order.

```
wxPIM.getMainHeaderConfig = function() {

  wxPIM.modeSwitchConfig = {
    view : "checkbox", label : "Desktop", labelWidth : 70, width : 110,
    value : (wxPIM.uiType === "mobile" ? 0 : 1), click : wxPIM.switchMode
  };

  if (wxPIM.uiType === "mobile") {

    return {
      view : "toolbar", id : "toolbar", height : 50,
      elements : [
        { view: "icon", icon: "bars",
          click : function() {
            if ($$("sidemenu").isVisible()) {
              $$("sidemenu").hide();
            } else {
              $$("sidemenu").show();
            }
          }
        },
        { id : "headerLabel", view: "label",
          label : "", defaultLabel : "wxPIM Day-at-a-glance"
        }
```

```
        ]
      };

    } else {

      return {
        view : "toolbar", id : "toolbar", height : 50,
        elements : [
          { view : "menu", width : 100, css : { "padding-top" : "4px" },
            data : [
              { value : "Modules", id : "Modules",
                submenu : wxPIM.registeredModules.sort()
              }
            ],
            on : { onMenuItemClick : wxPIM.launchModule }
          },
          { view : "toolbar", id : "taskbar", borderless : true, elements : [
          ] },
          { },
          wxPIM.modeSwitchConfig
        ]
      };

    }

  };
```

Of course, since the mode switch checkbox is going to be the same in either mode, you can pull that out and create the resultant wxPIM.modeSwitchConfig member for it, and since it's needed in this mainHeader.js file as well as in sideMenu.js, it makes sense to make it a member of the wxPIM object itself.

After that, you branch on the value of uiType, and when it's mobile, the config object returned is just what it was before in the original code. In desktop mode, though, that's when you need to do something different. In this case, though it's still a toolbar being built, now it's a toolbar with four elements: a menu that contains the list of modules (and note that you use the wxPIM.registeredModules collection for this, taking care to sort it so that the modules are always displayed in alphabetical order, which is another "fix" for the modularity issues from earlier), then a toolbar where the module task buttons

277

will go, and then a spacer that pushes the fourth element (the mode switch checkbox) over to the right. The taskbar toolbar begins with no elements, and you'll be adding buttons to it dynamically as modules are launched and closed.

Modifying the sidemenu

Next, you need to change the sidemenu to show the mode switch icon and re-arrange that bottom bar with it so that the home icon goes to the right. But, first things first, the data for the list needs to be built dynamically instead of statically as it was originally.

```
const listItems = [ ];
for (let moduleName of wxPIM.registeredModules) {
  listItems.push({ id : moduleName, value : moduleName,
    icon : wxPIM.modules[moduleName].getUIConfig().winIcon
  });
}
```

Once again, wxPIM.registeredModules comes to the rescue. Now, instead of the data attribute of the list being hard-coded module names, that data is built on the fly, again letting you be more modular. The data attribute just points to listItems now, but otherwise the list config is unchanged.

However, the footer row on the sidemenu is, of course, different and is now this:

```
{ cols : [
  wxPIM.modeSwitchConfig,
  { },
  { view : "button", type : "icon", label : "", icon : "home",
    align : "right", width : 32,
    click : () => {
      wxPIM.dayAtAGlance();
      $$("sidemenu").hide();
      $$("dayAtAGlance").show();
    }
  }
] }
```

The wxPIM.modeSwitchConfig that was built earlier is used, then a spacer, and then the same button config for the home icon as before.

278

That takes care of all the code that configures the UI. Now, you come to the two main attractions: launching modules and switching modes. The former is easily the biggest change from the original version of the code, and the latter is entirely new. Let's begin with launching modules.

The Big Change: Module Launching

Of all the changes required for the "desktop-ization" of wxPIM, the changes to the wxPIM.launchModule() are probably the biggest. But, I believe you'll find it all pretty logical. Read through this code, and then I'll walk you through it.

```
launchModule(inModuleName) {

  if (inModuleName === "Modules") { return; }

  if (wxPIM.uiType === "mobile") {

    if (wxPIM.activeModule) {
      wxPIM.modules[wxPIM.activeModule].deactivate();
    }

    wxPIM.activeModule = inModuleName;

    $$("sidemenu").hide();

    $$("headerLabel").setValue(inModuleName);

    wxPIM.editingID = null;
    wxPIM.isEditingExisting = false;

    $$(`module${inModuleName}-itemsCell`).show();
    $$(`module${inModuleName}-container`).show();

  } else {

    let moduleWindow = $$(`moduleWindow-${inModuleName}`);

    if (moduleWindow) {

      moduleWindow.show();
      return;

    } else {
```

```
      const moduleUIConfig = wxPIM.modules[inModuleName].getUIConfig();

  let toolbarHeight = $$("toolbar").$height;
  let vpWidth = document.documentElement.clientWidth - 100;
  let vpHeight = document.documentElement.clientHeight - 100 -
  toolbarHeight;
  let winWidth = moduleUIConfig.winWidth;
  let winHeight = moduleUIConfig.winHeight;
  if (vpWidth < winWidth) {
    winWidth = vpWidth;
  }
  if (vpHeight < winHeight) {
    winHeight = vpHeight;
  }
  const centerX = ((vpWidth - winWidth) / 2) + 50;
  const centerY = ((vpHeight - winHeight) / 2) + (toolbarHeight * 2);

  webix.ui({
    view : "ani-window", move : true, width : winWidth, height :
    winHeight,
    left : centerX, top : centerY,
    resize : true, id : `moduleWindow-${inModuleName}`, toFront : true,
    fullscreen : false,
    head : {
      view : "toolbar",
      cols : [
        { view : "label", label: moduleUIConfig.winLabel },
        { view : "icon", icon : "window-minimize",
          click : function() {
            $$(`moduleWindow-${inModuleName}`).hide();
            $$(`moduleTasbbarButton-${inModuleName}`).toggle();
          }
        },
        { view : "icon", icon : "window-maximize",
          click : function() {
            const win = $$(`moduleWindow-${inModuleName}`);
            win.config.fullscreen = !win.config.fullscreen;
```

```
          win.resize();
          if (win.config.fullscreen) {
            this.config.icon = "window-restore";
            win.setPosition(0, 0);
          } else {
            this.config.icon = "window-maximize";
            win.setPosition(centerX, centerY);
          }
          this.refresh();
          this.blur();
        }
      },
      { view : "icon", icon : "times-circle",
        click : function() {
          $$(`moduleWindow-${inModuleName}`).close();
          $$("taskbar").removeView(`moduleTasbbarButton-
          ${inModuleName}`);
        }
      }
    ]
  },
  body : moduleUIConfig
}).show();

const taskbar = $$("taskbar");
const moduleButton = webix.ui({
  id : `moduleTasbbarButton-${inModuleName}`,
  view : "toggle", type : "iconButton", width : 140, height : 50,
  icon : moduleUIConfig.winIcon, label : moduleUIConfig.winLabel,
  click : function() {
    const moduleName = this.config.label;
    if (this.getValue() === 1) {
      $$(`moduleWindow-${moduleName}`).hide();
    } else {
      $$(`moduleWindow-${moduleName}`).show();
    }
```

```
        this.blur();
      }
    });
    moduleButton.toggle();
    taskbar.addView(moduleButton);

  }

}

wxPIM.modules[inModuleName].refreshData();

wxPIM.modules[inModuleName].activate();

}
```

The first "problem" is that when the menu is clicked, the onMenuItemClick event is fired. This is fine; you need that to happen, except that it's true for the top-level item as well, namely, the *Modules* text. This, of course, isn't the name of a module, which is all you care about in this method, so you'll check to see whether the text you were passed is "Modules" and if so then just immediately return.

Once that check is passed, then what code path you travel depends on the current uiType. When it's mobile, the code is basically the same as before. However, when it's the new desktop mode, that's when it gets different.

In this mode, the first thing that needs to happen is you need to see whether the module is already "running." This just means whether a window for it exists already. If it does, then the task is easy: just call show() on the window (in case it's behind another), and that's it, you're done.

If no window already exists, though, then you need to build it. To do so, you need the UI config for the module, and that means a call to getUIConfig() of the module's class instance. Next, the code needs to figure out the size the window should be. The logic here is to first get the height of the toolbar up top and subtract a little bit of buffer space from both the height and width available in the browser window, taking the toolbar into account as part of the height. This effectively gives you the maximum size the window could be while still fitting in the available browser space. After that, you grab the winWidth and winHeight attributes on the UI config object that tell you how big the window should initially be. This way, each module can determine its optimal size as part of its design. These aren't Webix attributes; they are extra attributes unique to your code. Webix ignores them, so it's nice to keep everything all encapsulated like that. Once you have those, you make a comparison to those max sizes that were determined earlier and use either the specified `winWidth` and `winHeight` or the maximum values. This way, the window always fits without being cut off. Finally, with the window's dimensions known, you can now calculate the X and Y location so that the window is centered on the screen to start.

Now, it's time to build the window! The view used is the custom `ani-window` that you defined earlier in the `wxPIM` constructor. The window is defined to be `movable` and `resizable`, and `toFront` is set to `true`. What that last one does is ensure that when the user clicks anywhere in the window, it will be brought to the foreground. Without this, it may still sit behind another window, obscuring it, which isn't what you expect windows to do! I also explicitly set the `fullscreen` attribute to `false` to indicate to Webix that this window should not take up the entire available space, at least not initially (hint-hint!).

The head of the window is a `toolbar` that houses the label of the window as stated in the `winLabel` attribute of the config object, another additional attribute especially for wxPIM usage that Webix ignores. After that are three `icon` elements, one for minimizing the window, one for maximizing (or restoring when the window is maximized), and one for closing the window.

The handler for the minimize `icon` just needs to hide the window, and also it calls `toggle()` on the `taskbar button` for this window (which you get a reference to by constructing the appropriate ID for). The `button` is a `toggle button` that actually gets added after the window is built, as you'll see shortly, so it has a pressed state and a nonpressed state. As you'll see, it initially gets set in the pressed state when the window is launched so that it stands out from the others and indicates which window is "current," so when minimized, this state needs to be reversed.

The handler for the maximize `icon` is a little more involved. First, you need to tell Webix to make the window full-screen and then `reconfigure()` it, which results in it being re-drawn filling the available space. Then, based on whether the window is now full-screen or not, the `icon` needs to change to either the maximize icon or the restore icon. This way, the `icon` is effectively a toggle. The `refresh()` method of the `icon` needs to be called to reflect the change from `window-restore` to `window-maximize` (or vice versa), and then finally I call `blur()` on the `icon` because failing to do that leaves it with a slight background color difference that I just didn't think looked so good and certainly is not what you'd expect given what happens with a real desktop OS window.

The close `icon` handler is just a call to `close()` on the window, as well as a call to `removeView()` on the `toolbar` where the module task buttons are. Nothing else needs to be done to close a module.

Finally, the body of the window is the `moduleUIConfig` that was retrieved earlier. And with that, you have a fully constructed module window that you can show with a call to `show()`.

Note that the UI config for the window is the same as the UI config when in mobile mode, at least as far as the core code goes. Each module can, of course, determine what UI config to return given the current `uiType`, but the core code doesn't care; it treats it the same either way.

The final thing that has to happen that is specific to desktop mode is adding a taskbar button for the module. As I mentioned earlier, it's a `toggle button` with a `click` handler. The handler looks at the current state of the `toggle button`, which is either a 0 or a 1. When it's a 1, that corresponds to the pressed state, so you expect the module window to be hidden in that case, which is what a desktop operating system taskbar button does. If it's a 0, then the window needs to be shown. Either way, I again `blur()` off the button so as to not have it look weird and then `toggle()` the button so that its visual state is pressed when the window is current and showing, not pressed when it's hidden. Finally, `addView()` is called, passing the config for the button, and Webix adds the button for you.

After that, you have a few more tasks to accomplish, and they have to happen regardless of which UI mode you're in. First, a call to the module's `refreshData()` method ensures that the summary view shows fresh data. This is really important only when in mobile mode or when first showing a window in desktop mode because doing it when the window is already visible is redundant. But, it does no harm to do it, so it's easier to just make the call without checking any conditions. Finally, the `activate()` method gets called since that's the lifecycle you previously defined for your modules.

And with that, you can launch modules in either UI mode! But, how do you actually switch between modes? Well, that's next!

Switching Modes

Finally, you need to add some code for switching between desktop and mobile modes. Although wxPIM determines which mode to use when initially launched, the user may decide they'd prefer to use the other mode, and that's where that check box comes into play. When checked, it means use desktop mode; unchecked means mobile mode. When the `checkbox` is changed, `wxPIM.switchMode()` is called.

```
switchMode() {

  $$("sidemenu").hide();
```

```
for (let moduleName of wxPIM.registeredModules) {
  let moduleWindow = $$(`moduleWindow-${moduleName}`);
  if (moduleWindow) { moduleWindow.close(); }
}

wxPIM.activeModule = null;

$$("baseLayout").destructor();

switch (this.getValue()) {
  case 0 : wxPIM.uiType = "mobile"; break;
  case 1 : wxPIM.uiType = "desktop"; break;
}

wxPIM.start();

};
```

First, the sidemenu is hidden, regardless of whether it's showing or not (it might not even be active, as in desktop mode). Next, all open windows need to be closed. Again, nothing breaks if this code executes even in mobile mode because of course no window will be found then, so there's no need to branch on uiType here. Next, you ensure that there is no activeModule reference, which matters if you're switching to mobile mode (because that member doesn't come into play in desktop mode anyway).

Next, you get to be destructive! You need to tear down the entire current UI regardless of what mode you're in. Do you remember in baseLayout.js how you added an id to it? Well, here's why: you can now get a reference to the root element of your UI based on that ID and call the destructor() method on it, which is available on all Webix views and which destroys not only that view but also all its children. So, doing this makes Webix destroy the entire UI in one fell swoop! One command, so much destruction...it's like being in charge of a nuclear button!

Ahem.

Anyway, once the UI is destroyed, you, of course, need to build it back up again in whatever the new mode is. So, you look at the value of the checkbox. If it's 0, that's unchecked, so wxPIM.uiType is set to mobile; otherwise, the box is checked, and you set it to desktop instead. Then, all you need to do is call wxPIM().start(), which you'll recall is what kicks everything off and where the UI is built from. The core UI config code, of course, branches based on wxPIM.uiType (and all the module class instances are re-created as part of this too, so all state is reset), and that's really all it takes to switch modes!

285

With that, all the changes to the core code have been looked at. Now, let's move on to the changes in the modules themselves, and you'll work from the least amount of change to the greatest amount of change, picking up some new concepts in the process.

Module Changes: Notes

The first change that needs to be made to the notes module is to add a constructor so you can set the `isEditingExisting` and `editingID` members on the class instance.

```
constructor() {

  this.isEditingExisting = false;

  this.editingID = null;

}
```

Every module will have this now, as I mentioned earlier in the chapter. Rather than these variables being members of the wxPIM object, they are now members of each class so that each module tracks its state with regard to editing rather than it being a common thing. This is necessary to make desktop mode work properly. I'll skip repeating myself when I discuss the next three modules as this applies to all of them.

The next change needed is something in the UI config object, and it's something you've seen before.

```
winWidth : 500, winHeight : 500, winLabel : "Notes", winIcon : "file-text"
```

As with the constructor change, all modules have these non-Webix attributes as part of the UI config object (and as with those, I won't mention this again for the other modules). As you saw when I dissected the `launchModule()` method, the `winWidth` and `winHeight` attributes tell the core code what the initial dimensions of the window for this module should be, and `winLabel` tells it what the title test of the window should be. The `winIcon` attribute defines the FontAwesome icon that is shown in the `sidemenu` as well as on the taskbar buttons.

The next change is a small but important thing in the newHandler() method. Previously these two lines of code were found in it:

```
wxPIM.isEditingExisting = false;
wxPIM.editingID = new Date().getTime();
```

They are now altered to be these:

```
wxPIM.modules.Notes.isEditingExisting = false;
wxPIM.modules.Notes.editingID = new Date().getTime();
```

That should be an obvious change. Since you moved isEditingExisting and editingID into the class instance, you have to update them there now. In a similar way, this change is necessary for the editExisting() method as well, except there a new ID isn't generated; it uses the ID of the selected item. Once again, this is a change that applies in the same way to the rest of the modules, so I won't point this out again with them.

The final change is just something that needs to be added to the class.

```
dayAtAGlance() {
}
```

As you saw previously, every module gets a chance to participate in the day-at-a-glance screen, and that's by virtue of a call to this method. The notes module doesn't actually participate, though, so just an empty method is all you need to fulfill the contract that the core code expects a module to adhere to.

Module Changes: Contacts

While the notes module wasn't changed at all in terms of its UI design, let's do something a little different with the contacts app and try to use the space afforded in desktop mode a bit more efficiently. Figure 7-5 shows one way this can be accomplished.

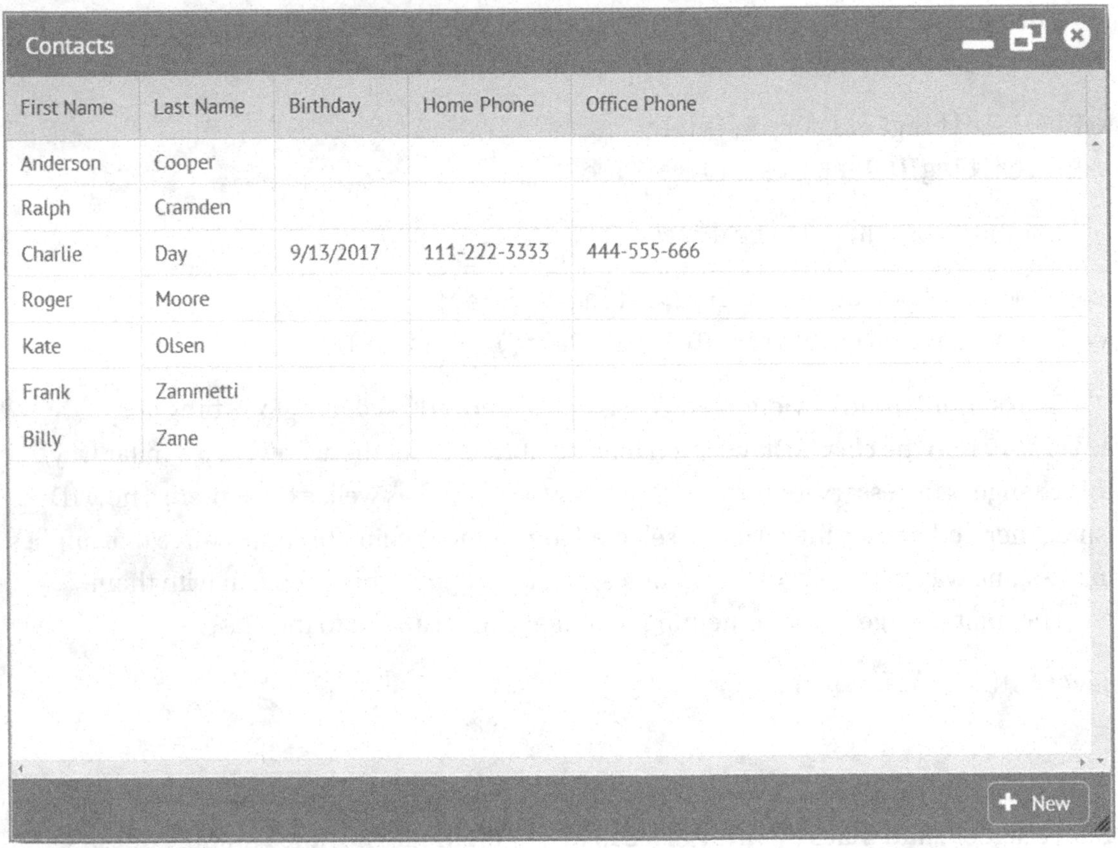

Contacts					⬓ ⧉ ⊗
First Name	Last Name	Birthday	Home Phone	Office Phone	
Anderson	Cooper				
Ralph	Cramden				
Charlie	Day	9/13/2017	111-222-3333	444-555-666	
Roger	Moore				
Kate	Olsen				
Frank	Zammetti				
Billy	Zane				
					+ New

Figure 7-5. A grid is more efficient with the available space

Instead of using a unitlist, let's instead use a datatable. The change to the code involves a branch on wxPIM.uiType, and the unitlist configuration is replaced with this:

```
function() {
  if (wxPIM.uiType === "mobile") {
    return { view : "unitlist", id : "moduleContacts-items",
      type : { height : 40 }, template : "#lastName#, #firstName#",
      uniteBy : (inObj) => {
        return inObj.lastName.substr(0, 1);
      },
      click : wxPIM.modules.Contacts.editExisting.bind(this)
    };
  } else {
    return { view : "datatable", id : "moduleContacts-items",
```

```
      resizeColumn : true, dragColumn : true,
      columns : [
        { id : "firstName", header : "First Name", minWidth : 100,
          sort : "string", adjust : true
        },
        { id : "lastName", header : "Last Name", minWidth : 100,
          sort : "string", adjust : true
        },
        { id : "birthday", header : "Birthday", minWidth : 100,
          sort : "date", adjust : true,
          format : function(inValue) {
            return new Date(inValue).toLocaleDateString();
          }
        },
        { id : "homePhone", header : "Home Phone", minWidth : 120,
          sort : "string", adjust : true
        },
        { id : "officePhone", header : "Office Phone",  minWidth : 120,
          sort : "string", adjust : true, fillspace : true
        }
      ],
      on : { onItemClick : wxPIM.modules.Contacts.editExisting }
    };
  }
}(),
```

A unitlist is still used in mobile mode, and its configuration is the same, but now in desktop mode, you use a datatable instead. I've pulled out the fields I think you would most want to see in such a datatable, and resizeColumn and dragColumn both set to true, respectively, allow the user to drag the divider between columns to change their size and to drag columns around to put them in any order they want. For the birthday column, the date needs to be formatted for display, and the plain old JavaScript toLocalDateString() method of the Date object does the trick. Setting adjust : true on all the columns instructs the datatable to find the largest item in each column, whether that is data or the column header itself, and automatically set the width of the column to that value, which avoids wrapping. All columns support sorting according to the sort type specified for each. Finally, setting fillspace to true makes the last Office Phone column fill whatever horizontal space remains in the datatable after all the columns have been rendered.

Aside from that change, the only other things different about the code in the new version of wxPIM are the changes common to all modules as previously described, so let's move on to the appointments module.

Module Changes: Appointments

The appointments module, like the notes module, has minimal changes to it. The UI isn't changed for desktop mode (that's only true for contacts and tasks), so it's really just the changes common to all modules that you're well aware of by now.

Aside from those common changes, the only thing different is the addition of the previously shown dayAtAGlance() method. So, you're basically done with appointments at this point!

Getting Responsive with It: Tasks

For the tasks module, I'm going to introduce a little bit of responsive design. Now, *responsive design* is a term that has different meanings for different people, but at the end of the day it all boils down to the same essential thing: a UI that responds to the device it's running on. Most usually that means adjusting the UI to use the available screen space effectively. This could mean that on a mobile device, your UI is a single column of content but on a larger desktop monitor it shifts to two columns.

It's also most typical that people mean a CSS-based solution when they talk about responsive design. You run into things such as breakpoints that define what the UI layout should be at various screen sizes (i.e., one column if the width of the display is 640 pixels or less, two columns if it's more; 640 is considered a *breakpoint*). But, there's absolutely nothing that says a responsive design has to be CSS-based, and in fact when your entire UI is built with JavaScript, as is the case with a Webix app, an argument can be made that it makes more sense to be responsive in a JavaScript-centric approach too.

The philosophical debate aside, the bottom line is adjusting to the available resources, so let's see what you can do about that with the tasks module. You already saw one approach to responsiveness in the contacts module: using a `datatable` rather than a `unitlist`, which allows for more data to be seen at a given time when in desktop mode. For the tasks module, though, let's do something different. You'll have the summary view and the details view side by side, as shown in Figure 7-6.

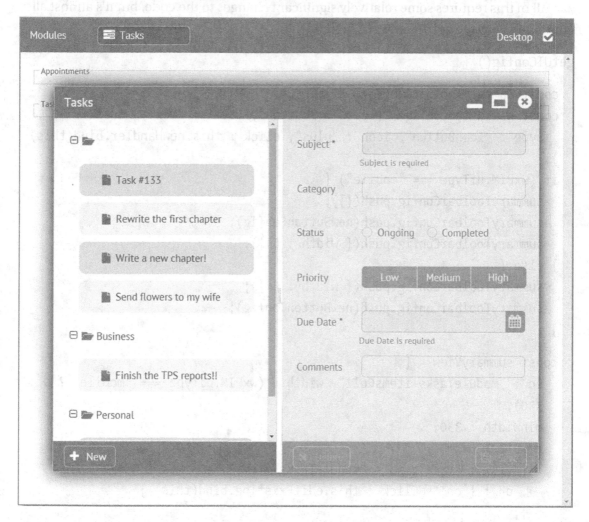

Figure 7-6. *A more efficient layout when there's space*

This allows the user to see both views simultaneously, which is usually thought of as being a more efficient way to view summary-detail data (if you've heard the term *master-detail view*, then you already know what you're building here). The user can still,

291

of course, resize the window as they see fit and can even maximize it, which allows them to see more or less data as they want. In effect, this layout is responsive in another way. It will resize based on the window size, and the space is distributed between the two columns to fit the size of the window. Also, you'll put a `resizer` element between the summary and details view so the user can further adjust the size between them as they see fit by dragging the `resizer` left and right.

All of this requires some relatively significant changes to the code, but it's almost all contained with the getUIConfig() method.

```
getUIConfig() {

  const summaryToolbarConfig = [ ];
  const newButtonConfig = { view : "button", label : "New", width : "80",
    type : "iconButton", icon : "plus", click : this.newHandler.bind(this)
  };
  if (wxPIM.uiType === "mobile") {
    summaryToolbarConfig.push({});
    summaryToolbarConfig.push(newButtonConfig);
    summaryToolbarConfig.push({ width : 6 });
  } else {
    summaryToolbarConfig.push({ width : 6 });
    summaryToolbarConfig.push(newButtonConfig);
  }

  const summaryView = {
    id : "moduleTasks-itemsCell", width : (wxPIM.uiType === "mobile" ? 0 :
    330),
    minWidth : 330,
    rows : [
      { view : "tree", id : "moduleTasks-items",
        on : { onItemClick : this.editExisting.bind(this) }
      },
      { view : "toolbar", cols : summaryToolbarConfig }
    ]
  };

  const detailsToolbarConfig = [
    { width : 6 },
```

```
  { id : "moduleTasks-deleteButton", view : "button", disabled : true,
    label : "Delete", width : "90", type : "iconButton",
    icon : "remove", click : () => { wxPIM.deleteHandler("Tasks"); }
  },
  { },
  { view : "button", label : "Save", width : "80",
    type : "iconButton", icon : "floppy-o",
    id : "moduleTasks-saveButton", disabled : true,
    click : function() {
      wxPIM.saveHandler("Tasks", [ "moduleTasks-detailsForm" ]);
    }
  },
  { width : 6 }
];
if (wxPIM.uiType === "mobile") {
  detailsToolbarConfig.splice(1, 0,
    { view : "button", label : "Back To Summary", width : "170",
      type : "iconButton", icon : "arrow-left",
      hidden : (wxPIM.uiType === "desktop"),
      click : () => {
        $$("moduleTasks-itemsCell").show();
      }
    },
    { }
  );
}

const detailsView = {
  id : "moduleTasks-details", minWidth : 350,
  rows : [
    { view : "form", id : "moduleTasks-detailsForm", borderless : true,
      elementsConfig : { view : "text", labelWidth : 100, bottomPadding : 20,
        on : { onChange : () => {
          $$("moduleTasks-saveButton")[$$("moduleTasks-detailsForm").
          validate() ?
            "enable" : "disable"]();
```

```
    } }
  },
  elements : [
    { name : "subject", label : "Subject", required : true,
      invalidMessage : "Subject is required",
      attributes : { maxlength : 50 }
    },
    { view : "text", name : "category", label : "Category",
      suggest : [
        { id : 1, value : "Personal" },
        { id : 2, value : "Business" },
        { id : 3, value : "Other" }
      ],
      on : {
        onItemClick : function() {
          $$(this.config.suggest).show(this.getInputNode());
        }
      }
    },
    { view : "radio", name : "status", label : "Status", value : 1,
      id : "moduleTasks-category",
      options : [
        { id : 1, value : "Ongoing" }, { id : 2, value : "Completed"
}

      ]
    },
    { view : "segmented", name : "priority", label : "Priority",
    value : 1,
      options : [
        { id : 1, value : "Low" },
        { id : 2, value : "Medium" },
        { id : 3, value : "High" }
      ]
    },
    { view : "datepicker", name : "dueDate", label : "Due Date",
      id : "moduleTasks-dueDate", required : true,
```

```
        invalidMessage : "Due Date is required"
      },
      { name : "comments", label : "Comments",
        attributes : { maxlength : 250 }
      }
    ]
  },
  { },
  { view : "toolbar", cols : detailsToolbarConfig }
  ]
};

const baseObj =  { winWidth : 800, winHeight : 600, winLabel : "Tasks",
winIcon : "tasks",
  id : "moduleTasks-container"
};

if (wxPIM.uiType === "mobile") {
  baseObj.cells = [ summaryView, detailsView ];
} else {
  baseObj.cols = [ summaryView, { view : "resizer", },detailsView ];
}

return baseObj;

}
```

The first change is an architectural one. Rather than one large JavaScript object, instead you have a number of objects that get composed at the end into the object returned by the method. This is a generally good approach anyway, but it's especially important (necessary really) when the structure is going to change a fair bit and vary based on some condition.

The first of these objects is one for the summary view's toolbar. There's a single button for creating a new item in either mode, but in mobile mode, that button is on the right, whereas in desktop mode it's on the left. That's so that in desktop mode, when the summary view toolbar and details view toolbar are both always visible, there's some visual separation between the New button and the detail view buttons.

Next, an object for the summary view is built. The `width` of the summary view is determined based on `wxPIM.uiType`. When in mobile mode, a width of 0 makes this view fill the available space. In desktop mode, it gets an initial width of 330. The `minWidth` is set to this value as well because any smaller and horizontal scrolling starts coming into play, which makes it a bit less usable. Note that the `toolbar` at the bottom is a reference to the one you built before this object, so you're starting to compose the things already, building up the object to be returned as you go.

Next up is the configuration for the details view `toolbar`. Similar to the summary view `toolbar`, it needs to change based on mode because in desktop mode there's no need for the Back To Summary `button`. Plus, in desktop mode, since there will be only two buttons instead of three, it makes sense to push them out to the two ends of the `toolbar` (hence the reason the New `button` needed to be on the left in desktop mode). Since in either mode the `toolbar`'s configuration really only differs by the presence of the Back To Summary view, I create the array of `toolbar` items as it appears in desktop mode, and then for mobile mode, I just `splice()` in the Back To Summary `button`. This avoids redundancy and possibly extra branching logic.

After that, the details view configuration is built, and this is essentially the same as it was in the original version, with the one change being the reference to the `toolbar` that was built before this rather than including that configuration inline.

Finally, with all these subobjects, so to speak, built and ready for use, it's time to construct the object that will be returned by this method. The `baseObj` is the object that will be returned, and it initially contains just the most basic configuration needed for this module, namely, the special items wxPIM uses to configure the `window`. Notice, though, that it has no content yet. That's where the `if` statement after that comes in. For mobile mode, you want this object to be a `multiview`. Remember that Webix implicitly creates a `multiview` if the configuration includes a `cells` array, so that gets added for mobile mode. For desktop mode, you're building a two-column layout instead, so you need to add a `cols` array. The addition of the `resizer` view in between the summary and details is all you need to do to allow for resizing those two elements. Webix takes care of creating the draggable handle between them as well as doing the resize when the user drags it.

There are just a few other minor changes necessary in this module, beginning with an additional line of code at the end of both the `newHandler()` and `editExisting()` methods.

```
$$("moduleTasks-details").enable();
```

The thing is that when the user clicks the New button or selects an item to edit, the details side of the window needs to be enabled or the user won't be able to do anything. That's where this statement comes into play.

The final change is at the end of refreshData(). Remember that refreshData() will be called when a task is added, modified, or deleted (as well as when activate() is called). In all those cases, the problem is that the detail side will usually be enabled and have data in it, but it won't be the right data potentially. So, you need to clear and disable the form.

```
$$("moduleTasks-detailsForm").clear();
$$("moduleTasks-details").disable();
```

With that last change in place, the new version of the contacts module is done!

A Few Leftover Bits: saveHandler() and deleteHandler()

With the modules taken care of, you're almost done with the changes to wxPIM now. All that remains are a few leftover bits that need to be modified to make it all work in the core code.

First, in both the wxPIM.saveHandler() and wxPIM.deleteHandler() methods there is this line:

```
itemData.id = wxPIM.editingID;
```

Well, as you know, the editingID is no longer a member of the wxPIM object itself; it's a member of each module's class instance. So, that line needs to be changed to this:

```
itemData.id = wxPIM.modules[inModuleName].editingID;
```

Finally, again in both methods, you want to be sure that the day-at-a-glance screen gets updated no matter what mode you're in. In the original mobile-only version, day-at-a-glance gets updated when you switch to it, so if you add a task in the tasks module, you'll see that task (if it's for the current day, of course) when you switch back to day-at-a-glance because it gets updated at that point. But, in desktop mode, day-at-a-glance is effectively the background over which module windows float. It's always visible, so if you add a task in the task module window, you expect to see it reflected in the background immediately. To accomplish that, all you need to do is add one line.

```
wxPIM.dayAtAGlance();
```

I do this right before the `webix.message()` call (though the order doesn't actually matter).

And with that change, you're done! wxPIM is now a mobile/desktop app that intelligently switches between the modes at startup and also allows the user to switch between the modes at will manually. It's a little more responsive, using the available space a bit more effectively, and at the end of the day you used probably 90 percent the same codebase, give or take. Not too shabby!

Summary

In this chapter, you modified the wxPIM application to work better in a desktop environment. In the process, you saw some approaches to creating a responsive Webix app, that is, a single codebase that reacts to its runtime environment and modifies its UI to suit that environment better. You saw some further usage of Webix components and helper functions, and most importantly you saw how with just a few considerations, the same underlying Webix codebase can run on mobile devices as well as on classic desktops.

In the next chapter, I'll introduce a server component into the mix so that wxPIM can become an even more useful application while at the same time demonstrating some important concepts in terms of client-server capabilities with Webix.

Taking wxPIM to the Cloud

In the two previous chapters, you built an application called wxPIM. You used the knowledge of Webix you built up in prior chapters and learned a few new things as you built the app. Now, wxPIM is a decent little app: it's nominally useful and works whether on a desktop or mobile device.

However, what happens if you want to use it on more than one device? Indeed, you can already, but the data you create won't be shared between them. That's a little bit of a deal-breaker, no?

To address that issue, you need a server. As the title of the chapter says, you need a cloud (since *everything* is a cloud these days if it's connected to other machines it seems!), and you need to hook wxPIM up to it.

Now, this is a book about Webix, not about building servers. But, fortunately, there's a tool out there that makes building serves remarkably easy, and best of all, it uses the same fundamental technology as you used when building wxPIM itself, namely, JavaScript. I am, of course, talking about the famous and popular Node.js, or just Node for short. In this chapter, you'll build a simple Node-based server to store your data on and then modify wxPIM to talk to that server. If you do this right, you'll be able to run wxPIM on multiple devices, save your data to the server, and access it on other devices as well.

Of course, if the name Node, REST, Express, and NeDB all already have strong meaning for you, then, by all means, skip ahead to the "Hooking wxPIM Up to the Server" section. But, otherwise, read on, and consider the next few sections an added bonus on top of learning Webix! (Hey, I like to give my readers *more* than they bargain for when I can!)

Building a Server with Node...Wait, What's Node?

Ryan Dahl. That cat has some talent, I tell ya! Ryan is the creator of a fantastic piece of software called Node.js, or just plain Node from here on out. Ryan first presented Node at the European JSConf conference in 2009, and it was quickly recognized as a potential game-changer, as evidenced by the standing ovation his presentation received.

© Frank Zammetti 2018
F. Zammetti, *Practical Webix*, https://doi.org/10.1007/978-1-4842-3384-9_8

Node is a platform for running (primarily, though not exclusively, server-side) code that is high-performance and capable of handling tons of load with ease. It is based on the most widely used language on the planet today: JavaScript. It's extremely easy to get started with and understand, yet it puts tremendous power in the hands of developers in large part thanks to its asynchronous and event-driven model of programming. In Node, almost everything you do is nonblocking, meaning code won't hold up the processing of other request threads. This, plus the fact that Node uses Google's popular and highly tuned V8 JavaScript engine to execute code (the same engine that powers their Chrome browser), makes it very high performance and able to handle a large request load.

It's no wonder that so many significant players and sites have adopted Node to one degree or another. Moreover, these aren't minor outfits either; I'm talking about names you doubtless know, including DuckDuckGo, eBay, LinkedIn, Microsoft, Walmart, and Yahoo as just a few examples.

Node is a first-class runtime environment, meaning you can do things like interact with the local file system, access relational databases, call remote systems, and much more. In the past, you'd need to use a "proper" runtime like Java or .NET to do all this; JavaScript wasn't a player in that space. With Node, this is no longer true!

To be clear, Node isn't in and of itself a server. You can't just start up Node and make HTTP requests to it from a web browser. It won't do anything in response to your requests by default. No, to use Node as a server, you have to write some (straightforward and concise, as you'll see) code that then runs inside Node. Yes, you effectively write your own web server and app server, if you want to split hairs (or potentially FTP, Telnet, or any other type of server you might want). That's a very odd thing to do as a developer, to say the least, and it does sound daunting! To be sure, it would be if you tried to write a web server from scratch in many other languages, especially if you want it to do more than just serve static content files. But not with Node!

But remember, acting as a server is just one capability that Node provides as a JavaScript runtime, and it can provide this functionality only if you, as a developer, feed it the code it needs to do so! In fact, a great many developer tools, and other types of apps, use Node as their runtime nowadays. Node really is all over the place!

Node also allows you to use the same language and knowledge on both client and server, something that was difficult to accomplish before. In fact, aside from Java and some Microsoft technologies, there never before has really been an opportunity to do so until Node came along. It's a pretty compelling opportunity.

Another key aspect of Node is a driving design goal of the project, which is keeping its core functionality to an absolute minimum and providing extended functionality by way of APIs (in the form of JavaScript modules) that you can pick and choose from as needed. Node gets out of your way as much as possible and allows you only to introduce the complexity you really need, when you need it.

In addition to all of this, getting, installing, and running Node are trivial exercises, regardless of your operating system preference. There are no complicated installs with all sorts of dependencies, nor is there a vast set of configuration files to mess with before you can bring up a server and handle requests. It's a five-minute exercise, depending on the speed of your Internet connection and how fast you can type!

All of this makes working with Node so much simpler than many competing options, while providing you with top-notch performance and load-handling capabilities. Moreover, it does so with a consistent technological underpinning as that which you develop your client applications.

That's Node in a nutshell! Please be aware that this section is in no way, shape, or form meant to be an exhaustive look at Node. There's so much more to Node than this, and if you're new to it, I very much encourage you to peruse the Node site for a while. But, for the purposes of this book, this level of understanding (plus a few additional items that you're going to get to next) should be sufficient.

Next, let's see about getting it onto your machine so that you can start playing with some code together.

Getting and Installing Node

Getting and installing Node couldn't be easier, and there's only one address to remember: `http://nodejs.org`. That's your one-stop shop for all things Node, beginning with, right on the front page, downloading it, as you can see in Figure 8-1.

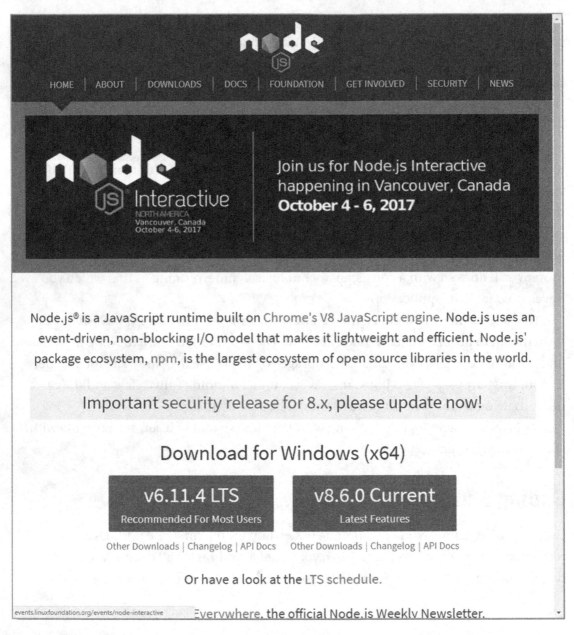

Figure 8-1. *Whatever the button label, you're probably not going to miss it!*

Although it really shouldn't matter for our purposes here, I do suggest using the LTS (Long Term Support) version. The LTS version tends to be more stable with fewer bugs, at the cost of not having all the latest and greatest features.

The download will install in whatever fashion is appropriate for your system. For example, on Windows, Node provides a perfectly ordinary and straightforward installer that will walk you through the necessary (and extremely simple) steps. On Mac OS X, a typical install wizard will do the same.

Once the install completes, you will be ready to play with Node. The installer should have added the Node directory to your path. So, as a first simple test, simply type **node** at a command prompt and press Enter. You should be greeted with a > prompt. Node is now listening for your commands in CLI mode. To test it, type the following:

```
console.log("test");
```

Press Enter, and you should be greeted with something like what you see in Figure 8-2 if running on Windows. (On Mac OS X or *nix, it should look substantially the same, accounting for platform differences.)

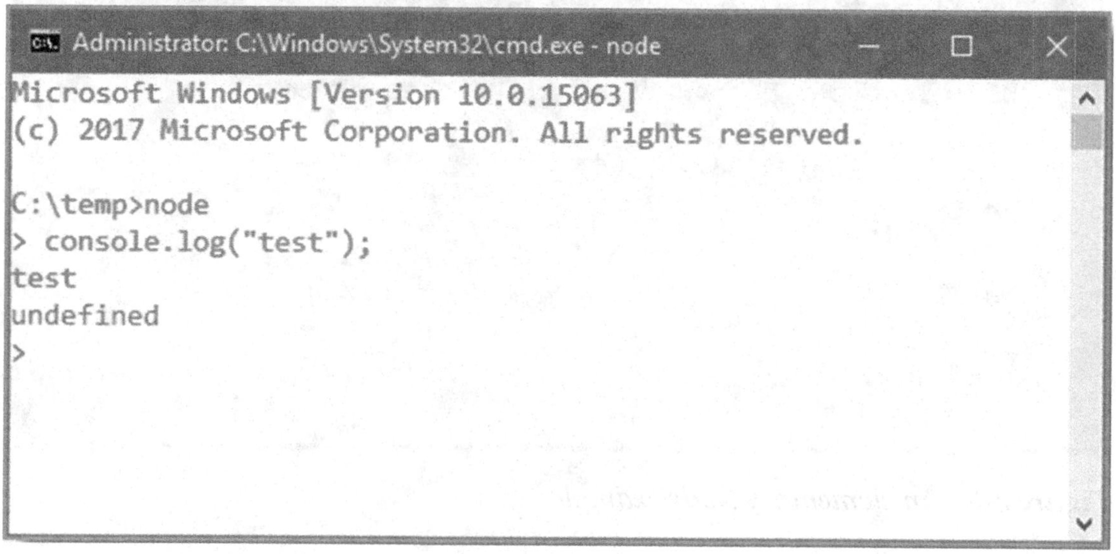

```
Administrator: C:\Windows\System32\cmd.exe - node                    —    □    ✕

Microsoft Windows [Version 10.0.15063]
(c) 2017 Microsoft Corporation. All rights reserved.

C:\temp>node
> console.log("test");
test
undefined
>
```

Figure 8-2. Say hello to my little friend, Node!

Interacting with Node in CLI mode is fine, but it's limited. What you really want to do is execute a saved JavaScript file using Node. As it happens, that's easy to do! Simply create a text file named listing_08-01.js, for example, and type the code shown in Listing 8-1 into it and save it.

Listing 8-1. A Quick Node Test

```
var a = 5;
var b = 3;
var c = a * b;
console.log(a + " * " + b + " = " + c);
```

To execute this file, assuming you are in the directory in which the file is located, you simply need to type this:

```
node listing_08-01.js
```

Press Enter after that, and you should be greeted with an execution, such as the one you see in Figure 8-3 (in which I've also displayed the JavaScript file to be executed).

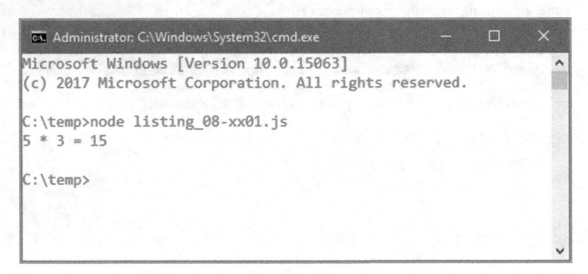

Figure 8-3. *An elementary Node example*

Now, clearly this little bit of code is unexceptional, but it does demonstrate that Node can execute plain old JavaScript just fine. You can experiment a bit here if you like, and you will see that Node should execute any basic, plain old JavaScript that you care to throw at it.

Even if that were all Node did, it would be pretty cool and useful for many things. Of course, that's far from all that Node can do! I'm here to talk about writing server software, and Node makes that a trivial exercise indeed.

My First Node Server

When I say that Node makes writing server software trivial, that may well be the understatement of the year! Perhaps the simplest example (that actually does something anyway) is what you can see in Listing 8-2.

Listing 8-2.   A Simple Web Server in Node

```
var http = require("http");
var server = http.createServer(function (inRequest, inResponse) {
  inResponse.writeHead(200, { "Content-Type" : "text/plain"} );
  inResponse.end("Hello from my first Node server!");
});
server.listen(80, "127.0.0.1");
```

Type that into a file, save it as `listing_08-02.js`, and then launch it from a command line the same way you did for the previous example. Now fire up your favorite web browser, and visit `http://127.0.01`. You'll be greeted with the text "Hello from my first Node server!" If that isn't a little bit amazing to you, then you've probably seen the Flying Spaghetti Monster travel one too many times around your neighborhood and have been totally desensitized to the amazing!

Obviously, this is a simplistic example, but it should get the basic idea across well enough. But, what exactly is going on in that simple example at a code level? As it happens, quite a bit actually, and most of it is key to how Node works.

The first concept is the idea of importing modules. In the example code, `http` is a module. This is one of the core Node modules, and, as such, it is compiled directly into the Node binary. Therefore, you won't find a separate JavaScript file for it in the Node installation directory. This is true of all the Node core modules, all of which you can find in the Node documentation on the Node site. To import any of them, you just `require()` them by name.

You can create your own modules too just by adding other `.js` files and `require()`'ing them. This gets a little more involved, with discussions of things like scope and exports, but for the purposes of this book you won't need to do that, but I wanted to at least mention it in case you really are completely new to Node so that you can find the appropriate section in the Node docs to describe this.

The `require()` function returns an object that is essentially the API provided by the module. This object can include methods, attributes, or whatever you want. In fact, it could conceivably be just a variable with some data in an array. More times than not, though, it will be an object with some methods and attributes. In the case of `http` in this example, one of the methods the object returned is `createServer()`. This method creates a web server instance and returns a reference to it. The argument you pass to this method is a function that serves as a request listener, that is, the function executed any time a request is made to the server.

Creating a web server alone won't actually do anything. It won't respond to requests until you do a little more work. The `createServer()` method returns a reference to the web server instance, which contains the method `listen()`. That method accepts a port number on which the server should listen and, optionally, the hostname on which to listen. In the example, the standard HTTP port 80 is specified, along with the standard local machine address 127.0.0.1. Once you call this method, the server will begin listening for requests (assuming nothing else is already using that port on your system, that is!), and for each request that comes in, it will call the anonymous function passed to `createServer()`.

This callback function (callback functions being the most common mechanism by which Node provides nonblocking functionality) receives two arguments, `inRequest` and `inResponse`, which are objects representing the HTTP request and response, respectively. In this simple example, all this callback function does is first write an HTTP header to the response object specifying a good outcome via an HTTP 200 response code. You also pass, as the second argument to `writeHead()`, an object that defines response headers. In this case, the Content-Type header is set to text/plain to indicate a simple text response. Finally, the `end()` method is called on the response object, passing the response you want to send back. This completes the handling of a given request.

As you can see, creating a server with Node is exceedingly simple, in its most basic form at least. However, there's an even easier way to do so, and it's in fact probably the most common way of writing a Node server, and that's by using the very popular Express module. But, before you go there, let's discuss something else first: NPM.

Node's Partner in Crime: NPM

NPM, which stands for Node Package Manager, is a companion app that installs alongside Node. With it, you can download packages, which are just JavaScript modules (and any supporting stuff they might need) from a central package registry, which you can find at `https://www.npmjs.com`.

Using NPM is simple: it's simply another command to run from a command prompt, just like Node. For example, if you want to see what modules have been installed into the global cache, you can execute the following:

```
npm -g ls
```

The global cache is one place modules can be installed to. This makes them accessible to any project that uses Node. You can also install modules in a specific project, and this is usually where you do want to install them. For example, let's say you create a directory named `MyFirstNodeProject`. In it, you execute the following:

```
npm install express
```

If you do that, you'll find that a directory called `node-modules` has been created, and inside it will be a lot of...well, a lot of stuff you typically don't need to worry about too much! In short, though, it's all the code that makes up the Express package (which I'll cover shortly) plus whatever packages Express itself depends on (and whatever *they* might depend on, and so on). NPM takes care of fetching all of those dependencies for you. You'll also notice a file named `package-lock.json` has been created, and for our purposes here you don't need to worry about that except to know not to delete it as NPM needs it to do its job.

Now, in all of this, I did skip one step that clearly is optional but is, in fact, typical, and that's initializing a new project. With most Node/NPM projects, you'll also have a file named `package.json` in the root directory of the project. This provides information to NPM and Node about your project that it needs to do certain things. While you can write this file by hand or even go without it, it's a good idea to have it, and it's a good idea to let NPM create it for you, which you can do by executing this command:

```
npm init
```

If you are following along, please make sure the directory you run this from is empty (delete node_modules and package-lock.json if present). This will trigger an interactive process that walks you through the creation of the package.json file, something like you see in Figure 8-4.

```
Administrator: C:\Windows\System32\cmd.exe

C:\temp\MyFirstNodeProject>npm init
This utility will walk you through creating a package.json file.
It only covers the most common items, and tries to guess sensible defaults.

See `npm help json` for definitive documentation on these fields
and exactly what they do.

Use `npm install <pkg>` afterwards to install a package and
save it as a dependency in the package.json file.

Press ^C at any time to quit.
package name: (myfirstnodeproject)
version: (1.0.0)
description: Testing
entry point: (index.js)
test command:
git repository:
keywords:
author: Me
license: (ISC)
About to write to C:\temp\MyFirstNodeProject\package.json:

{
  "name": "myfirstnodeproject",
  "version": "1.0.0",
  "description": "Testing",
  "main": "index.js",
  "scripts": {
    "test": "echo \"Error: no test specified\" && exit 1"
  },
  "author": "Me",
  "license": "ISC"
}


Is this ok? (yes) y

C:\temp\MyFirstNodeProject>
```

Figure 8-4. *Initializing a project with NPM*

Opening the generated `package.json` file should look something like this:

```
{
  "name": "myfirstnodeproject",
  "version": "1.0.0",
  "description": "Testing",
  "main": "index.js",
  "scripts": {
    "test": "echo \"Error: no test specified\" && exit 1"
  },
  "author": "Me",
  "license": "ISC"
}
```

Now, let's say you want to add that Express package to this project. Running the same install command as before will do that, but it will also update the `package.json` file, adding this element:

```
"dependencies": {
  "express": "^4.16.1"
}
```

The reason this is important is that now, let's say you want to give this project to someone else. You typically do not want to give them all the dependencies your project requires, all the content of node_modules. Instead, they can re-create it using the `package.json` file just by doing this:

```
npm install
```

That will read the `package.json` file and automatically install all the dependencies! Now, the person you're working with has the same development environment as you as far as project dependencies go for this project without having to do any leg work themselves! Pretty sweet, right?

As you can guess, there's quite a bit more to NPM than just what I've shown here, but these are the real basics that will allow you to understand the code for the server that you're going to write in support of wxPIM. And, in fact, I'm just about ready to discuss that, but before I do, there's one last bit of foundational knowledge I need to make sure you have, namely, REST.

Taking a Very Active Break with REST

REST, which stands for Representational State Transfer, is an architectural approach to providing web services. The basic idea is that a given URL represents a resource, and a client can interact with that resource using standard HTTP methods such as PUT, GET, POST, and DELETE (which correspond to the well-known CRUD methods of Create, Retrieve, Update, and Delete). This is all independent of what technology the service is written in.

For example, let's say you want to provide access to a bank account resource. The URL might be as follows:

```
http://www.fakebank.com/accounts/checking/123456789.json
```

If you access this URL with an HTTP method of GET, you will retrieve checking account 123456789, assuming it exists, of course. The format of the response, in this case, would be JSON since that's the extension used. Some RESTful web services, as many people refer to this model as, allow you to request that the response be in XML, JSON, or other formats, while some don't give you a choice (in which case you might not have an extension there at all).

The response is said to be a "representation" of the checking account resource, which is where the "Representational" portion of REST comes from. Likewise, if you wanted to update an attribute of this account, you would POST back to the same URL, and the contents of the POST body would be the JSON for the account with the changes in it (and this covers the "State Transfer" part of the name). To create a new account, use the HTTP PUT method and leave off the account number part of the URL; to delete the account, just use the DELETE method without sending any content (and, most likely, without the JSON extension part of the URL).

Note that the HTTP methods are usually referred to as verbs, since they specify an action, and the corresponding operations I've described here are typical but not set in stone. You may encounter a service that uses other HTTP methods for the various operations the API of the service supports, but what I describe here is what you're likely to see most of the time.

I mentioned verbs there, and it's an important distinction. Notice here is that the URL doesn't include anything like getAccount?acctNum=123456789, like you might typically see in a normal URL. Instead, the HTTP method conveys to the service what action you want to be performed, while the URL includes the noun, or the object (or type of object), that is being operated on.

REST is a pretty simple model for web services but one that has gained a ton of traction precisely because it is so simple! It's easy to write clients in a variety of technologies, and creating RESTful service providers is no more difficult. It builds on the standards we all know and love and use every day (HTTP) and can make use of the same sorts of security mechanisms used in such environments.

You already know enough of Node to create such a service interface, but it can be even easier, if you can believe it, and that's thanks to one specific module, Express, and that's what you're finally getting to now!

Hurry It Up, Kid: Express It!

Express (https://expressjs.com), which is perhaps the most popular Node module around, is a minimal framework for creating web applications that offers developers a set of robust features that eliminates a lot of boilerplate-type code from your application code. Express offers a large set of APIs, utility methods, and what it calls middleware to provide many of the common things modern web applications need. Being a minimal, thin framework means that Express provides excellent performance on top of everything else.

Express is especially useful for, but is in no way specific to, writing RESTful API code. If you look back at the previous sample server code, you'll notice that there's no mention of HTTP methods there. In fact, every request of any type will be handled by the one callback function supplied. That means if you want to implement a RESTful service, that callback will need to interrogate the request object, determine the HTTP method, and then branch accordingly. That's not especially difficult to do, but it's code you have to write. Then, since REST is based on URL structure, you'll need to write code to parse the URL to figure out what operation to perform. Again, it's not rocket science, but it's work you have to do yourself.

Using Express avoids all of that. Instead, you write code like this:

```
const app = express();

app.get("/cars/:vin", function(inRequest, inResponse) {

  // Return a car object with the specific VIN number

});
app.listen(8080);
```

Here, you create an Express application, which is the basis of everything you do with Express. Then, you tell the app that for a GET request to a URL in the form `/cars/:vin`, execute the given function. The `:vin` part of the URL tells Express that after `/cars` in the URL will come a value that you want to have presented in the collection of parameters that Express parses out of the URL and you want to name it `vin` (which you can access in the function by doing `inRequest.params.vin`). In case you are unaware, VIN is short for "vehicle identification number" and is the unique number that identifies every car manufactured. So, assuming you have a database of VIN numbers, a GET request to this particular URL can return an object representing the car associated with the VIN number specified. Finally, you just have to start up the Express app by telling it what port to listen on. That's it! No parsing the URL yourself, no handling different request methods, not even creating a server yourself. Express takes care of all those details for you!

As with Node and NPM, there's quite a bit more than Express can do, and you'll see some of it when you write the server code. But for the most part, this example shows you almost everything you need. I will, of course, describe the additional parts, but before that you have one final helping hand to look at that you'll need to write the wxPIM server, called NeDB.

Third-Party Data Help: NeDB

Since the whole point of writing a server for wxPIM to talk to is to store the data somewhere beyond local storage in the browser, you obviously need a mechanism to save that data on the server. There are a great many options for doing so in a Node application, from just writing plain-text files on the file system to interacting with an Oracle database. However, for our purposes here, I wanted something with a simple API and something that doesn't require setting up yet another server. The module I found that fits the bill on all counts is NeDB (`https://github.com/louischatriot/nedb`) by Louis Chatriot.

NeDB has an API that seeks to emulate the popular MongoDB, which is a document-based database that has no schema. MongoDB and by extension NeDB are not relational in nature, instead storing (usually) JSON-based objects (called *documents*) and then allowing you to query them based on their attributes.

While MongoDB is its own server that a Node-based app can connect to, NeDB is JavaScript-based and is just a module added to a Node app. NeDB also stores its data in plain text files that you can open in a text editor if you want, which is nice in case you ever need to recover anything. It has (most) of the important features of MongoDB, certainly everything you'll need: creating items, updating them, finding them and deleting them, and allowing you to do so across different collections of items.

To give you a quick flavor of working with NeDB, here's a simple example:

```
const db = new nedb({ filename : "people.db", autoload : true });

db.insert({ firstName : "Billy", lastName : "Joel" },
  function (inError, inDocument) {
    if (inError) {
      console.log("Error" + inError);
    } else {
      db.findOne({ firstName : "Billy" },
        function (inError, inDocument) {
          if (inError) {
            console.log("Error" + inError);
          } else {
            console.log(inDocument);
          }
        }
      );
    }
  }
);
```

You create an instance of a database by providing NeDB with the file name of that database and also tell NeDB to load it at that point automatically. Then, you can call the insert() method, passing it an object to insert and a callback function. The callback function can do whatever makes sense. In this case, I just retrieve the document that was just inserted and log it to the console. Remember that NeDB is almost always asynchronous, so you'll need to deal with callbacks (or use a Promise-based approach if you prefer). The findOne() method does exactly that: finds a specific single document based on some query, here based on the firstName attribute. Of course, if there's a chance there's more than one document with a firstName of Billy, then chances are you want to use the find() method instead, which returns an array of matching documents.

For the purposes of this server, you won't need too much more NeDB than this, but know that it provides a very rich API, so if you need a simple database module that doesn't have any outside dependencies (as in no additional server to run), then NeDB is, in my opinion, one of the best choices available in the world of Node development.

Writing the Server

Before you really get into the code behind the server, I want to make a quick disclaimer. There are two things that won't be dealt with here: security (and by extension any notion of multiple users) and robust data synchronization. For the former, it's simply not needed for what you're doing in this book. For the latter, data synchronization is a complex and tricky topic that, again, isn't really required in this book. Instead, I'll be implementing a simple data synchronization scheme that I'll admit right up front isn't production-ready. But, as a learning exercise, I believe it's more than sufficient.

With that said, let's get down to business!

First things first, being a Node application that has a few dependencies, you're going to need a properly set up `package.json` file. It just so happens I've got one ready to go.

```
{
  "name" : "wxPIM",
  "version" : "1.0.0",
  "description" : "wxPIM app from the book Practical Webix",
  "repository" : "https://github.com/fzammetti/wxpim",
  "main" : "server.js",
  "author" : "Frank W. Zammetti",
  "license" : "MIT",
  "dependencies" : {
    "body-parser" : "*",
    "express" : "*",
    "nedb" : "*"
  }
}
```

As you can see, it's just like the basic `package.json` that NPM generated for the earlier example (with values appropriate for this project inserted, of course), but now with a few dependencies listed. You know what `express` and `nedb` are now. The `body-parser` dependency is another module that handles the parsing of incoming request bodies. You'll need this because when you perform POST and PUT requests for creating and updating data items, respectively, the data will be sent as a string of JSON in the body of the request. Parsing a request body is a little more involved with Node than you might imagine, so it's far better to use some good, vetted, and existing code to do that, so `body-parser` it is.

One quick note: did you notice the "*" as the value for the three dependency attributes? Those values specify the version of each dependency you want NPM to pull down when you do an npm install command. The values here are known as SemVer values, short for "semantic versioning." SemVer is a fairly in-depth topic, but it's also not especially relevant for our purposes here. But, so as to not leave you hanging, the string "*" is a SemVer value that means that any version satisfies the dependency. You're saying that any version of express and nedb could be used by our project. However, in practice, what happens is that NPM will pull down the *latest available major release* version. It's a shortcut to say "gimme the latest stable version of this dependency."

Now, you can move on, finally, to the server code, as housed in the (surprise!) server.js file. You'll go through this in chunks, beginning with this bit:

```
const bodyParser = require("body-parser");
const express = require("express");
const nedb = require("nedb");
const path = require("path");
```

The first thing you need to do is to import the modules that will be used to write the server. The body-parser you know about, and express and nedb should be obvious. The path module is a module that contains useful utility functions for dealing with file system paths. And, it just so happens, that's used in the next chunk of code, among other things:

```
const app = express();
app.use(bodyParser.json());
app.use("/", express.static(path.join(__dirname, "../app/v3_add_Server")));
app.use("/webix", express.static(path.join(__dirname, "../../webix")));
```

A shown in the previous examples, the first step to using Express is to instantiate it, and what you get back is a skeleton Express app that you can build upon as necessary. The app.use() method is one way to build upon it. Express has a notion of something called *middleware*. Middleware consists of functions that get inserted into the request/ response cycle of the app. In other words, think of a request coming into an Express-based server application. There may be a number of things you want to happen to the request. Maybe you want to log its content, then check it for some security token (aborting if not found probably), then parse the request URL to get a map of parameters on it, and finally process the request in whatever application-specific code you've written. If you imagine all those steps as a pipeline that the request goes through, each of the steps can be considered middleware. Express lets you build up this pipeline by adding whatever middleware makes sense. You could certainly write all that logic in your application code, but that's probably not a great idea, certainly not the most efficient approach. Using preexisting middleware (or writing your own that you can reuse time and again) is probably a better idea, and the middleware approach allows for this, as well as changing the processing flow of requests quickly and easily without changing much code at all.

Here, the first step you want to happen in the pipeline is for the body of the incoming request to be parsed and translated to a JSON object. So, you tell Express that by calling `app.use()` and passing it an instance of the middleware to execute, the return value of `bodyParser.json()` in this case. This piece of middleware will execute for all requests because there is no path specified.

However, what if you want some middleware to execute only for some specific path? That's entirely doable: you just need to tell Express what the path is by passing it as the first parameter to `app.use()`. There's two such calls after the first, and these use a built-in bit of middleware, `express.static()`. This tells Express that for a specific path, / and / webix here, the request should be served as static content. In other words, a request URL in the form `/test.htm` will return the file `test.htm` without executing any application-specific code. This is necessary for this app because the wxPIM code needs to be served when the initial request to `<server_ip>/` is requested. Express intelligently assumes that if there's nothing after that, then the `index.html` will be the default. Since the Webix code and resources need to be loadable too, a second `app.use()` call is made to cover those.

The middleware for both of those is returned by the call to `express.static()`. The argument to that function is a file system path, but here is where that path module comes into play. Using `path.join()`, and telling it to join `__dirname` with a relative path specification, results in a true, absolute file system path being generated. The variable `__dirname` is something Node supplies that corresponds to the path to the script that was executed, so that's `server.js` in this case. The `path.join()` function takes care of the system-specific details of creating the path so that the code can move from server to server, and as long as the location of the application code and Webix code stays the same relative to the `server.js` file, `path.join()` can create an absolute path that `express.static()` needs to work.

With the modules imported and the Express processing pipeline set up, it's time to think about data, and that means creating/opening some databases with NeDB.

```
const databases = {
  appointments : new nedb({ filename : `${__dirname}/appointments.db`,
  autoload : true }),
```

```
  contacts : new nedb({ filename : `${__dirname}/contacts.db`, autoload :
  true }),
  notes : new nedb({ filename : `${__dirname}/notes.db`, autoload : true }),
  tasks : new nedb({ filename : `${__dirname}/tasks.db`, autoload : true })
};
```

I've created a single object with four attributes, one for each database associated with each wxPIM module.

(C)RUD: Create (POST Handler)

The reason I house the databases in an object keyed by name is because it will allow us to write generic code, as you can see in the first of five functions (one for each HTTP method POST, GET, PUT and DELETE, plus on extra that you'll get to soon):

```
const postHandler = function(inRequest, inResponse) {

  let [collection, id, item] = commonOpening("POST (create)", inRequest);

  const db = databases[collection];
  db.insert(item, function (inError, inDocument) {
    if (inError) {
      commonErrorHandler(inError, inResponse);
    } else {
      inResponse.status(201);
      inResponse.send(JSON.stringify(inDocument));
    }
  });

};
app.post("/data/:collection", postHandler);
```

This handler handles POST requests (which corresponds to the *C*, Create, in CRUD), as you can tell by the fact that the final line is to tell Express to use it for post requests, but only for URLs in the form /data/:collection. The :collection token means that Express will look for a single value after /data/ in the URL and will grab that value and put it in the inRequest.params map. The term *collection* here corresponds to the name of a wxPIM module, which matches up with the database members in the databases object (in all lowercase, though).

317

Terms of endearment.   When speaking of REST, especially in the Express world, you may hear the term *routes* and *endpoints*. Route means the part of the URL following the server name and the base part that identifies the API. So, if you make a GET request to this server app at `127.0.0.1/data/notes/1234`, the route is `notes/1234` (and the API itself is said to reside at `127.0.0.1/data`). An endpoint represents a specific operation within an API, so that really refers to the HTTP method that's used. To put it another way, a route is the name you use to access an endpoint, and the endpoint specifies the operation to perform on the item that name specifies (and of course, the URL is the combination of the two, plus the server path to the API itself).

The first thing this function does is call a common helper function, `commonOpening()`, which is this:

```
const commonOpening = function(inMethodDescription, inRequest) {

  const collection = inRequest.params.collection;
  const id = inRequest.params.id;
  const item = inRequest.body;
  console.log(
    `${inMethodDescription}\ncollection: ${collection}\n
    id: ${id}\nitem: ${JSON.stringify(item)}`
  );
  return [ collection, id, item ];

};
```

The goal here is to return the `:collection` token value, as well as the ID of an item and the parsed POST body as an object. There's also some logging so you can see a request coming into the server on the console.

Now, it's important to realize that this function is used by all the request handlers, even though for some, not all of the data items it pulls out of the request are present. For example, for this POST handler, there's not going to be an ID on the URL; there's only going to be a collection. But, that's fine. You'll just get null values for the things that aren't applicable. Later, you'll see that for a DELETE request, you have no POST body, and that's likewise not a problem. Using this common code, though, reduces duplication, and Don't Repeat Yourself (DRY) is usually a good principle to follow, so I have!

After that, you can finally see why the databases are contained in an object. You can use the :collection value as an index into that object to get a reference to the correct database for the module. This way, this POST handler will work for any wxPIM module and doesn't need to know what they are (only the databases code needs to know about modules, but that's a little harder to avoid frankly).

Once a reference to the correct database is obtained, then it's just a matter of making a simple db.insert() call on it, passing it the parsed POST body in the variable item, which is whatever item the wxPIM client app is trying to create (an appointment, contact, note or task) and giving it a callback function.

The callback function, as you saw previously, first checks for an error, and if one occurs, it calls the commonErrorHandler() function.

```
const commonErrorHandler = function(inError, inResponse) {

  console.log(inError);
  inResponse.status(500);
  inResponse.send(`{ "error" : "Server error" }`);

};
```

This again avoids repeating too much code. If any error occurs, you send back an HTTP 500 error response and a response body that is a bit of JSON that the client can display to the user.

If no error occurs, then you send back an HTTP 201 (created) and the created object, in case there are new members added to it that the client may need (in fact there is: NeDB adds an _id attribute, though the client code doesn't actually need this). This is a best practice RESTful design in terms of both response code and what gets returned.

C(R)UD: Read (GET Handler)

The next bit of code you find in server.js is the *R* in CRUD, Read, or the GET HTTP request method handler.

```
const getHandler = function (inRequest, inResponse) {

  let [collection, id, item] = commonOpening("GET (read)", inRequest);

  const db = databases[collection];
  const callback = function (inError, inDocuments) {
```

```
    if (inError) {
      commonErrorHandler(inError, inResponse);
    } else {
      inResponse.status(200);
      inResponse.send(JSON.stringify(inDocuments));
    }
  };
  if (id) {
    db.findOne({ id : id }, callback);
  } else {
    db.find({}, callback);
  }

};
app.get("/data/:collection/:id?", getHandler);
```

As you can see, it's substantially the same as the POST handler, a theme you'll see repeated for the remaining method. The commonOpening() function is used again to get the name of the collection to operate on, the ID of the item to get, and the POST body as the item (which of course isn't relevant for this operation, but commonOpening() gets it anyway). This time, there are *two* types of request: getting a single specific item or getting all items for a specified collection. That's where the if branch after the callback is defined comes into play. Notice that the callback isn't passed inline to the NeDB method this time; it's assigned to the callback variable instead. That's because which NeDB method is called depends on whether the URL included an ID or not, but either way, the same callback handler should be used. If it did include an ID, then the findOne() method, with the first argument being the match criteria to find the document with the specific ID, is what you need because the caller requested a specific item. If there was no ID, however, then the caller wants all items in the collection, so the find() method, with no match criteria, is used instead. But, for either, the same callback function is used; that's why it's separate this time, as compared to the POST handler. An HTTP 200 (ok) response code with the document(s) in the body is the response in either case.

Note how the path passed to the app.get() method specifies both :collection and :id? as tokens. The ? character has special meaning: it tells Express that the token is optional. Without that, Express wouldn't recognize a request to get all because it would expect two tokens while only one would be passed (there's no :id when requesting all items in a collection).

CR(U)D: Update (PUT Handler)

Next up is the PUT method handler, which handled the *U* in CRUD, Update.

```
const putHandler = function (inRequest, inResponse) {

  let [collection, id, item] = commonOpening("PUT (update)", inRequest);

  const db = databases[collection];
  db.update({ id : id }, item, { returnUpdatedDocs : false },
    function (inError, inNumAffected, inAffectedDocuments, inUpsert) {
      if (inError) {
        commonErrorHandler(inError, inResponse);
      } else {
        getHandler(inRequest, inResponse);
      }
    }
  );

};
app.put("/data/:collection/:id", putHandler);
```

Once again, it's almost identical in most ways to the previous two. Of course, this time, it's the update() method of the database object that gets called, and it is passed a query, the ID of the item to update, and the updated item itself. The third argument tells the method that you do not want the document returned. The reason for this is that instead you're going to call the getHandler() method. I ran into some issues when trying to use the returned document; some sporadic corrupt documents were being returned. I suspect it's a NeDB bug, but the solution was simple enough: just use the code you already know works in the getHandler() method!

As with the GET handler, the URL that maps to this function includes two tokens, one for the collection and one for the ID of the item to update, but this time the ID is *not* optional, so there's no question mark involved.

CRU(D): Delete (DELETE Handler)

To complete the set of four CRUD methods, you, of course, need an HTTP DELETE handler, and that's up next.

```
const deleteHandler = function (inRequest, inResponse) {

  let [collection, id, item] = commonOpening("DELETE (delete)", inRequest);

  const db = databases[collection];
  db.remove({ id : id }, { }, function (inError, inRemovedCount) {
    if (inError) {
      commonErrorHandler(inError, inResponse);
    } else {
      inResponse.status(200);
      inResponse.send(id);
    }
  });

};
app.delete("/data/:collection/:id", deleteHandler);
```

Of course, this is extremely similar to updateHandler() because like that method, deleting requires a specific ID be specified, and it is passed as the query argument first. The second argument, an empty object, is used to specify options for the removal. NeDB supports a multi-option here (which is, in fact, the only one supported at the time of this writing) to allow for deleting multiple matching documents. But since that's not something you need since you're specifying a unique ID to delete, that's just an empty object. Finally, app.delete() is called to map this function to the DELETE HTTP method with a path that includes :collection and :id tokens, as you'd (ideally at this point!) expect.

The response from this function is an HTTP 200 and the ID of the deleted item, which is a typical convention for REST DELETE operations.

And, As an Added Bonus...

That takes care of the four CRUD operation handlers, but there's one additional function that I alluded to earlier that you need, and that's one to get *all* the data in *all* collections at once. This will be used whenever wxPIM starts up, so all the data on the server can be retrieved and stored in local storage in one request.

```
app.post("/getAllData", function(inRequest, inResponse) {

  let [collection, id, item] = commonOpening("POST (getAll)", inRequest);
```

```
const returnObject = { };

let collectionsToLoad = item.length;

for (let collectionName of item) {
  databases[collectionName.toLowerCase()].find({},
    function (inError, inDocuments) {
      if (inError) {
        commonErrorHandler(inError, inResponse);
      } else {
        returnObject[collectionName] = inDocuments;
        collectionsToLoad = collectionsToLoad - 1;
        if (collectionsToLoad === 0) {
          inResponse.status(200);
          inResponse.send(JSON.stringify(returnObject));
        }
      }
    }
  );
}

});
```

You'll notice first that I wrote this a little differently than the other four: the handler function is now an anonymous function passed to app.post(). There's no reason this is better or worse really; it's nothing beyond aesthetics and the code style you prefer. The only thing I'd say is that if you think or know you will need to call a handler method directly, as I did with getHandler() being called from updateHandler(), then you really can't use this inline anonymous function style.

But, regardless of style, the function isn't too complex. It handles a POST request to the path /getAllData. Note that you might expect it to be something like /data/getAll so that it's part of the base API, and that would be a reasonable expectation. However, that would clash with the previous POST handler because remember that it expects a collection name after the /data route, so /data/getAll would treat getAll as the collection name, and you'd have a problem since there is no such collection. By giving this function its own API route, that problem is avoided.

The POST body here will contain an array of module names, which remember means *collection* on the server side, which is really a synonym of *database*. That array is iterated over, and for each, the name is lowercased so that it matches what's in the databases object, and then the find() method is called with no query on each database object, which returns to you all items in that database.

Now, this means you'll have four asynchronous operations running at once, once for each database. For each, the returned documents are added to the returnObject object. When all of them are complete, a response needs to be rendered by the server. However, since the calls are asynchronous, you don't know which order they'll finish in, so how do you know when to render the response? Easy: you count down, starting from the number of items in the incoming array, until you hit zero in the callback. The order then doesn't matter because whichever callback invocation results in the countdown reaching zero, that's the one that fired last and so it knows to render the response, which is just a JSON serialization of returnObject, which then will contain all the data for all modules. You could write this in a Promise-centric way as well if you prefer that style of asynchronous coding.

Just one small bit of code remains in server.js, and it's the code that kicks it all off.

```
app.listen(8080, function () {
  console.log("wxPIM server listening on port 8080")
});
```

Yep, it's just like you saw in the earlier example! Once this executes, the server is up and running, and wxPIM has a remote API to call to persist its data!

Hooking wxPIM Up to the Server

With the server code fully investigated, you can now look at the changes required to the wxPIM version you've developed over the past two chapters and make the changes necessary to connect the client app to the server. It turns out to not be all that much, but it does introduce some new Webix capabilities, so let's dive right in!

Modules: A Small but Necessary Change

Virtually all of the changes are in the core code, save one minor but important change in all four modules. Previously, in the newHandler() of each module was this line of code:

```
wxPIM.modules.Appointments.editingID = new Date().getTime();
```

Now, that line is changed to the following:

```
wxPIM.modules.Appointments.editingID = "" + new Date().getTime();
```

This was needed because NeDB seemed not to be able to find documents when the IDs were numbers. So, by concatenating the time value with an empty string, JavaScript coerces the value to a string, which makes the queries with NeDB work as expected. Like I said, it's a very minor thing but critical to making this work, and this is literally the only change to any module's code!

Starting a Little Differently

To begin looking at the core code changes, you first have a small but important change in the start() method in core.js.

```
start() {

  for (let moduleName of wxPIM.registeredModules) {
    wxPIM.modules[moduleName] = new wxPIM.moduleClasses[moduleName]();
  }

  webix.ui(this.getBaseLayoutConfig());

  webix.extend($$("baseLayout"), webix.ProgressBar);

  webix.ui(this.getSideMenuConfig());

  wxPIM.getAllData();

}
```

There are two changes here. The first is the line that adds a ProgressBar to the base layout using the webix.extend() method. This will be needed when you call the server. Since those requests are asynchronous, and because you want to keep this code as simple as possible, I'll use the "block the user from doing anything until the code is finished" approach and mask the screen when a request is in flight. The ProgressBar will show a spinning icon during that period to give the user some indication that work is occurring. Blocking the user isn't typically a great user experience (UX), but it is simple and effective, so it's suitable for our purposes here.

Before You Go Any Further, Let's Talk About Good Ol' AJAX

AJAX is a technique that came to life, so to speak, at the hands of one Jesse James Garrett in an essay he wrote in February 2005. There, he coined the term AJAX, which stands for Asynchronous JavaScript and XML. The interesting thing about AJAX, though, is that it doesn't have to be asynchronous (but virtually always is), doesn't have to involve JavaScript (but virtually always does), and doesn't need to use XML at all (but probably doesn't 99+ percent of the time).

Ajax is, at its core, an exceedingly simple, and by no stretch of the imagination original, concept: it is not necessary to refresh the entire contents of a web page for each user interaction, or each "event," if you will. When the user clicks a button, it is no longer necessary to ask the server to render an entirely new page, as is the case with the "classic" Web. Instead, you can define regions on the page to be updated and have much more fine-grained control over user event handling as a result. No longer are you limited to simply submitting a form to a server for processing or navigating to an entirely new page when a link is clicked.

The interesting thing about Ajax is that it is in no way, shape, or form new, and it actually wasn't even when Mr. Garrett coined the term. A few years ago, when AJAX was still somewhat new, I liked to say that you could always tell who has done AJAX before and who hadn't because those who had are mad that it was a big deal and they didn't get credit for "inventing" it themselves!

Nowadays, the term AJAX isn't used as much as before. People tend to talk about "out-of-band requests" or simply "asynchronous requests," and as I alluded to earlier it's virtually never XML nowadays. It's almost always JSON. But, the core concept remains the same: call the server, get some data, and use it in some way without repainting the entire screen. That's ultimately the point.

However, there are still remnants of AJAX it floating around, and one of the places you can find such remnants in in Webix itself, where you find the `webix.ajax()` function. This is the singular function that allows the client application to interact with the server.

When you call `webix.ajax()`, you get back an object that has a number of methods on it for configuring the call to the server, plus some methods for actually executing that call. There are also some shortcut methods available if you're making typical GET and POST requests, so which call syntax you use comes down to what your needs are. I'm going to use the more verbose approach in the wxPIM server code because I think it's slightly easier to see what's going on.

And, rather than give you any contrived examples here, because it's not at all fundamentally complicated, you'll just look at the real use of webix.ajax() in the code.

Back to That getAllData() Method

With AJAX generically out of the way, you can look at the second change in the start() method, which is the call to wxPIM.getAllData(). This implements our very simplistic form of synchronization, as you can see here:

```
getAllData() {

  wxPIM.maskUI();
  webix.ajax()
    .timeout(10000)
    .headers({ "Content-Type" : "application/json" })
    .post("/getAllData", JSON.stringify(wxPIM.registeredModules))
    .then(function(inResult) {
      localStorage.clear();
      const allModuleData = inResult.json();
      for (let moduleName of wxPIM.registeredModules) {
        const moduleDataArray = allModuleData[moduleName];
        const moduleDataObject = { };
        for (let i = 0; i < moduleDataArray.length; i++) {
          const nextItem = moduleDataArray[i];
          moduleDataObject[nextItem.id] = nextItem;
        }
        localStorage.setItem(`${moduleName}DB`, webix.
        stringify(moduleDataObject));
      }
      localStorage.setItem("dataLoaded", true);
      wxPIM.unmaskUI();
      wxPIM.dayAtAGlance();
    })
    .fail(function(inXHR) {
      $$("baseLayout").hide();
      webix.message({
        type : "error", text : "Server not available, wxPIM cannot start"
```

```
        });
    });

}
```

The first step is to block the UI with the `ProgressBar` that was added to the base layout. This is done with a call to `wxPIM.maskUI()`.

```
maskUI(inModuleName) {

  $$("baseLayout").disable();
  $$("baseLayout").showProgress({ type : "icon" });
  if (wxPIM.uiType === "desktop") {
    for (let moduleName of wxPIM.registeredModules) {
      let moduleWindow = $$(`moduleWindow-${moduleName}`);
      if (moduleWindow) {
        moduleWindow.disable();
        if (moduleName === inModuleName) {
          moduleWindow.showProgress({ type : "icon" });
        }
      }
    }
  }

}
```

First, the base layout is disabled, so no user input is possible, and the `ProgressBar` on it is shown. If you're in mobile mode, then you're done at this point, but if in desktop mode, then there's more work to do. The problem is that the module windows aren't part of the base layout, which means that the `ProgressBar` on it won't block the windows. It doesn't do much good to block the base layout if the user can still interact with a module window! So, you iterate the collection of modules and look for a window for each. If one is found, then it's disabled. That covers all windows. Then, when you find the window corresponding to the name of the module that was passed in, then you show the `ProgressBar` on it (which is added when the window is launched, just like it's added to the base layout). In the case of calling this from `getAllData()`, there is no module name passed in, but that's fine—no harm, no foul.

Small launchModule() change.   As mentioned, there is a small change in launchModule() related to this. The change is simply that when webix.ui() is called to create the window, now the returned reference is captured in a variable win. Then, rather than immediately calling show() on it anonymously, a call to webix.extend() is first made to add the ProgressBar, just like is done to the base layout. Only after that is win.show() called. The reason for this is that if you call show() before the extend() call, then an error occurs, and the window doesn't get built properly. Since show() was previously called directly on the reference returned by webix.ui() anonymously, this change was necessary; otherwise, there would have been no way to call extend() on it first and avoid that error.

Once that's done, you can go ahead and call the server using that webix.ajax() method I mentioned. All of the AJAX calls that are made from here on out will have some common configuration: setting a timeout and headers. Because the UI is being blocked, you don't want there to be a long timeout in case of problems. I decided on ten seconds, though you could argue for a lesser or greater value. It's also necessary to ensure that the server knows that you're sending in JSON in the POST body, so the Content-Type header needs to be set. Without this, the content won't be parsed properly by Express body-parser middleware.

After the timeout() and headers() methods are called, it's time to make the request, and that's done through one of the methods of the object returned by webix.ajax(), which correspond to HTTP methods: del() (for DELETE), get(), patch(), post(), or put(). You provide these methods with the URL to send the request to, which here is that /getAllData route you created earlier. Then, in this case, you need to send an array of module names in the POST body so that object is serialized to JSON and provided as the second argument to the post() method.

The return value from any of these methods is a promise, so you can then attach a then() handler for successful responses and a fail() handler for error responses. Assuming no errors occur, the first step in the then() handler is to clear local storage. Remember, this is a "cheap" method of synchronization here, so you're literally just replacing whatever data you have locally with what the server gives you, making the server the canonical source of wxPIM data at all times.

After that, you, of course, need to populate local storage with what the server sent back, so the array of module names is iterated, and for each, the data from the returned object is pulled out based on the name. Each item in the data array is attached to an initially empty object using the id field of each array element as the key in the new object, and finally, that object is stored in local storage. That ensures the data structure that the client-side wxPIM code depends on is there.

When all the data has been stored, then it's just a simple matter of calling wxPIM. unmaskUI() to reenable the UI.

```
unmaskUI() {

  $$("baseLayout").enable();
  $$("baseLayout").hideProgress();
  if (wxPIM.uiType === "desktop") {
    for (let moduleName of wxPIM.registeredModules) {
      let moduleWindow = $$(`moduleWindow-${moduleName}`);
      if (moduleWindow) {
        moduleWindow.enable();
        moduleWindow.hideProgress();
      }
    }
  }

}
```

It's exactly like wxPIM.maskUI() except of course you're calling enable() on the base layout and all windows and hiding the ProgressBar components on each. Finally, a call to wxPIM.dayAtAGlance() is made to populate that screen, like would normally happen at this point even without the call to the server.

Now, in the case of a failure, you take drastic but simple and effective measures: hide the ProgressBar, hide the *entire* UI, and tell the user that wxPIM couldn't start. This is far from being a robust approach, but this isn't an app you'll be selling to people for real-world use, so it doesn't need to be production-ready (and besides, this gives you an opportunity to enhance the app later as an independent learning exercise!).

Saving to the Server

Next up is the common wxPIM.saveHandler() method, which naturally needs to make an AJAX call to the RESTful API that is the wxPIM server code.

```
saveHandler(inModuleName, inFormIDs) {

  const itemData = { };
  for (let i = 0; i < inFormIDs.length; i++) {
    const formData = $$(inFormIDs[i]).getValues();
    webix.proto(itemData, formData);
  }
  itemData.id = wxPIM.modules[inModuleName].editingID;

  delete itemData.$init;

  wxPIM.maskUI(inModuleName);

  const thenHandler = function(inResult) {
    const moduleData = wxPIM.getModuleData(inModuleName);
    moduleData[itemData.id] = itemData;
    localStorage.setItem(`${inModuleName}DB`, webix.stringify(moduleData));
    wxPIM.modules[inModuleName].refreshData();
    $$(`module${inModuleName}-itemsCell`).show();
    wxPIM.dayAtAGlance();
    wxPIM.unmaskUI();
    webix.message({ type : "error", text : "Item saved" });
  };

  const failHandler = function(inXHR) {
    wxPIM.unmaskUI();
    webix.message({
      type : "error", text : "Server not available, data changes not
      currently possible"
    });
  };

  const callURL = `/data/${inModuleName.toLowerCase()}`;
  const callTimeout = 10000;
```

```
const callHeaders = { "Content-Type" : "application/json" };
const callBody = JSON.stringify(itemData);

if (wxPIM.modules[inModuleName].isEditingExisting) {
  webix.ajax()
    .timeout(callTimeout)
    .headers(callHeaders)
    .put(`${callURL}/${itemData.id}`, callBody)
    .then(thenHandler)
    .fail(failHandler);
} else {
  webix.ajax()
    .timeout(callTimeout)
    .headers(callHeaders)
    .post(callURL, callBody)
    .then(thenHandler)
    .fail(failHandler);
}

}
```

Things are the same early on: the same sort of form merging you already know about is still done, but the changes start with masking the UI, as you saw in wxPIM.getAllData(). Next, you define a success and failure handler, which corresponds to thenHandler and failHandler. You have to remember that this method handles both creating a new item and updating an existing one, so there's two different calls that can be made from here, a POST for creating and a PUT for updating. But, the basic logic in the then() handler and fail() handler is the same in both cases, so they get defined and stored in the thenHandler and failHandler references. Likewise, the URL starts off the same (but with the ID of the item added when doing an update), so the callURL variable contains that common base. To avoid repeating too much code, the callTimeout, callHeaders, and callbody variables are likewise created independently of the actual call.

Then, with all those variables populated with the appropriate value, the code interrogates the isEditingExisting member of the current module. If it's true, then the if branch is followed, resulting in a put() call. This is where the ID is added to the base URL to create the complete appropriate URL for that operation. If a new item is being created, then the else branch executes, making a post() request.

Upon a successful call, the `thenHandler` code fires. You can update local storage only once the response comes back successfully from the server; otherwise, you would have a synchronization problem, so that's the first step done in the callback. In fact, the code in the callback is essentially the same as before you added the server component to this app, save for hiding the mask and reenabling the UI. So, as before, the module is given a chance to update its data (its summary screen more specifically), and then the day-at-a-glance screen is asked to refresh itself as well in case this new or updated item is to be displayer there.

Similarly, the `failHandler` code simply unmasks and reenables the UI and tells the user the change couldn't be saved. Nothing is saved to local storage in that case, and the user can retry the save if they want. Otherwise, they can treat the app as if it's in a read-only mode.

Deleting from the Server

The final difference in the core code, meaning the last thing you need to do to make wxPIM server-aware, is a similar change to `wxPIM.saveHandler()` but this time in the `wxPIM.deleteHandler()`.

```
deleteHandler(inModuleName) {

  webix.html.addCss(webix.confirm({
    title : `Please Confirm`, ok : "Yes", cancel : "No", type : "confirm-
    warning",
    text : `Are you sure you want to delete this item?`, width : 300,
    callback : function(inResult) {
      if (inResult) {
        wxPIM.maskUI(inModuleName);
        webix.ajax()
          .timeout(10000)
          .del(`/data/${inModuleName.toLowerCase()}/${wxPIM.
          modules[inModuleName].editingID}`)
          .then(function(inResult) {
            const dataItems = wxPIM.getModuleData(inModuleName);
            delete dataItems[wxPIM.modules[inModuleName].editingID];
            localStorage.setItem(`${inModuleName}DB`, webix.
            stringify(dataItems));
```

```
        wxPIM.modules[inModuleName].refreshData();
        $$(`module${inModuleName}-itemsCell`).show();
        wxPIM.dayAtAGlance();
        wxPIM.unmaskUI();
        webix.message({ type : "error", text : "Item deleted" });
      })
      .fail(function(inXHR) {
        wxPIM.unmaskUI();
        webix.message({
          type : "error", text : "Server not available, data changes
          not currently possible"
        });
      });
    }
  }
}), "animated bounceIn");

}
```

This code is the same as before until you get inside the callback. Masking and disabling the UI has been added again, and now a webix.ajax() call is made to the server to do the delete, this time using the del() method, which corresponds to the HTTP DELETE method. Since there's just one type of call here, the code is simpler than in wxPIM.saveHandler() since there's no branching involved. All the configuration for the call is therefore inlined, as are the then() and fail() handlers. Upon a successful response, the data is again deleted from local storage, the module is given a chance to refresh its data and summary screen, and the same goes for day-at-a-glance. The UI is returned to its usable state, and a message is shown to the user. If a failure occurs, the same message is given to the user indicating they appear to be in an offline state, and no data changes occur.

With that, wxPIM is now fully server-capable!

Summary

In this chapter, you took a small detour from Webix to learn about some server-side technologies including Node, NPM, Express, RESTful APIs, and NeDB. Then, you took a detour right back into Webix to learn how to hook wxPIM up to the server. You saw how easy it is to make calls to remote systems from a Webix app.

In the next chapter, you'll take the next logical step, which is making wxPIM a true mobile app using the popular Cordova (aka Phonegap) tool.

Packaging wxPIM with PhoneGap

Now that wxPIM is feature-complete on both the client and server sides, it's time to talk about truly mobilizing this application.

That's where a new piece of technology comes into play: PhoneGap. With this tool, you'll be able to transfer the app into a native application (more or less) that will run across multiple mobile platforms including Android and iOS.

While it's entirely possible merely to put the client app on a web server and have people access it with their web browser, that's not a true native app experience, like many people expect these days. You can't just go and download your app from the app store on your device, such Google Play for Android or the App Store for iOS. That's a piece of the puzzle that you need to supply, and PhoneGap is precisely what you need to pull off that trick!

The Problems with Mobile Development

Mobile development has historically been a bit tricky if you had it in your head to support multiple platforms. If you wanted an app to run on Android, iOS, Windows Phone, and so on, you faced a Herculean task. The only real option for a long time was to write multiple applications using native SDKs specific to each platform. You'd write your app in Objective-C for iOS, in Java for Android, in .NET for Windows Phone, and in C++ for BlackBerry. Sure, you could design the code of the application in such a way that rewriting it for each platform was slightly easier (that's just good architecture after all), but it was still essentially rewriting it for each platform, so a little easier or not, it was still a major chore.

© Frank Zammetti 2018
F. Zammetti, *Practical Webix*, https://doi.org/10.1007/978-1-4842-3384-9_9

This is a form of fragmentation; the market itself is fragmented with the multiple platforms available. This fragmentation is fantastic for consumer choice, but it *does* make life difficult for a developer, unless you choose not to support some platforms, and that's usually not a great idea if you want to reach the widest possible audience. Of course, the market has largely narrowed to two main players, iOS and Android, but there *are* still other players out there that you may want to consider, and certainly the future could find new players on the field at any time.

However, rewriting code for each platform is becoming less and less the approach that most developers take in favor of (arguably, at least) better choices such as cross-platform libraries that let you write a single codebase that runs on multiple platforms (well, mostly a single codebase anyway). Libraries such as Corona, Ionic, and React Native, for example, allow you to do this, and they do so rather well in many situations.

In this context, the combination of HTML, JavaScript, and CSS can also be viewed as such a cross-platform tool. It's not always thought of like that, but that's what it is in effect. You target this "platform" made up of these three technologies, and as long as a mechanism is available on a given "physical" platform to execute your application (read: a web browser), it will generally work across platforms. As it happens, a web browser is exactly that mechanism! Using these technologies, you can avoid a number of forms of fragmentation all at once.

Before I talk about that, though, let's look at the forms of fragmentation you're trying to avoid in the first place, that is, the forms of fragmentation that come along with actual native development that make it harder than you'd like it to be.

Fragmentation of User Experience

Another problem with mobile development across multiple platforms is that of providing a consistent user experience. Each platform has its own UI design and patterns that the native development methodologies provide an application. That means the application will look, feel, and function differently in terms of its UI from one platform to another. While there are means by which a developer can to some extent work around this default behavior, it is usually frowned upon. Creating an app that follows the iOS modes of operation and UI metaphors and running it on Android isn't typically the best answer even when you can pull it off.

Still, it's a starting point at least, and for some apps, it'll be acceptable, but it's still a form of fragmentation that you as a developer need to at least consider.

Fragmentation of Features

It's also true that not all platforms are created equal in terms of features (though the gap there too has narrowed to a significant degree). Android, for example, has the notion of home screen widgets while iOS does not. If your application's basic functionality depends on widgets, the experience will be different, perhaps drastically so, on iOS (and it might not even be possible to bring your app to a given platform because of it).

This means your application may have considerably different capabilities running on one platform than it does on another platform by necessity. Especially for users who might jump between platforms, that's not going to endear them to your application, more so if they lose features they depended on previously.

Fragmentation of Development Tools

Another problem is that of the various development tools. Developing an iOS application, for example, requires you to have a Mac. If you're more of a Windows user, like I am, that's a bit of a problem. Even if you're a Mac user, you still need to have Xcode installed to do iOS development. Even though you can do Android development just fine on a Mac, you don't need to have Xcode installed for that. There can be vast differences in the platforms and tools you need to develop for various mobile platforms; that's the basic point here. And, that's before even talking about the vastly different APIs that each platform presents.

If you want to develop for multiple platforms, then the situation becomes worse. Each platform has its own SDK if nothing else, and you'll need to install them all for the platforms you want to support. That aside, you'll still need to learn different languages, APIs, and platform-specific tools. While it's true that a capable developer can generally jump between technologies without too much difficulty, there's no question that it slows them down and sometimes leads to less optimal designs. Something that works great in Objective-C might not work as well in Java, architecturally speaking. Being able to optimize a design across technologies is a huge task no matter how capable you are, and the best developer in the world may not be able to overcome some challenges because of the intrinsic differences between mobile platforms.

Enter the White Knight: PhoneGap

Now let's go back to what I proposed earlier, that is, building an app with HTML, JavaScript, and CSS that runs in a browser on a mobile device (because in theory that *should* avoid all of that fragmentation). HTML, JavaScript, and CSS are all standards-based technologies, which means that aside from some relatively minor differences here and there between browsers, an app written using them will generally look, feel, and function consistently across platforms. That sure sounds like the Holy Grail of mobile development, doesn't it? Especially if you narrow the scope a bit to HTML5, which to most people actually means the combination of HTML5, CSS3, and the latest version of JavaScript you can make a strong case for it being exactly that.

There's still a significant problem to deal with, though: the "native experience." What I mean by that is the experience that a user has of downloading an app to their device from an online store that appears to run like any other native app written with Objective-C for iOS or Java for Android, for example. Yes, they can point their web browser at a URL and launch your app, and in some ways, that's arguably better as it ensures that they always run the latest code. However, it's not the same thing, and people seem to prefer not having to do that. (I make this statement based on the popularity of apps.)

Is there a way to accomplish that goal with these technologies? Of course, there is: PhoneGap.

What Is It?

PhoneGap is a framework that allows you to use standardized web technologies to build mobile applications. In short, you more or less build your application using HTML5 as you always would and then "package" it using PhoneGap to create a native application. This application can be built to target multiple platforms, and it can then be offered for download in each platform's online app store. The application, to the end user, looks and works just like any other application. It gets an icon in the launcher, for example, which launches the app without opening the web browser.

Not only does PhoneGap provide this native "wrapper" around your HTML5 application code, but it also provides a robust collection of JavaScript APIs that you can (optionally) use to gain access to the native device capabilities that your HTML5-based application running in a web browser otherwise wouldn't have access to use. Things such as gyroscopes, accelerometers, GPS, databases, and more, are made available to you via these APIs. While you certainly can write an application that doesn't use them, you often will want to incorporate them in order to provide all the capabilities that users expect from a modern mobile app.

The underlying goal of PhoneGap is to offer, effectively, a runtime that provides parity across platforms. Develop a PhoneGap application using standard HTML5 technologies, one that targets the PhoneGap APIs where necessary, and the result is that your app will work the same across all supported platforms without you having to lift a finger to achieve that goal. In other words, it's Nirvana!

A Brief History of PhoneGap

PhoneGap was birthed at an event in San Francisco named iPhoneDevCamp in 2008 as a means to deal with the issue that many developers run into when starting iOS development, which is that Objective-C can be challenging or, at the very least, unfamiliar even to experienced developers. Although somewhat less true today because of the popularity of iOS development, it was certainly true in 2008. At that point in time, it was called PhoneGap. It quickly gained popularity because it provided experienced web developers with an avenue into native iOS development using technologies with which they were already comfortable, rather than having to learn Objective-C and a completely new way of doing things. Then, in 2009, Cordova (still known as PhoneGap) won the People's Choice Award at O'Reilly Media's Web 2.0 conference. That's when people really started to take notice, and it was the catalyst for PhoneGap usage to explode quickly.

Though originally created by a company named Nitobi, PhoneGap was purchased by Adobe in 2011. Shortly thereafter, Adobe contributed the PhoneGap codebase to the Apache Software Foundation where it lives now under the name Cordova.

Don't let this confuse you! In simple terms, Cordova is the underlying open source library, while PhoneGap, still very much alive and kicking under the Adobe banner, is the most commonly used distribution of Cordova, so to speak. Perhaps a better way to put it is that it is analogous to how WebKit relates to Safari: WebKit powers Safari, and, in the same way, Cordova powers PhoneGap. Yes, that also means there could be other competing versions of Cordova, and it also means that PhoneGap could have different capabilities than the basic distribution of Cordova.

As a developer, you can choose to use "naked" Cordova if you like, or you can use PhoneGap specifically. The differences will, by and large, not be huge, aside from some differences in tooling. For the sake of simplicity, you're going to use PhoneGap because that gives you the ability to use something that Adobe provides called PhoneGap Build, which will make life much easier for you here. We'll get to that shortly, but before then, let's cover something else: how PhoneGap does what it does.

How Does This Black Magic (Basically) Work?

I've been using the term *native app* a bit loosely here with regard to PhoneGap. In fact, PhoneGap apps are actually "hybrid" apps, not true native apps. The difference is that a hybrid app runs within a WebView, which handles rendering the UI, rather than the native toolkit of the underlying OS platform.

A WebView is something that nearly all modern mobile OSs have. Some platforms have different names for it, but probably the most common one is WebView. Whatever it's called, it's a specific UI component that can be embedded directly into the UI of a true native application. Typically, this is used to show things such as online help content or registration pages—any web site really that the application needs.

This is done without launching a separate web browser, and I'm sure you can see how that's a handy capability for any app to have! A WebView differs from a web browser in that it doesn't have typical web browser controls such as the back, forward, and home buttons. Instead, it's just the viewport portion of a browser—the blank canvas onto which HTML is rendered. Beyond being simply handy for a native app, though, it's the key to PhoneGap!

At the most basic level, PhoneGap is not much more than a small native app with a UI that is nothing but a full-screen WebView control within which your HTML5 web app is launched. From there on, your app works as if it were running in a web browser, which, of course, it actually is, as far as the HTML and JavaScript that make up your app are concerned! Remember, though, it's a web browser that doesn't look like a web browser to the user since it doesn't have the usual navigation controls or other "chrome" around the rendering surface of a typical browser. The canvas on which your app renders its UI is the entire screen of the mobile device effectively, just as is the case for a native app.

It's really one of the more clever ideas to come along, but it's also quite simple and obvious after the fact, which, of course, is a hallmark of any great idea! There is, of course, slightly more to it than that. Every WebView control allows for one other key capability: the ability of JavaScript code to call native code, be it C/C++, Objective-C, or Java, depending on the OS. It presents these calls as part of a large JavaScript API that you can use, or not use at all; it's completely up to you. Since this book isn't about PhoneGap, it's about Webix, I won't go into much detail on these APIs, just like I didn't go into the vast API provided by Node or Express. However, near the end of this chapter, I will use an API to enhance wxPIM, just to give you a little bit of a view into what the APIs have to offer.

A Simpler Build Approach: PhoneGap Build

Creating a PhoneGap app isn't hard. You essentially build it like any other web app you would build and then you use the command-line tools provided by PhoneGap (or just Cordova if you want to stay completely open source). Either of those provides a robust command-line interface (CLI) that allows you to take that simple web app and package it up into a native app.

The problem with that, though, is that it requires all that native tooling I talked about earlier. You need the SDKs for the platforms you want to support installed, plus whatever IDEs or tools they require, and that assumes you're on the appropriate desktop platform to install any of it in the first place! It can be quite a nightmare to get a proper cross-platform mobile development platform set up. It's time and effort even if it goes smoothly or it could be a huge pain in the tuchus, as my mom likes to say!

Thankfully, there is a much simpler solution that takes virtually all of this pain away: PhoneGap Build. PhoneGap Build is a cloud-based solution offered by Adobe that allows you to upload your application's source code, plus a small XML configuration file that provides some details needed by the servers that then builds your application for a number of platforms and ultimately makes download links available to you. You simply upload an archive of your app, and after a few minutes, you'll be able to download versions for various supported mobile platforms.

It really is a fantastic service that removes virtually all the pain of building for multiple mobile platforms. Let's dive in, shall we?

Get Ready: Signing Up

The first thing you'll need to do is to sign up for a PhoneGap Build account. To do so, visit `https://build.phonegap.com` and click the big Get Started! button next to the floating robot over the scrolling sky. (I know, it sounds crazy, but that's what's there, and it actually looks cool!) When you click the button, the page will automatically scroll to a section that outlines your plan choices, as shown in Figure 9-1.

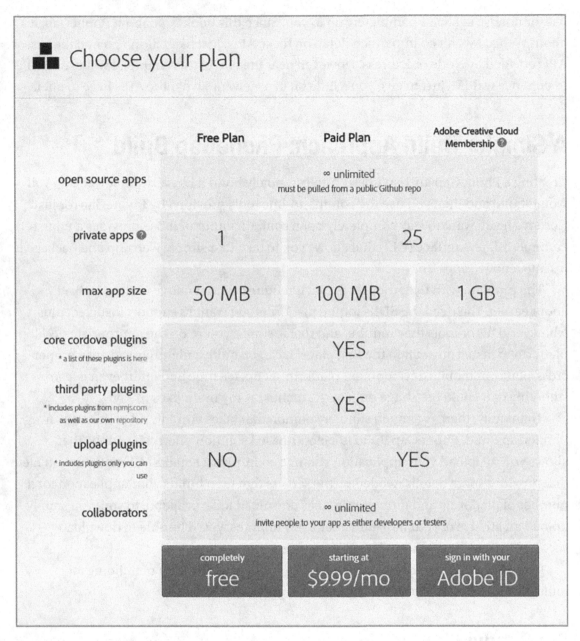

Figure 9-1. *PhoneGap Build plan options*

If you happen already to have an Adobe ID, then you are all set! Simply sign in with your credentials for that service, and you're good to go. You will have the ability to create 25 separate private apps within PhoneGap Build, and you can then manage and build them independently. You'll also have the ability to have unlimited open source apps.

The difference between a public app and a private app in this context is simply where the source code of your app is found. If your code can be found on GitHub or some other publicly available Git repository, then it is public. Otherwise, it's private. For your needs here, you'll be dealing with a private app, so there's no need to get set up with Git and no need for you to have any knowledge of it if you don't want to. The number of private apps allowed is the big differentiating factor in the PhoneGap Build plans available to you. For your purposes here, a single private app is fine, but if you need more, then that's when you'll need to fork over some cash to Adobe.

Of course, you can remove an existing private app to make room for another at any time, and so as long as you're working on only one app at a time, then the free option would be sufficient. The free service also, from my experience, is subject to longer lines in terms of queuing for a build to occur. In other words, you might wait five minutes for your build to complete instead of 30 seconds if you have a paid plan (though *most* of the time the build speed actually *is* measured in seconds). That's a small price to pay in my mind. Either way, for what you need to do here, it's perfectly fine.

Once you select your plan, you'll be asked to sign into an existing Adobe account or to create a new one (you can also log in with Facebook or Google credentials if you prefer).

Once you create the account or log in, then you'll find yourself staring at a screen very much like the one shown in Figure 9-2, which is your personal app console. At this point, you can do a number of things. First, you can create a new private app by supplying the URL to a Git repository (or connect to your GitHub account if you have one) or upload a ZIP archive of your application. If you already have an app uploaded, as I do in the screenshot, you can update the code (if I'm creating a new build) or request PhoneGap Build to rebuild all the available versions (iOS, Android, and Windows Phone). You can also click the icons for each of the supported platforms to download the packaged application for that platform. There's even a QR code you can scan with your phone to access the download link (because typing is for suckers!)

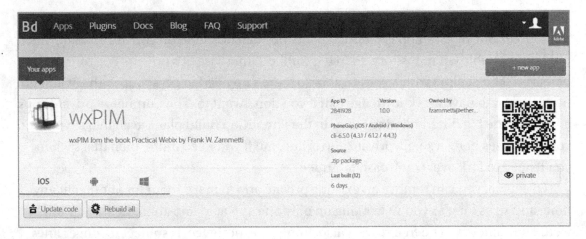

Figure 9-2. *Your app console*

Really, for what you're doing in this book, that's just about all you need to know about PhoneGap Build, well, except for one very important thing that allows it to work at all: the configuration file.

Get Set: The Configuration File

The configuration file, which you'll name `config.xml` and place in the root directory of the app alongside the `index.html` file that serves as the app's starting point, is where you specify metadata about your application that informs PhoneGap Build about various parameters it needs to build your application. Most of the information you can put in this file is optional, and you can get away with a small subset of all that is available to you. Listing 9-1 is the `config.xml` file for wxPIM. As you can see, it is rather spartan.

Listing 9-1. The config.xml File for wxPIM

```
<?xml version="1.0" encoding="UTF-8"?>
<widget xmlns="http://www.w3.org/ns/widgets"
  xmlns:gap="http://phonegap.com/ns/1.0"
  id="com.etherient.wxPIM"
  version="1.0.0">

  <name>wxPIM</name>
  <description>wxPIM fom the book Practical Webix by Frank W. Zammetti
  </description>
```

```
<author href="http://www.zammetti.com" email="fzammetti@etherient.
com">Frank W. Zammetti</author>
<preference name="phonegap-version" value="cli-6.5.0" />
<plugin name="cordova-plugin-vibration" spec="2.1.5" />
```

`</widget>`

The first required element is the `<widget>` element. This must be the root element that lets PhoneGap Build know you're following the widget specification, which the config file is based on. This element has a number of attributes, but only `id` and `version` are required.

The `id` attribute is the unique identifier of your application, which must be unique across all apps built using PhoneGap Build. The way you ensure this without meeting up with every other developer in the world and coming to some sort of arrangement is to use reverse-domain name naming. This is typically seen in Java package names, and it is simply your domain name backward, plus an app name. For example, I own the domain name `etherient.com`, so `com.etherient.wxPIM` fits the bill. Now I only have to ensure the final portion of that, `wxPIM`, is unique within the domain I control. I'm not averse to arguing with myself at times, but I'm sure even I can manage this level of cooperation with myself!

The `version` attribute is a free-form field, but typically the value is in the common major.minor.patch form, as you can see.

The `<name>` and `<description>` elements, children of the root `<widget>` element, are not actually required by the widget spec, but the PhoneGap Build documentation calls them out as required by the build servers. The `<author>` element is similarly not required, not even by the build servers, though it's a good element to include anyway.

The `<preference>` element is how you define various options to direct the build servers what to do. None are required, but at a minimum, the `phonegap-version` option should usually be specified so that you know what version of the library the build servers will build your code with.

Finally, the `<plugin>` element tells PhoneGap Build that your app is going to use a PhoneGap plug-in, which are JavaScript modules that expose various native device capabilities through a JavaScript API. In this case, you're going to use the vibration plug-in so you can make the device vibrate under certain conditions that you'll see shortly.

There's quite a lot more you can specify in the config file, including things like images for icons and splash screens and plug-ins to use (plug-ins being extra PhoneGap libraries that provide more capabilities to your app), but that's going beyond the scope of this book. If you're interested, and certainly I hope you are at this point, the PhoneGap Build documentation provides all the details (and there are even GUI tools available to create the config file if you prefer; search online for *configap* to find one).

Go: Starting the Build

With a `config.xml` file written and added to the root of your application, it's time to kick off a build. The first step to doing this is a simple one: create a ZIP archive from your application's directory. This needs to include all your application code, including libraries (like Webix).

Note when I say "zip up that directory," I mean you should zip up the contents of the directory, not the directory itself. Put another way, after you zip it up, copy the archive file to an empty directory somewhere else and try to extract it. When you do so, you should not see a new directory created in the empty directory. Instead, you should see the contents of the root of the application "spill out," so to speak, directly into the previously empty directory into which you're extracting the archive.

With the archive created, you can send it off to PhoneGap Build. To do so, click that New App button on the app console, which will lead to a screen like in Figure 9-3.

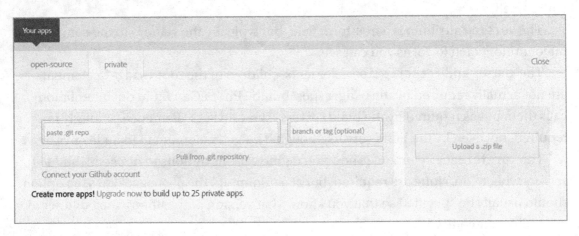

Figure 9-3. Adding a new app

Here, I've clicked the Private tab since that's the kind of app I want to send. And, given that you have a ZIP file to upload, the Git repo part doesn't matter; only that big "Upload a .zip file" does. Once you click that button and select the ZIP file, you'll be greeted by a progress bar for a few seconds before finding yourself back on the app console screen with the new app listed.

But, at this point, nothing has been done other than shipping the archive off to the build servers. To initiate the build, you click the Ready to Build button that you'll find is available. Once you do, it shouldn't really take more than ten seconds or so for an app the size of wxPIM to be built.

Crossing the Finish Line: The Output Files

After the build completes and you're back at the app console screen, you can click the name of your app to see details about it, as shown in Figure 9-4.

Figure 9-4. *wxPIM details*

Each of the supported platforms uses its own native bundle formats, but all of them are archives containing platform-specific code. On iOS, the format is IPA. For Windows Phone, it's an APPX file. For Android, the answer is an APK.

Notice in Figure 9-4 that the iOS build has failed, as indicated by the error icon. If you click the Error button, it will explicitly tell you that this is because you need to provide a signing key for iOS. While Android and Windows Phone support signing keys as well, they aren't required for development and so don't cause an error. I'll touch on this in the next section.

At this point, you can download the bundle for each platform using the buttons next to each (except for iOS) and install those bundles onto a real device, or an emulator, and begin testing your app.

From here you can also upload a new archive via the Update code button, or you can trigger a rebuild with the "Rebuild all" button. You can also rebuild for a specific platform with the Rebuild button next to each, and you can select signing keys with the drop-downs (which also include functionality to add those keys).

PhoneGap Build also has the notion of "collaborators," others that are working on a project with you. The Collaborators tab lets you maintain this list of people and provides them with the ability to, for example, download builds. You can also view and maintain plug-ins that your app uses on the Plugins tab (if any are used, obviously). Finally, the Settings tab allows you to control some things about your app. This includes enabling debugging capabilities to your app and enabling hydration (something beyond the scope of this book, but in short, it's a means to allow you to easily push new builds to testers quickly). You can also switch an app between being public and private (subject to the limitations of your account type of course), and you can delete the app entirely from here as well (to make room for a different single private app if you're using a free account, for example).

Getting Files onto Your Device

As described in the previous section, the native bundles for each platform for which your app was successfully built are easily downloadable from the app info page or the Install page. However, that tells you nothing about how to get that bundle onto a real device or an emulator. Let's talk about that now, shall we?

Deploying to Android Devices

For Android, the answer is quite simple: plug in your device and copy the APK to the device like you would any other file. When that's done, use whatever file manager you prefer and execute the APK. That will trigger an application installation like any other, providing you do one thing first: enable the "Unknown sources" option, which allows for the installation of apps from sources other than the Play store. This option is under Security in your devices' settings.

Another approach, and the technique I personally use most because it is arguably the simplest and most convenient, at least in my mind, is to create a share to a network directory on my PC. Next, I make sure that the APK is present in that directory, and then I use a file system browser on my device, such as FX File Explorer, ES File Explorer, or Astro File Explorer (all of which critically include SMB capabilities) to browse to that share and directly launch the file. This approach is nice because I don't have to bother with USB cables, making sure that drivers are installed, or any of that. I also don't have to worry about uploading to a web server (of course, the web server could be running locally, which would make that approach not much different from this one frankly). It's still a two-step process, as all of these are, but now it's very straightforward. In addition, when I'm testing on multiple devices, it's easy since the same APK is always at the same location, and I can browse to it any time I like to install it.

If you are already familiar with Android development and have the Android SDK installed, then you can use ADB (Android Debug Bridge, a command line tool for interacting with an Android device) to push the APK to your device. But, since that requires installing some development tools to work and you're trying to avoid that as much as possible, I'll leave that to an exercise for you if you'd like to explore that option on your own.

Deploying to iOS Devices

To deploy to an iOS device, you'll need a few things.

- First, you'll need a Mac because the development tools you'll need to accomplish the next few steps (OpenSSL and most likely Xcode) are available only on a Mac. (OpenSSL isn't Mac-only, but Apple only allows you to complete these steps on a Mac, and Xcode is most definitely Mac-only.)

- Then, you'll need to sign up for the iOS developer program ($99 per year). This will give you access to the Apple Developer Portal.

- Next, you'll need to obtain an Apple developer certificate using the Keychain Access application.

- After that, you'll need to register the devices you want to be able to deploy to on the Apple Developer Portal.

- Once that's done, you'll need to create a provisioning profile, also through the Apple Developer Portal.

- With that accomplished, you'll be able to use the certificate you created as a signing key on PhoneGap build.

- Finally, with a build successful using the key, you'll then be able to plug in your i-device and push the app to it for testing using the developer tools you installed.

And if that sounds like a lot of effort, you are 100 percent correct!

It's not really *that* difficult once you walk through the steps, but if it's your first time, it can seem very daunting—so daunting, in fact, that I'm not going to try to cover it all here! Instead, I'm going to point you to one address.

```
http://docs.phonegap.com/phonegap-build/signing/ios
```

That's the PhoneGap Build page that describes the steps and provides links to everything you'll need. The bottom line is that if you want to deploy an app build with PhoneGap Build to iOS, unlike Android or Windows Phone, you'll need to pay for the privilege, and you'll need to run the iOS development gauntlet to at least some degree to be able to do so.

A Few Necessary Code Changes and Enhancements

If you take the wxPIM app code as it exists right now and submit it to PhoneGap Build, assuming you add the `config.xml` file, it won't work. That's because there are a few changes that are necessary. The first is that since you need to include everything your app needs in the archive, which includes Webix, that means that in `index.html`, the paths to Webix need to be updated. Fortunately, that's as easy as changing the Webix CSS and JS file imports to the following:

```
<link rel="stylesheet" href="webix/webix.css" type="text/css"
media="screen" charset="utf-8">
<script src="webix/webix.js" type="text/javascript" charset="utf-8"></
script>
```

Now, the Webix source is copied into the root directory of the project, and that minor issue is taken care of.

Something else you need to do is to add a new import.

```
<script type="text/javascript" src="phonegap.js"></script>
```

That brings in the core PhoneGap code that is required to use any of PhoneGap's capabilities, like the vibration API. In fact, you can leave the app as it is now and build it, and it will ostensibly work, but you won't be able to use any PhoneGap capabilities. Note that the PhoneGap Build documentation says that you should *not* include this file. However, in practice, using the vibration API, or indeed *any* PhoneGap plug-in, seems to depend on this import being present. I'm not certain if this is a bug in PhoneGap Build, though that's my guess, and either way, at the time of this writing, this import is required.

That isn't quite enough, though, because up until now you've been either loading wxPIM directly off the file system or getting it from the Node server. This presents a problem because the AJAX code doesn't know the address to the Node server now. To deal with that, you'll add a prompt where the user can enter the server address at startup. To do so, the following code is added to the start() method in the core.js file, right at the end:

```
const serverAddress = localStorage.getItem("serverAddress");
if (!serverAddress) {
  wxPIM.promptForServerAddress();
} else {
  // Get all data from server.
  wxPIM.getAllData();
}
```

The server address will be stored in local storage, so if it isn't found at startup, then you need to prompt for it via a call to wxPIM.promptForServerAddress(), which is this:

```
promptForServerAddress() {

  wxPIM.maskUI();
  const win = webix.ui({
    view : "ani-window", move : false, width : 260,
    position : "center", resize : false, id : "serverAddressWindow",
    toFront : true,
    fullscreen : false, head : "Information needed",
    body : { height : 140, rows : [
      { borderless : true, height : 30, template : "Please enter server
      address",
```

```
      css : { "text-align" : "center", "padding-top" : "10px", "padding-
      bottom" : "10px" }
   },
   { view : "text", id : "serverAddressText", css : { "padding-bottom" :
   "10px" } },
   { view : "button", label : "Ok",
     click : () => {
       localStorage.setItem("serverAddress", $$("serverAddressText").
       getValue());
       $$("serverAddressWindow").close();
       wxPIM.unmaskUI();
       wxPIM.getAllData();
     }
   }
 ] }
});
win.show();

}
```

This shows a window asking the user for the server address. After that, the window is closed, and `wxPIM.getAllData()` is called, which you'll notice is what is done if the address was found in `start()`. Of course, what if the server address isn't correct or isn't reachable? Well, that's where some changes to `getAllData()` come into play.

```
getAllData() {

  wxPIM.maskUI();

  const failOrExceptionHandler = function(inObj) {
    navigator.vibrate(3000);
    localStorage.removeItem("serverAddress");
    $$("baseLayout").hide();
    webix.message({
      type : "error", text : "Server not available, wxPIM is in read-only
      mode"
    });
  };
```

```
    try {
      webix.ajax()
        .timeout(10000)
        .headers({ "Content-Type" : "application/json" })
        .post(`${localStorage.getItem("serverAddress")}/getAllData`,
          JSON.stringify(wxPIM.registeredModules)
        )
        .then(function(inResult) {
          const serverAddress = localStorage.getItem("serverAddress");
          localStorage.clear();
          const allModuleData = inResult.json();
          for (let moduleName of wxPIM.registeredModules) {
            const moduleDataArray = allModuleData[moduleName];
            const moduleDataObject = { };
            for (let i = 0; i < moduleDataArray.length; i++) {
              const nextItem = moduleDataArray[i];
              moduleDataObject[nextItem.id] = nextItem;
            }
            localStorage.setItem(`${moduleName}DB`, webix.
              stringify(moduleDataObject));
          }
          localStorage.setItem("serverAddress", serverAddress);
          wxPIM.unmaskUI();
          wxPIM.dayAtAGlance();
        })
        .fail(failOrExceptionHandler);
    } catch (inException) {
      failOrExceptionHandler(inException);
    }

  }
```

The basic logic here is that you make the call to the server to get all data like always, but now you have the possibility of a failure *or* an exception. Both are treated the same: the server can't be reached for some reason, whether it's a network problem or the user fat-fingered the address. To reduce code, you have a single handler for both, the failOrExceptionHandler function. If this executes, then the server address is removed from local storage, and a slightly altered message from the last version of wxPIM is shown. The user can then reload the app to enter the server address again, but note that the UI is *not* hidden this time like before. This allows them to use the app in read-only mode. (If they try to mutate data, assuming the server still can't be reached, they'll get the failure message like before.)

You'll also see a call to navigator.vibrate() in that handler code. This is using the PhoneGap vibration API and causes the device to buzz for three seconds (assuming the device has haptic feedback capabilities; if it doesn't, this line will simply do nothing). This is just a little extra alert to the user that the server wasn't reachable.

Of course, if the AJAX request is successful, then everything just continues as before...well, *almost*! Since the procedure here is to clear local storage before filling it with the data retrieved from the server, you have a problem because that includes the server address! So, before the clear, the address is saved and then set again after the clear and the data load.

Another required change in wxPIM is in the common saveHandler() and deleteHandler() methods, which are just prepending the server address to the URL, the same as is done in getAllData(). Other than these changes, wxPIM works as expected as a PhoneGap-ified app.

One final change must be made to make this all work, and it's in the constructor. Previously, the last line of the constructor was as follows:

```
webix.ready(this.start.bind(this));
```

Now, however, in the world of PhoneGap, you have to change that to the following:

```
document.addEventListener("deviceready", this.start.bind(this), false);
```

The reason this change is necessary is because you can't use PhoneGap APIs like vibration until the device tells you it's ready for that, and PhoneGap provides a deviceready event to signal that. To ensure the API hasn't been used before, then you no longer use webix.ready() since that, it turns out, fires before deviceready does (at least some of the time), so you delegate to PhoneGap's event instead to ensure you don't really start the app until it says you're good to go. (The app being used before is unlikely given it wouldn't occur until the UI is built and the user enters a server address and clicks the button on the dialog, but this is still something you should try to avoid.)

With that, wxPIM is now PhoneGap-ready and is a true mobile app, at least as close as you're going to get without having to deal with Objective-C, Java, and all the *other* stuff that comes with doing true native development!

Summary

In this chapter, you took wxPIM and created a "native" app out of it using the popular PhoneGap tool. You saw how this allows you to have a package specific to a mobile platform like Android or iOS that can be installed like any other application from that platform's app store. You also saw how the APIs that PhoneGap provides can be used to enhance an application running in such a mode and how PhoneGap Build allows you to do builds in the cloud without mucking about with native SDKs and tooling installation.

In the next chapter, you'll see a whole new side of Webix as we developer another whole app that is nothing at all like wxPIM: a game!

The Fun Side of Webix: A Game!

All work and no play makes Jack a dull boy (and a murderer at a snowy resort lodge, as we learned in *The Shining*). With luck, you'll avoid that fate, but the point stands: if you don't stop to smell the roses every now and again, you tend to not have as good a life as you should. This is true for web development and Webix too! (You didn't think I would be able to pull this back to relevance, did you?)

Throughout this book, you've seen Webix through the prism of writing actual useful code and applications. But, nothing says that's all you can do with Webix. No, you can do something more frivolous, something more fun, something like, say, write a game!

Games are a great project for any developer to undertake because they touch on so many different disciplines in programming, from graphics and sound to AI, data structures, algorithmic efficiency, and so on. In my position as a lead architect, I'm sometimes asked by developers how they can sharpen their skills. My answer is always the same: write a game! I don't believe any other project allows the diversity and creativity and, therefore, opportunity for learning.

Plus, by their very nature, games are *fun* to write!

In this chapter, you'll use Webix to write a game. The benefit in terms of this book is that you'll get to see a few new Webix facilities and see others in ways you maybe haven't before. In the end, you'll learn while ideally having fun.

Let's kick things off by figuring out what kind of game to make and coming up with what every great game needs: a story!

© Frank Zammetti 2018
F. Zammetti, *Practical Webix*, https://doi.org/10.1007/978-1-4842-3384-9_10

The Story So Far

The inhabitants of Gorgona 6 are a cosmic contradiction: a technologically advanced civilization that is simultaneously technologically backward! For example, they visited their own moon before figuring out that they should put wheels on luggage and, more importantly for the purposes here, they can build fast, sleek spaceships, but they are pretty wimpy ships that can't survive much of anything! Just a bump into a space rock is enough to do them in (and being a peaceful people, the Gorgonians never develop weapons of any sort).

This is problematic because their star system has a vermin problem: it's lousy with space-born critters and dangers! They have the gargantuan space fish of the third moon of Valtrax; the naturally occurring sentient machine beings of protoplanet 10101110; space zombies (but who *doesn't* have space zombies, amiright?), and your basic rogue asteroids tumbling about. These things gum up the works of the shipping lanes and pleasure cruise trails (though how anyone can derive pleasure from a cruise where your piece of garbage ship could be destroyed at any moment by the slightest impact is yet another contradiction embodied by the Gorgonians).

Fortunately, there is a solution to these problems: on the outskirts of the solar system is an alien crystal that emits an unknown type of energy that kills the space vermin, at least for a little while. The Gorgonians have figured out how to collect this energy, little by little. So, they send out ships that are essentially space tankers (but being Gorgonian ships, they at least *look* cool!) to collect the energy and return it to the home world.

Your job, as one of the brave pilots of the "crystal tanker fleet," is to make your way through the space vermin to extract energy from the crystal and then bring it home. When you collect enough energy, the vermin are destroyed, and you're a Gorgonian hero!

At least for a little while.

You get some points or something for doing this, of course! Let's call 'em *space credits* with which you can maintain your Gorgonian lizard-licking habit.

And that, friends, is how you conceive a simple game that you can code up with web technologies, obviously including Webix. I mean, I'll say up front that if you're expecting *Call of Duty*, *Halo*, or *Destiny* levels of gameplay, then you're going to be sorely disappointed. This ain't gonna be no AAA title, and it's not a game you'll want to be playing over and over again (probably—hey, you *could* wind up loving it I suppose!). But it'll be a good learning experience, which of course is the goal here.

Let's get to it; the vermin need destroying!

The Basic Layout

So, what does this game look like? Well, if you've ever played a game with, say, a frog that hops across lanes of traffic of various types to get to a goal on the other side...well, this game may or may not be conceptually similar to that. To be more precise, Figure 10-1 shows what it looks like.

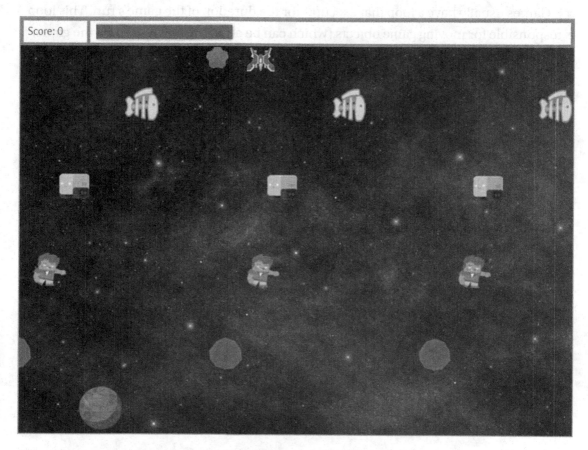

Figure 10-1. *Maybe we should call it Spacershipper?*

Your ship starts at the bottom of the screen, near the home world. You use the cursor keys to move through the lanes of vermin (asteroids, zombies, sentient machines, and space fish, starting from the bottom). When you reach the top, you touch the crystal, and the energy bar at the top fills. Then, you return through the vermin, touch your home world, and the energy is transferred, at which point all the vermin explode, you get some points, and the vermin come back so you can do it all over again. Of course, you explode if you touch anything but the crystal or your home world.

Like I said, it's not exactly a complex, top-tier game, but it *is* a game!

361

Basic Application Architecture

In many respects, this is a simple application to architect. As with most web apps, it starts with an `index.html` file that loads all the resources, including a single CSS file and a number of JavaScript source files. There is a main class, `WXGAME`, which contains the `webix.ready()` call in its constructor, as you've come to expect from a Webix app.

Games usually have a loop that executes for the duration of the game's run. This loop is responsible for moving game objects (which can be anything that makes up the game, like the crystal, planet, player's ship, and vermin in this game), checking for collisions, updating scores, and so on. `WXGAME` is no exception, as you'll see when you get to `main.js`. But, in terms of architecture, the key is the main game loop, so keep that in mind for later.

You also, of course, need some graphics, and there are a number of image files in an `img` directory. The files are named consistently: XX-Y, where XX is the type of graphic (enemy, explosion, planet, player) and Y is the frame number because these objects are animated. So, for example, to show an explosion on the screen, you'll need to show images `explosion-0.png`, `explosion-1.png`, `explosion-2.png`, `explosion-3.png`, and `explosion-4.png` in rapid succession. The one exception are the enemy files, which are actually named XXZ-Y where Z is just a number from 1 to 4 (because there's four types of enemies: space fish, sentient machines, zombies, and asteroids). There's also a static background image, named, unsurprisingly enough, `background.png`.

I'll go through each file, in an order that I think will make sense, but just to give you a bird's-eye view, Figure 10-2 shows the files you'll be looking at.

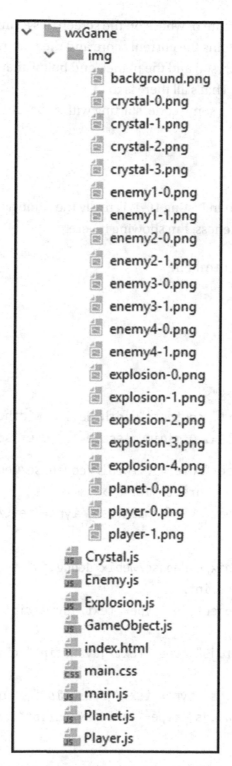

Figure 10-2. *The directory structure and files for this project*

In terms of the architecture of what's on the screen, it's a simple setup: a `toolbar` of content at the top that contains the current score and the energy bar that fills and unfills as the player contacts the crystal and the planet, and below that is the playfield area where the action happens. That's all there is to it!

Now, let's start exploring some code, starting with `index.html`.

index.html

The `index.html` file, shown in Listing 10-1, is really the same as any you've seen before, but for the sake of completeness, I'm showing it here.

Listing 10-1. The index.html File

```
<!DOCTYPE html>

<html>

  <head>

    <meta charset="UTF-8">
    <meta name="viewport" content="width=device-width,height=device-
    height,initial-scale=1.0,minimum-scale=1.0,user-scalable=yes">

    <link rel="stylesheet" href="../webix/codebase/webix.css" type="text/
    css" media="screen" charset="utf-8">
    <link rel="stylesheet" href="main.css" type="text/css" media="screen"
    charset="utf-8">

    <script src="../webix/codebase/webix_debug.js" type="text/javascript"
    charset="utf-8"></script>
    <script src="GameObject.js" type="text/javascript" charset="utf-8"></
    script>
    <script src="Player.js" type="text/javascript" charset="utf-8"></
    script>
    <script src="Enemy.js" type="text/javascript" charset="utf-8"></script>
    <script src="Crystal.js" type="text/javascript" charset="utf-8"></
    script>
```

```
<script src="Planet.js" type="text/javascript" charset="utf-8"></
script>
<script src="Explosion.js" type="text/javascript" charset="utf-8"></
script>
<script src="main.js" type="text/javascript" charset="utf-8"></script>

<title>wxGame</title>

</head>

<body></body>

</html>
```

Really, except for all the JS files aside from main.js being imported, it's exactly the same as before. All the interesting stuff is in the JavaScript files. Before you get to those, though, let's see what's in main.css (hint: not much!).

main.css

The main.css file contains a grand total of one class, as you can see in Listing 10-2.

Listing 10-2. It Doesn't Get Much Simpler Than main.css!

```
.cssPlayfield {
  background-image : url("img/background.png");
  overflow : hidden;
  position : relative;
}
```

As you can probably guess, this class will be applied to the main playfield area to provide the space background. This class also tells you that any overflowing content will be hidden, which is important so that your vermin will smoothly move off one edge of the playfield and can then be brought back from the other side. To put it another way, content will be "clipped" at the edges of the playfield area. Also, as you'll see, all the game objects are positioned absolutely, which means they need to be children of a positioned element. That's the purpose of setting position:relative here.

main.js

The main.js file is where the core code is, including that main game loop I mentioned. I'll walk you through this code in sections to make it more easily digestible, beginning with this bit:

```
"use strict";

class WXGAME {
}
const wxGame = new WXGAME();
```

I'm cheating a little here and showing you the high-level structure of the code. There's obviously a lot more code in this file, but it's all in that WXGAME class. Showing it this way shows that it's a single class and a single instance of that class that you're dealing with.

Now, in terms of the code inside the class, it begins with the constructor.

```
constructor() {

  this.score = 0;

  this.enemies = [ ];
  this.player = null;
  this.crystal = null;
  this.planet = null;

  this.KEY_UP = 38;
  this.KEY_DOWN = 40;
  this.KEY_LEFT = 37;
  this.KEY_RIGHT = 39;

  this.explosionCount = 0;
  this.explosions = { };

  for (let i = 0; i < 360; i = i + 45) {
    this[`CSS_ROTATE_${i}`] = webix.html.createCss({
      "transform" : `rotate(${i}deg)`,
      "-webkit-transform" : `rotate(${i}deg)`,
      "-moz-transform" : `rotate(${i}deg)`,
```

```
    "-o-transform" : `rotate(${i}deg)`,
    "-ms-transform" : `rotate(${i}deg)`
  });
}

webix.ready(this.start.bind(this));

}
```

First up, you have a member to record the player's score. After that are four members that are references to the game objects: all the enemies on the screen, the player's ship, the crystal, and the planet. Whenever you write a game, two things you need to keep in mind are optimization and performance. One thing this means, especially in JavaScript, is to cache references to things you'll frequently be accessing, especially in the main game loop, so you don't need to incur the overhead of a lookup every time. That's the reason for these members.

After those are four pseudoconstants (since there's no real constants in JavaScript) that store the key codes associated with the up, down, left, and right arrow keys. You'll need them when you handle keypress events to determine what to do.

Next up are two variables for dealing with explosions. At any point in time, there could be multiple explosions on the screen (when you return all the energy to the planet, all the vermin explode, for example), and that means you'll need to keep track of how many there are, which is why you need `explosionCount`. The `explosions` object will store a reference to each of those explosions as they occur. (Remember, an explosion is a sequence of animation frames, and it takes time to cycle through those frames, and then there is work to do when each completes, as you'll see.)

Next up, you see something new from Webix land: the `webix.html.createCss()` method. This method allows you to create a new CSS class, which will be inserted into the DOM and which you can then apply to DOM nodes. In this case, the image of the player's ship always faces up, but when they are moving, you need it to point in different directions, 45 degrees apart (up, down, left, right, up+left, up+right, down+left, and down+right). So, you'll use CSS to rotate the static image, and for each possible rotation direction, you'll create a CSS class to apply. That's what's happening here. The `transform` CSS style allows you to perform all sorts of various transformations on an object, `rotate` being just one of them. The interesting thing about `webix.html.createCss()`, though, is that you don't specify the name of the CSS class. Webix controls that (though, critically, it does return it from the call). But, of course, in order to apply this class, you need to know that name. So, you'll record that name as a member of a CSS_ROTATE_X member on the wxGame instance, where X is the rotation degrees. So, when you want to rotate the ship so that it points to the right when the player moves it right, you will apply the class name stored in wxGame["CSS_ROTATE_90"] (since that's a 90-degree rotation from its static image pointing upward).

Finally, you have the familiar webix.ready() call, which fires wxGame.start():

```
start() {

  webix.ui({
    type : "clean",
    cols : [
      { },
      { width : 800, type : "clean",
        rows : [
          { },
          { type : "clean", height : 600,
            rows : [
              { view : "toolbar", id : "header", height : 40,
                elements : [
                  { id : "score", width : 90, view : template", template :
                  "Score: 0000" },
                  { view : "chart", type : "barH", padding : 5,
                    value : "#count#", id : "energyBar", color : "green",
                    xAxis : {
                      start : 0, end : 100, step : 1, lines : false,
                      color : "#ffffff"
                    },
                    data : [ { id  : "energy", count : 0 } ]
                  }
                ]
              },
              { id : "playfield", css : "cssPlayfield" }
            ]
          },
          { }
```

```
      ]
    },
    { }
  ]
});

this.playfield = $$("playfield").$view;

for (let y = 0; y < 4; y++) {
  for (let x = 0; x < 3; x++) {
    this.enemies.push(new Enemy({
      type : y + 1, x : x, y : y, playfield : this.playfield
    }));
  }
}

this.player = new Player({ playfield : this.playfield });
this.crystal = new Crystal({ playfield : this.playfield });
this.planet = new Planet({ playfield : this.playfield });

this.player.animate = webix.wrap(this.player.animate, this.
transferEnergy.bind(this));

document.onkeydown = this.keyHandler.bind(this);
document.onkeyup = this.keyHandler.bind(this);

setInterval(this.run.bind(this), 100);

}
```

First, the basic screen structure is built. Here, you're just using the basics of Webix that by now you've come to know (and, I'd bet, love!). To make life simpler (trying to make the game responsive to the screen size is a much more difficult endeavor), I've decided on an 800×600 viewport in which to make the game. So in essence, you have a columnar layout with three columns and two spacers flanking an 800-pixel wide area. Inside that center area goes three rows: a spacer, the top bar where the score and energy bar go, and then the main play area with a height of 600. That first spacer is needed to push it all down, so you wind up with the viewport centered on the page.

The top bar is a Webix `toolbar` with two elements: a simple text area (via a Webix `ui.template` component) for the score and a horizontal bar chart for the energy bar. The data for the bar chart is a single series with an ID of energy, which is relevant because you'll need that in order to update the value of the chart later.

You'll note that the playfield area doesn't have any content, just an ID and the `cssPlayfield` style class applied to provide the background and overflow clipping. That's as it should be. Everything that shows up there will be drawn separately by the game code.

After the construction of the layout, you have some more work to do. First, a reference to the playfield is retrieved. To be more specific, the DOM node that encapsulates the playfield is retrieved, which you can get for most any Webix component via its `$view` property. This is done for speed; you'll need this reference a lot throughout the code, and you don't want to have to look it up each time with `$$()`.

Next, it's time to create some enemy vermin! Looking back at Figure 10-1, you can see that there are four rows of them with three vermin in each. So, there are two loops: the y loop for the rows and the x loop for the vermin in each row. For every enemy, an instance of the `Enemy` class is created and is added to the `enemies` array on the `wxGame` instance. Each enemy is of a specific `type`, numbered 1 through 4, which just so happens to be what the y loop is when you add 1 to it. The x and y config values are not x and y on the screen but x and y in terms of which row (y) and enemy on that row (x) each is. These will be used to construct a unique ID for each enemy, as you'll see shortly. To create an enemy and put them on the screen, a reference to the `playfield` is required, so that is passed in to the `Enemy` constructor as well.

After that, you need to create the other game objects, namely, the player, crystal, and planet. You'll get into the game objects themselves in the next section, but for now it's enough to know that each is an object that encapsulates things like the animations frames each needs, the logic behind flipping between them, and things such as moving, showing, and hiding the objects.

After that comes a new Webix facility, the `webix.wrap()` function. What this does is allow you to "wrap" a function and have another execute before it does. In other words, it intercepts the execution of the target function. In this case, for reasons that will become clear later, I need to execute some additional code whenever the `animate()` method of the `player` object is called. I didn't want to put the logic in that function because that function is actually part of a common base class that `Player` extends from. While I certainly could have overridden `animate()` in the `Player` class, in good object-oriented form, taking care to call `animate()` on the superclass too, of course, that wouldn't have given me an opportunity to show you `webix.wrap()`, would it? This probably isn't the best way to do it (overriding `animate()` arguably is), but this works and is a good demonstration of `webix.wrap()`, which just requires you to pass a reference to the function to wrap, and the function to wrap it with, in that order. The `transferEnergy()` function, as its name implies, is used to transfer energy to and from the ship (and, at the risk of sounding like a broken record: as you'll see later).

Next, you need some event handlers for key up and key down events, and `keyHandler()` is that handler. I call `bind()` on it to ensure the `this` reference in it points to the `wxGame` instance.

Finally, it's time to kick off that main game loop I mentioned earlier, and `setInterval()` does that. I decided on 100ms as the interval here because in my testing, most modern machines with a modern browser can handle that speed without issue. Note that there are more complex methods to deal with the situation when it can't, called *time-based animation*, but that's beyond the scope of this book and for a simple example like this isn't really necessary. The `run()` method is the main game loop (which I also `bind()` to the `wxGame` instance), and that's the next stop.

Over and Over Again: run()

The main game loop is actually quite simple, as you can see here. Note that most of the functions called here will be examined after this, but I think the names are pretty clear, and you shouldn't, I expect, have any difficulty understanding this code conceptually even if you don't know all the details beyond the functions it calls just yet.

```
run() {

  this.player.move();

  this.player.animate();
  this.crystal.animate();

  for (let e in this.explosions) {
    if (this.explosions.hasOwnProperty(e)) {
      this.explosions[e].animate(this.explosions);
    }
  }
```

```
for (let i = 0; i < this.enemies.length; i++) {
  this.enemies[i].animate();
  this.enemies[i].move(this.playfield);
  if (wxGame.collision(this.enemies[i])) {
    this.explosions[`e${this.explosionCount}`] = new Explosion({
      playfield : this.playfield, explosionNumber : this.
      explosionCount++,
      x : this.player.xLoc - 10, y : this.player.yLoc - 5
    });
    this.adjustScore(-50);
    this.player.energy = 0;
    $$("energyBar").updateItem("energy", { count : 0 });
    this.player.hide();
    this.player.toStartingPosition();
  }
}

this.player.touchingCrystal = wxGame.collision(this.crystal);
this.player.touchingPlanet = wxGame.collision(this.planet);

}
```

A few tasks need to be accomplished with each 100ms iteration of this method, beginning with moving the player. As you'll see next, the keyHandler() method doesn't actually move the player in response to keypresses; it only sets flags to tell us which way to move it. The move() method of the player is what looks at those flags and actually moves the player, but that's coming a bit later.

The crystal and player game objects are animated, but that doesn't happen by itself; you have to write code for that, and that code is inside the animate() method of those objects, so they get called next.

The same is true for the enemies, which is where that enemies array comes into play as it gives us an easy way to loop through the enemies and animate them. Enemies also have to move, of course, so their move() method is also called.

Next, things get a little more complicated because any time the player collides with an enemy, an explosion needs to occur. So, the wxGame.collision() method is called to determine when a collision occurs. Since collisions can only occur between a player and an enemy, you only have to pass a reference to each enemy to check the player against. When this function returns true, then an Explosion game object needs to be created. There can be more than one explosion on the screen at once (not because the player can collide with more than one enemy—it can't because of the spacing between the enemies—but when the player brings energy back to the planet, all of the enemies explode simultaneously). So, the explosionCount member is used to number each explosion (and used to generate a unique ID for each). The explosion's location needs to be offset a little from the player's coordinates (the actual screen coordinates, that is, which the xLoc and yLoc attributes of the player tells you) because of the geometry of the graphics used. There's no magic here; it's just trial and error to get it to look like it's centered on the player! Unlike the enemies, x and y in this case do mean real screen location (which means left and top style attributes correspondingly since all these game objects are just img elements, as you'll see later).

In addition to exploding, the player needs to lose a few points too, so a call to the adjustScore() method does that, which accepts a positive number to increase the score or a negative number to decrease it. Also, any energy the ship is carrying should be cleared out, so player.energy is set to zero. This also means that the energy bar needs to be emptied immediately, so its value is set to zero. To update the chart, you need to alter its data, which is where the updateItem() method comes in. This takes an ID and a hash of values to set and updates a specific data item in the collection of data items the chart is rendering. Since you have only a single series in this chart, though, you have only a single data item, and it's the one with an ID of energy, and its count property is the property that the chart uses to render itself, so it's a pretty obvious call. One last thing needs to happen, which is that the player must be hidden until the explosion animation cycle completes, plus the player needs to be returned to its starting position. The hide() method takes care of the first part, and the aptly named toStartingPosition() takes care of the second.

Two more tasks need to be accomplished with each game loop iteration, and that's to see whether the player is touching the crystal or the planet. The same sort of call to collision() as was done to check for collisions with the vermin is done, and a flag is set on the player for either condition, which will be used in some other code later.

Up and Down: keyHandler()

As you saw earlier, the keyHandler() method is bound to both the key up and key down events, and that code is as follows:

```
keyHandler(inEvent, inKeyDown) {

  const evt = (inEvent) ? inEvent : (window.event) ? window.event : null;
  const keyCode = (evt.charCode) ? evt.charCode:
    ((evt.keyCode) ? evt.keyCode : ((evt.which) ? evt.which : null));

  switch (keyCode) {
    case this.KEY_UP: this.player.dirUp = inKeyDown; break;
    case this.KEY_DOWN: this.player.dirDown = inKeyDown; break;
    case this.KEY_LEFT: this.player.dirLeft = inKeyDown; break;
    case this.KEY_RIGHT: this.player.dirRight = inKeyDown; break;
  }

}
```

The first line ensures that you have an event object because not all browser types pass one in to the handler; some require the handler to get it from the window object. The second line then uses that object to determine the key code of the key that was pressed or released. These two lines are relatively standard and nothing Webix-specific.

The switch statement then looks to see whether the key code is one of the four defined in the constructor corresponding to the four cursor keys. For any match, one of the dirXX flags on the player instance is set. As previously mentioned, these flags will be used in the player's move() method, which you just saw is called from run().

When Worlds Collide: collision()

Most video games, including this one, require the ability to detect when two images (two game objects) run into each other. For instance, you need to know when your player's ship hits one of the enemy vermin. There are numerous collision detection algorithms, but many of them are not available to you in a browser setting because they require access to pixel-level data. For instance, checking each pixel of one image against each pixel of another, while giving 100 percent accurate detection, isn't possible in a browser (at least not without using the canvas element).

374

Instead, a simpler method is available to you than what is used here: bounding boxes. This is a simple method that basically just checks the four bounds of the objects. If the corner of one object is within the bounds of the other, a collision has occurred.

As illustrated in the example in Figure 10-3, each game object has a square (or rectangular) area around it, called its *bounding box*, which defines the boundaries of the area the object occupies. Note in the diagram how the upper-left corner of object 1's bounding box is within the bounding box of object 2. This represents a collision. You can detect a collision by running through a series of simple tests comparing the bounds of each object. If any of the conditions are untrue, then a collision cannot possibly have occurred. For instance, if the bottom of object 1 is above the top of object 2, there's no way a collision could have occurred. In fact, since you're dealing with a square or rectangular object, you have only four conditions to check, any one of which being false precludes the possibility of a collision.

This algorithm does not yield perfect results. For example, in this game, you will sometimes see the ship "hitting" an object when they clearly did not touch (most obvious with the asteroids). This is because the bounding boxes can collide without the object itself actually colliding because the graphics aren't all themselves perfect squares or rectangles. This could only be fixed with pixel-level detection, which, again, is not available to you. However, the bounding boxes approach gives an approximation that yields "good enough" results in many cases, including this one, so all is right with the world.

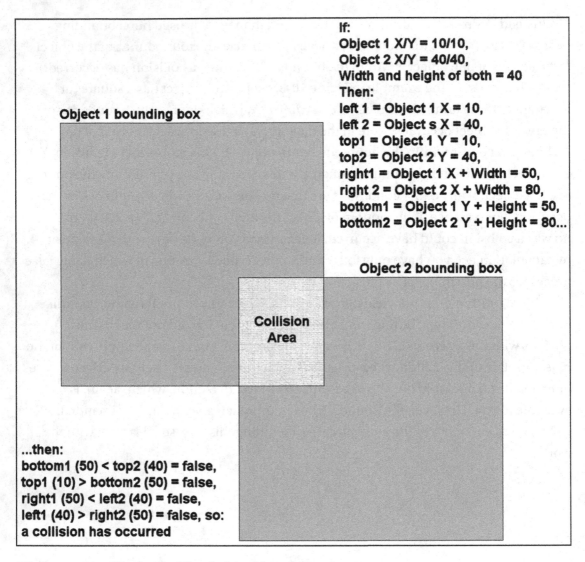

If:
Object 1 X/Y = 10/10,
Object 2 X/Y = 40/40,
Width and height of both = 40
Then:
left 1 = Object 1 X = 10,
left 2 = Object s X = 40,
top1 = Object 1 Y = 10,
top2 = Object 2 Y = 40,
right1 = Object 1 X + Width = 50,
right 2 = Object 2 X + Width = 80,
bottom1 = Object 1 Y + Height = 50,
bottom2 = Object 2 Y + Height = 80...

Object 1 bounding box

Object 2 bounding box

Collision
Area

...then:
bottom1 (50) < top2 (40) = false,
top1 (10) > bottom2 (50) = false,
right1 (50) < left2 (40) = false,
left1 (40) > right2 (50) = false, so:
a collision has occurred

Figure 10-3. *The basic idea behind bounding boxes*

The actual code behind the collision() therefore becomes pretty straightforward.

```
collision(inObject) {

  if (!this.player.isVisible || !inObject.isVisible) { return false; }

  const left1 = this.player.xLoc;
  const left2 = inObject.xLoc;
  const right1 = left1 + this.player.pixWidth;
  const right2 = left2 + inObject.pixWidth;
```

```
const top1 = this.player.yLoc;
const top2 = inObject.yLoc;
const bottom1 = top1 + this.player.pixHeight;
const bottom2 = top2 + inObject.pixHeight;

if (bottom1 < top2) {
  return false;
}
if (top1 > bottom2) {
  return false;
}
if (right1 < left2) {
  return false;
}
return left1 <= right2;

}
```

If the player isn't visible, as determined by examining its isVisible attribute, or if the player isn't visible, then there's no need to check for a collision because game objects are only ever not visible when they're exploding. After that, you get the values to be compared, which means the coordinates of the top, bottom, left, and right bounds of the player and the test object. Finally, it's just the four simple checks described to tell you if a collision has occurred.

To and From: transferEnergy()

Transferring energy from crystal to ship, or from ship to planet, occurs every time the animation frame of the player changes. Or, more precisely, it *can* occur because whether it *does* occur or not depends on whether the ship is in contact with either object (and whether there's energy to transfer, of course). As you'll recall, the animate() method of the player object is called with every tick of the main game loop, which is the run() method, and since the webix.wrap() method was used to intercept the call to animate(), that means transferEnergy() will also be called with each game loop iteration.

```
transferEnergy() {

  if (this.player.touchingCrystal && this.player.energy < 100) {
    this.player.energy = this.player.energy + 5;
    $$("energyBar").updateItem("energy", { count : this.player.energy });
    if (this.player.energy === 100) {
      while (this.crystal.randomlyPosition()) { this.crystal.
      randomlyPosition(); }
    }
  } else if (this.player.touchingPlanet && this.player.energy > 0) {
    this.player.energy = this.player.energy - 5;
    $$("energyBar").updateItem("energy", { count : this.player.energy });
    if (this.player.energy === 0) {
      while (this.planet.randomlyPosition()) { this.planet.
      randomlyPosition(); }
      this.blowUpAllEnemies();
      this.adjustScore(100);
      $$("energyBar").updateItem("energy", { count : 0 });
    }
  }

}
```

The first branch of the if statement covers the case when the player is touching
the crystal, as the player.touchingCrystal flag denotes. It also accounts for when the
player touches the crystal even though their energy is full, in which case you skip the
work here too. If both conditions are met, though, then with each tick of the game loop
you add 5 to the player's energy stores, and you also set the value on the bar chart to the
player's current energy value, which causes it to fill up. When the energy reaches 100,
then the crystal is randomly repositioned. Why the while loop, you ask? That's because
each call to crystal.randomlyPosition() could result in the crystal being positioned
still in contact with the ship. You don't want that. So, the while loop will keep calling
crystal.randomlyPosition() until it returns false, which means the crystal is not in
contact with the ship.

The second if branch is for when the player is touching the planet. There, the
player's energy is reduced by 5 each iteration, and when it hits zero, it's the planet this
time that needs to be repositioned. Then, all the enemies need to explode, which is what

blowUpAllEnemies() does. The player has to score some points here, so adjustScore() is called. Finally, the energy bar has to be cleared again, so its value is set to zero, as previously described.

Making It Worth It: adjustScore()

The adjustScore() method you've seen called a few times now, and it's just about as simple as you've probably imagined it was.

```
adjustScore(inAmount) {

  this.score = this.score + inAmount;
  if (this.score < 0) {
    this.score = 0;
  }
  $$("score").setHTML(`Score: ${this.score}`);

}
```

In fact, the only interesting bit here is the use of setHTML(), which is a method of the ui.template component that allows you to set any arbitrary HTML in the component you want.

Winning: blowUpAllEnemies()

One final method is present in main.js, and that's the method called when the player returns all the energy to the planet and that blows up all the enemies.

```
blowUpAllEnemies() {

  for (let i = 0; i < this.enemies.length; i++) {
    const enemy = this.enemies[i];
    enemy.hide();
    enemy.moveTo(enemy.startingX, enemy.startingY);
    this.explosions[`e${this.explosionCount}`] = new Explosion({
```

```
      playfield : this.playfield, explosionNumber : this.explosionCount++,
      x : enemy.xLoc, y : enemy.yLoc
    });
  }

  webix.delay(function() {
    for (let i = 0; i < this.enemies.length; i++) { this.enemies[i].show();
}
  }, this, [ ], 1000);

}
```

This works a lot like how the explosion is created when the player collides with an enemy, but here you need one explosion per vermin. Each is positioned according to the location of the vermin (and it doesn't really need those adjustments like was done for the player explosion because the geometry of the graphics lines up pretty well without it). Every enemy is hidden before its corresponding explosion is created, and it is also moved back to its original starting position via the call to its moveTo(), passing it the startingX and startingY members attached to each enemy (which are populated when the enemy is created, as you'll see shortly).

Now, that's great for blowing up the vermin, but the game has to continue after that, which means they need to be shown again. How do you do that? Well, in the interest of showing you another new Webix function, I've gone with usage of the webix.delay() function. This works a lot like the JavaScript-standard setTimeout() function, but with some additional features. First, this function takes the code you want to execute, which here is simply an iteration over the array of enemies, calling show() on each. The second argument is what scope that code should execute in, meaning what the this keyword points to when it executes. The third argument is an array of arguments to pass to the code, which is just an empty array here since you don't need to pass any. Finally, the last argument tells webix.delay() how long to wait until calling the code, in milliseconds. Since there are five frames of animation for an explosion and since each frame takes 100 milliseconds (because that's how long there is between main game loop ticks, and the frames are flipped from there), that means you have to wait at least 500 milliseconds before showing the vermin again. I doubled that for good measure, so 1,000 milliseconds, or one second, is it.

Object Orientation for Fun and Profit: The Game Object Hierarchy

By this point, you've examined the core game code, but that's only part of the equation. Throughout, you've seen reference to the various game objects, namely, crystal, explosion, planet, player, and enemy. Next, you'll look at those classes, beginning the hierarchy they are built from, shown in Figure 10-4.

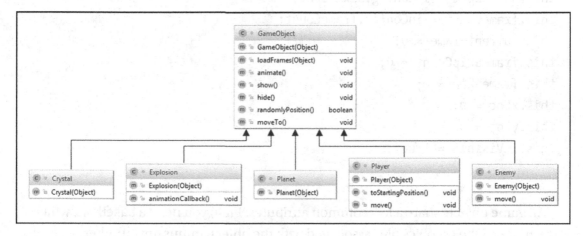

Figure 10-4. *The object hierarchy of game objects*

The five game objects are each represented by a class, and each of them extends from a common base GameObject class. This structure allows you to push as much of the common code that each object shares into that base class. It's always good to not repeat yourself, right? So, let's begin by looking at the GameObject class in detail and start to see the code behind the functions that you saw called upon from the core code.

GameObject.js

As with the WXGAME class in main.js, GameObject.js defines a class named GameObject, so it begins the same.

```
class GameObject {
}
```

However, in this case, there is no instantiation of a single instance like with WXGAME because this is a base class that all the other game objects extend from, not something that is instantiated on its own. As with most classes, this one opens with a constructor.

```
constructor(inConfig) {

  this.baseName = inConfig.baseName;
  this.pixWidth = inConfig.pixWidth;
  this.pixHeight = inConfig.pixHeight;
  this.frameCount = inConfig.frameCount;
  this.currentFrame = 0;
  this.frameSkipCount = 0;
  this.frameSkip = 0;
  this.xLoc = 0;
  this.yLoc = 0;
  this.isVisible = true;

}
```

All game objects share a few common attributes. First, you need a baseName, which is the name of the graphics files associated with the object, minus any numbers (i.e., just crystal, not crystal-1 and crystal-2 like the image files are named). Next, the object needs to know its width and height, and that's what pixWidth and pixHeight are for. Then, since all game objects, except for the planet, are animated, the code will need to know how many frames of animation there are, and frameCount denotes that. All of these are passed into the constructor via the inConfig object.

After those, you have some attributes that are the same for all game objects, at least to start, and so aren't passed in. The currentFrameCount is used internally to keep track of what animation frame is visible. The frameSkipCount and frameSkip attributes are used to slow the animation down. If you changed frames with every game loop tick, every 100ms in other words, the animations would look kind of manic! You'll see how these are used later, but that's their purpose. Finally, isVisible obviously tells you whether the object is currently visible and all objects start out visible by default.

Pixar Would Be Proud: loadFrames()

After the constructor, there needs to be a method that can load all the frames of animation for a given object. That's exactly what loadFrames() is for.

```
loadFrames(inConfig) {

  for (let i = 0; i < this.frameCount; i++) {
    const id = `${this.baseName}${inConfig.n}${i}`;
    const img = webix.html.create("img",
      { id : id, src : `img/${this.baseName}-${i}.png`,
        width : this.pixWidth, height : this.pixHeight
      }
    );
    img.style.position = "absolute";
    img.style.left = `${inConfig.x}px`;
    this.xLoc = inConfig.x;
    img.style.top = `${inConfig.y}px`;
    this.yLoc = inConfig.y;
    if (inConfig.hidden) {
      img.style.display = "none";
    }
    if (inConfig.z) {
      img.style.zIndex = inConfig.z;
    }
    webix.html.insertBefore(img, null, inConfig.playfield);
    this[`frame${i}`] = webix.toNode(id);
  }

}
```

As you saw, frameCount tells you how many frames there are, so the code loops with that value. Each animation frame winds up being a separate DOM node, and since you need to be able to access each, that means each must have a unique id, so the id value is constructed using the baseName and the loop count at the end. There's also an inConfig.n value that is optional and is inserted even before the frame number. This is specifically for explosions since there can be more than one of those at a time, so each needs to have an extra value in the id, and that's where inConfig.n comes into play.

So, for example, the player will wind up with two nodes, one with an id of player1 and the other player2, and an explosion will have an ID of explosion11, exposion12, and so on.

Speaking of creating a DOM node, that's exactly the next step! The webix.html.create() function lets you do that easily. The first argument is the type of element to create, an <img> element in the case of game objects. As you can see, that previously described unique id is included in the second argument, which is an object containing all the attributes associated with the element. These are any attributes that an <img> take can take, so src is one that is clearly necessary! The baseName again comes into play here to construct that src attribute value (so img/player-1.png, for example).

Once the element is created, you can set some style attributes on it. (Yes, you could do this by specifying a style attribute in the second argument to webix.html.create(), but that means building a string, and I find this style of coding it cleaner.) The element is positioned absolutely, and its left and top attributes are set using the inConfig.x and inConfig.y values passed in. You also store those as xLoc and yLoc for easier access later (which saves you from having to access DOM node attributes, so it's a little faster this way). The game object could be hidden initially via the inConfig.hidden attribute, and if so, then display is set to none. There's also a concern with z-index in that the player should always be on top, even if it's not created last (which it can't be because some other code depends on it having been created earlier). It's only a concern for the player, but being able to pass inConfig.z to set zIndex lets you deal with it consistently in all cases.

Next, you have two new Webix functions. First, all you've done so far is create an <img> element in memory. It's not actually on the screen at this point. In fact, it's not even in the DOM yet. So, you need to insert it into the DOM, and that's where webix.html.insertBefore() comes into play. You pass this function the object to insert, then a reference to the DOM node to insert the new one before (its "sibling," so to speak), and then a parent node if the sibling doesn't exist. In this case, you just want to append the element to the playfield node, which is passed in as inConfig.playfield, and not actually before any other element, so that's why null is the second argument. The third kicks in, and you get an append, as the last child, of the playfield node.

Finally, you need to have a reference to every <img> element created for each animation frame. While you could have gotten that reference from the call to webix.html.create(), since it returns the reference to the new node, I instead decided to use webix.toNode() to show you something new. This function allows you to get a reference to any DOM node by ID. Here, the reference is stored as an attribute of the game object instance, with each frame being a new attribute named frameX, where X is the frame number. That will allow later code to access these DOM nodes quickly and easily. In fact, the next thing you're going to look at makes use of that!

Make It Move: animate()

Animating a game object is fairly simple and, as you know, is triggered by a call to each object's animate() method from the run() method.

```
animate(inCollection) {

  if (!this.isVisible) { return; }

  this.frameSkipCount++;
  if (this.frameSkipCount < this.frameSkip) {
    return;
  }
  this.frameSkipCount = 0;

  this[`frame${this.currentFrame}`].style.display = "none";
  this.currentFrame++;
  if (this.currentFrame === this.frameCount) {
    this.currentFrame = 0;
    if (this.animationCallback) {
      this.animationCallback(inCollection);
    }
  }
  this[`frame${this.currentFrame}`].style.display = "";

}
```

First, you abort if the object isn't currently visible because why do the work of animating it if it can't be seen? If that check is passed, then the frameSkipCount member is increased, and until it equals the frameSkip value, no animation is done. This means that a certain number of main game loop ticks can be skipped before an object's animation frame is changed, effectively slowing the animation.

Once it's time to animate, the first thing to do is to hide the current frame. Remember that each frame is a separate DOM node, so only one can be showing at any given time for a given game object. The attribute name is formed using the currentFrame value, and from there it's a simple matter of setting its display style attribute to none.

Next, currentFrame is bumped up. When it equals frameCount, then it's time to restart the animation cycle. There's also the opportunity for some code to be executed when the animation cycle completes via a callback attribute of the game object that can optionally be set. This is specifically for explosions, as you'll see later. When the callback function is called, it is passed the inCollection argument that is passed to animate(), which is only ever done for explosions and is the collection of all explosions (and again, why that is will become apparent when you look at the Explosion class).

Finally, the new animation frame is shown by getting a reference to it through those frameX attributes I described earlier. Setting the style attribute to an empty string, which is the default for that attribute, makes it visible.

Yes, I See You: show()

There is also a show() method on every game object, and it's simple.

```
show() {

  for (let i = 0; i < this.frameCount; i++) {
    this[`frame${i}`].style.display = "";
  }
  this.isVisible = true;

}
```

It's just a matter of setting the style attribute of each animation frame <img> node to an empty string and of course marking the object as visible too.

Playing Hide (But Not Seek?): hide()

Where there's a show() method, there's likely to be a hide() method, and you won't be disappointed to know that there in fact is!

```
hide() {

  for (let i = 0; i < this.frameCount; i++) {
    this[`frame${i}`].style.display = "none";
  }
  this.isVisible = false;

}
```

I'm gonna go out on a limb here and say that doesn't need an explanation.

A Little Randomness in Your Day: randomlyPosition()

The crystal and the planet get randomly positioned at the start of the game, and when energy transfer is complete to and from them, that's where the randomlyPosition() method comes in.

```
randomlyPosition() {

  const min = Math.ceil(70);
  const max = Math.floor(730);
  this.xLoc = Math.floor(Math.random() * (max - min + 1)) + min;

  for (let i = 0; i < this.frameCount; i++) {
    this[`frame${i}`].style.display = "none";
    this[`frame${i}`].style.left = `${this.xLoc}px`;
  }

  const didCollide =  wxGame.collision(this);
  if (!didCollide) {
    for (let i = 0; i < this.frameCount; i++) {
      this[`frame${i}`].style.display = "";
    }
  }

  return didCollide;

}
```

First, a random number between 70 and 730 (inclusive) is chosen. These values result in the object never going off either edge of the playfield area. Once you have a location, every animation frame is hidden and then moved to the new location. Only the left style attribute needs to be changed since this is only randomizing the horizontal location; the vertical location never changes.

Once that's done, you need to see whether the object now collides with the player. If not, then animation frames are all shown (which doesn't matter for the planet since there's only one frame, and for the crystal this will be undone with the next game loop tick and only a single frame shown). The collision result is returned so that those while loops you saw earlier can kick in and randomlyPosition() will be called again (and again, and again, and…) until a noncollision location is determined. This isn't the most efficient way to go about doing this, but it's pretty simple and does the job well enough.

Go Where I Tell You: moveTo()

The final common function that all game objects should provide is being able to move them to a specific location on the screen directly, which is what moveTo() is for.

```
moveTo(inX, inY) {

  for (let i = 0; i < this.frameCount; i++) {
    this[`frame${i}`].style.left = `${inX}px`;
    this[`frame${i}`].style.top = `${inY}px`;
  }

}
```

This simply takes in X and Y values, which are set as the left and top style attributes, respectively, of every animation frame for the object. Its visibility isn't impacted, there are no worries about collision, and it's just an immediate move. This is primarily present for the enemies, as you'll see soon.

That done, your look at the GameObject class is concluded. Now let's move on to some specific game objects, starting with the Crystal class.

Crystal.js

The Crystal class is one of the simpler game object classes, but it's a good starting point because the others are not much more complex and, except for the Enemy class, look pretty similar to start.

```
"use strict";

class Crystal extends GameObject {

  constructor(inConfig) {

    super((function() {
      return webix.extend(inConfig,
        { pixWidth : 32, pixHeight : 30, frameCount : 4, baseName :
        "crystal" }
      );
    }()));

    super.loadFrames({
      x : 0, y : 2, playfield : inConfig.playfield, hidden : true
    });

    this.randomlyPosition();

  }

}
```

The constructor starts with a call to the constructor of the superclass, GameObject. The trick here is that the inConfig object that's passed into the constructor needs to have some additional information added to it specific to this game object. Of course, that's a problem because the super() call must be the first thing in the constructor of a JavaScript class. So, to deal with that, I've used the immediately invoked function pattern here. That is, an anonymous function is created and then immediately called, and the return value from this function becomes the argument passed to super(). What this anonymous function does is take inConfig and extend it using the webix.extend() function. This takes a target object as the first argument, so inConfig, and then "extends" it by taking all the attributes of a second object and adding them to the target. The return value is the target object but now including all the attributes of the second (which here is just an object defined inline containing `pixWidth`, `pixHeight`, `frameCount`, and `baseName`). If you look back on `main.js`, you'll see that for all game objects, `inConfig` contains `playfield`, while enemies also include a `type` and `x` and `y` attributes, which is why this is all done.

After the `super()` call, the `loadFrames()` method that you saw in the base class is then called. That gets all the animation frames loaded up, inserted into the DOM, and references stored on the object being constructed here.

Finally, in the case of the crystal, it needs to be randomly positioned. Note here that there's no need to care about collision checks because the crystal would never collide with the player at this point. At this point, the `Crystal` instance is fully constructed. There's no more code in this class because the base `GameObject` class includes any additional functionality it needs.

Note that for the remainder of the game object source files, I'll just be showing the methods each contains. I'll skip the `"use strict"` and opening `class XXX extends GameObject` line for brevity. But rest assured, they are indeed there!

Planet.js

Let's look at the `Planet` class next since like the `Crystal` class, it is quite simple.

```
constructor(inConfig) {

  super((function() {
    return webix.extend(inConfig,
      { pixWidth : 64, pixHeight : 64, frameCount : 1, baseName : "planet"
}
  );
}()));

  super.loadFrames({
    x : 0, y : 492, playfield : inConfig.playfield, hidden : true
  });

  while (this.randomlyPosition()) { this.randomlyPosition(); }

}
```

Yep, it's almost identical to the Crystal class except for one detail. The randomlyPosition() method is wrapped in a while loop so that it can be retried until a position is chosen that doesn't collide with the player. This also means that the player *must* have been *created* before the planet is; otherwise, the call to collision() in randomlyPosition() will fail. As with the Crystal class, there's no more code beyond this as GameObject handles everything else.

Explosion.js

The Explosion class is next, and it starts off very much like Crystal and Planet do.

```
constructor(inConfig) {

  super((function() {
    return webix.extend(inConfig,
      { pixWidth : 50, pixHeight : 50, frameCount : 5, baseName :
      "explosion" }
    );
  }()));

  this.explosionNumber = inConfig.explosionNumber;

  super.loadFrames({
    x  : inConfig.x, y : inConfig.y, n : inConfig.explosionNumber,
    playfield : inConfig.playfield, hidden : true
  });

}
```

One difference here is that each explosion is given a number, which is used to create the unique id of the DOM node, as you saw in loadFrames(). The number is attached to the Explosion instance being constructed, and it is also passed to loadFrames() as the n attribute. In addition, an explosion is initially hidden.

Finally, you have a game object class with some additional functionality! Recall earlier that when the explosion's animation cycle concludes, a callback function is called. Now it's time to see what happens in that function.

```
animationCallback(inCollection) {

  for (let i = 0; i < this.frameCount; i++) {
    const id = `explosion${this.explosionNumber}${i}`;
    webix.html.remove(webix.toNode(id));
  }

  delete inCollection[`e${this.explosionNumber}`];

  if (!wxGame.player.isVisible) {
    wxGame.player.show();
  }

}
```

As it happens, not all that much! First, explosions aren't like the crystal or player or even the enemies in that they are shown and then aren't needed anymore; they don't need to hang around. So, you have to clean up the DOM nodes for each of the `<img>` tags associated with each animation frame. The `webix.html.remove()` function is used for that. You hand it a reference to a DOM node, which you get with the previously shown `webix.toNode()` function, and remove it. That's all well and good. It cleans up the DOM nicely, but you still have a game object hanging around. To avoid leaking memory, that is removed from the `wxGame` instance, which is where that `inCollection` being passed as an argument comes into play. That's an object where a reference to each explosion is stored, so it's a simple matter of deleting the attribute from that object associated with the constructed attribute name for this explosion (e1, e2, e3, etc., depending on however many explosions there are).

One final task is needed: showing the player if they are currently hidden. This occurs only when the explosion is shown as a result of the player running into an enemy, but it does no harm when the explosion is the result of all enemies exploding.

Enemy.js

The Enemy class is the first you hit that is a bit more complex, and that's because there's more logic involved in creating them and positioning them. That work all happens in the constructor.

```
constructor(inConfig) {

  super((function() {
    return webix.extend(inConfig,
      { pixWidth : 48, pixHeight : 48, frameCount : 2 }
    );
  }()));

  const x = inConfig.x;
  const y = inConfig.y;
  const type = inConfig.type;
  for (let i = 0; i < this.frameCount; i++) {

    const id = `enemy${x}${y}${i}`;
    const img = webix.html.create("img",
      { id : id, src : `img/enemy${type}-${i}.png`,
        width : this.pixWidth, height : this.pixHeight
      }
    );
    img.style.position = "absolute";
    img.style.display = "none";
    this.moveDirection = "right";

    if (type % 2 === 0) {
      this.moveDirection = "left";
      this.frameSkip = 2;
    }
    let leftAdjust = 0;

    if (type === 1) { leftAdjust = 0; this.moveSpeed = 10; }
    if (type === 2) { leftAdjust = 80; this.moveSpeed = 6; }
    if (type === 3) { leftAdjust = 120; this.moveSpeed = 14; }
    if (type === 4) { leftAdjust = 200; this.moveSpeed = 8; }

    this.xLoc = x * 300 + leftAdjust;
    this.startingX = this.xLoc;
    img.style.left = `${this.xLoc}px`;
    this.yLoc = y * 120 + 60;
```

```
    this.startingY = this.yLoc;
    img.style.top = `${this.yLoc}px`;
    webix.html.insertBefore(img, null, inConfig.playfield);
    this[`frame${i}`] = webix.toNode(id);

  }

}
```

If you compare this to `loadFrames()` in the base `GameObject` class, you'll see a lot of similarity, and usually duplicate code is to be avoided. However, here, I felt there was enough difference to warrant copying it and then modifying it as necessary.

After the usual `super()` call, you get to work creating each of the animation frames, just like in `loadFrames()`. First, the x, y, and `type` attributes from `inConfig` are grabbed into local variables to make things more concise. Then you loop by `frameCount` and create an `<img>` for each using `webix.html.create()` as before. The `id` of each is a little different here in that it consists of the base name (which you know here is enemy), followed by the x and y values and the loop iteration variable. That ensures you have a unique `id` for each where x and y correspond to the column and row they're logically in on the screen relative to each other. Each `<img>` is positioned absolutely like always and is also hidden. That way, the player won't see the initial movements as you get them all created and into place (they might not have, depending on how fast the browser works anyway, but better safe than sorry).

Next, you need to determine how fast and in what direction each enemy moves. You start off assuming they're moving to the right, but for types 2 and 4 you change that to the left (so that each row of enemies alternate movement direction) and also adjust the animation speed via the value of `frameSkip` so that types 2 and 4 animate a little slower. That just adds some visual variety to the proceedings.

Next, you need to account for the starting horizontal location of each enemy. If you picture the screen, each row of enemies is a different type, starting with 1 at the top. For each row, each enemy starts a little more to the right than the row above it. This creates consistent gaps between the enemies as they move. That's where the `leftAdjust` variable comes into play. The value is determined based on the enemy type, and the values are just trial-and-error, but what I thought looked good and, critically for gameplay purposes, presented enough space to be not impossible yet small enough gaps that it wouldn't be a piece of cake to get through. In addition, the speed of each row is determined in the same way. Each row of vermin moves at a different speed, which means how many pixels they move horizontally, as determined by the value of the moveSpeed attribute attached to the object instance.

With all that determined, it's a simple matter of positioning the <img> setting the left and top style attributes to the values of xLoc and yLoc. These are calculated from the leftAdjust value and the x and y values (the multiplied values are again trial-and-error based on the gaps I wanted between them). In addition, the starting location for each is recorded as startingX and startingY so that after the player returns all the energy to the planet and the enemies blow up, you can reposition them in the right place without running through all the logic again. Finally, the enemy is inserted into the DOM with webix.html.insertBefore() and a reference stored to it via a call to webix.toNode().

With the enemy constructed, the other thing that this class needs to supply is a move() function, called on every iteration of the main game loop, to move each enemy.

```
move() {

  if (!this.isVisible) { return; }

  if (this.moveDirection === "right") {
    this.xLoc = this.xLoc + this.moveSpeed;
    if (this.xLoc >= 850) {
      this.xLoc = -50;
    }
  } else {
    this.xLoc = this.xLoc - this.moveSpeed;
    if (this.xLoc <= -50) {
      this.xLoc = 850;
    }
  }

  this["frame0"].style.left = `${this.xLoc}px`;
  this["frame1"].style.left = `${this.xLoc}px`;

}
```

Of course, this logic needs to be done only if the enemy is visible. If it's not, then the explosions are occurring, so there's no need to move them in that case. If it is visible, though, then the moveDirection is interrogated to see whether to increase or decrease the xLoc attribute value. When moving right, there is a point where the vermin has moved off the edge of the playfield to the right far enough, and you need to position it off the playfield to the left so that it appears to "wrap around" and move across the playfield again. That value is 850, and the same sort of logic applies when moving left except that the value is now -50 to trigger a reset off the right edge of the playfield. These values are of course based on the edges of the playfield (0 and 800, since the width is 800) plus (or minus) 50, which accounts for the width of a vermin. That way, it's always completely unseen when it hits those reset points. Finally, regardless of which direction the vermin are moving and regardless of whether it wrapped around the opposite side or not, the enemy is repositioned.

Player.js

The final class you need to examine is Player, and it starts off very much like Crystal and Planet did.

```
constructor(inConfig) {

  super((function() {
    return webix.extend(inConfig,
      { pixWidth : 40, pixHeight : 34, frameCount : 2, baseName : "player"
}
    );
  }()));

  super.loadFrames({
    x : 0, y : 0, playfield : inConfig.playfield, hidden : true, z : 100
  });

  this.toStartingPosition();

  this.dirUp = false;
  this.dirDown = false;
  this.dirLeft = false;
  this.dirRight = false;

  this.energy = 0;
  this.touchingCrystal = false;
  this.touchingPlanet = false;

}
```

You again have a call to super(), followed by a call to loadFrames(). In the case of the latter, the z attribute is passed so that the zIndex style attribute will be set (any value higher than zero would have worked here; I just like a nice, round century!). This ensures that the player always appears on top of other game objects, which only really matters for the crystal and planet, but it just doesn't look right for the ship to be behind those! After that is a call to the toStartingPosition() method, which you'll be looking at next. But, before that, you have a couple of additional attributes on this class. The four dirXX attributes are the flag values that you saw set in the WXGAME.keyHandler() method. This tells you which direction the player is moving. The energy attribute is how much energy the ship currently has onboard, and touchingCrystal and touchingPlanet are the flags that tell you whether the ship is currently touching the crystal or planet, respectively, so that WXGAME.transferEnergy() knows when to do its work, as you saw earlier.

Now, moving on to that toStartingPosition() method:

```
toStartingPosition() {

  for (let i = 0; i < this.frameCount; i++) {
    const frame = this[`frame${i}`];
    this.xLoc = 376;
    frame.style.left = `${this.xLoc}px`;
    this.yLoc = 512;
    frame.style.top = `${this.yLoc}px`;
  }

}
```

Well, that's clearly nothing too complicated! Each animation frame <img> element is moved to some hard-coded values that correspond to centering the player on the bottom of the playfield area.

The final bit of code in this class, and in fact the last bit of code to examine for this project, is the move() method. This method moves the player with each run() execution.

```
move() {

  if (!this.isVisible) { return; }

  const xMoveSpeed = 5;
  const yMoveSpeed = 5;
  let xAdj = 0;
```

```
  let yAdj = 0;
  let degrees = 0;
  if (this.dirUp && !this.dirDown && !this.dirLeft && !this.dirRight) {
    yAdj = -yMoveSpeed;
    degrees = 0;
  } else if (this.dirUp && !this.dirDown && !this.dirLeft && this.dirRight)
{
    xAdj = xMoveSpeed;
    yAdj = -yMoveSpeed;
    degrees = 45;
  } else if (!this.dirUp && !this.dirDown && !this.dirLeft && this.
  dirRight) {
    xAdj = xMoveSpeed;
    degrees = 90
  } else if (!this.dirUp && this.dirDown && !this.dirLeft && this.dirRight)
{
    xAdj = xMoveSpeed;
    yAdj = yMoveSpeed;
    degrees = 135;
  } else if (!this.dirUp && this.dirDown && !this.dirLeft && !this.
  dirRight) {
    yAdj = yMoveSpeed;
    degrees = 180;
  } else if (!this.dirUp && this.dirDown && this.dirLeft && !this.dirRight)
{
    xAdj = -xMoveSpeed;
    yAdj = yMoveSpeed;
    degrees = 225;
  } else if (!this.dirUp && !this.dirDown && this.dirLeft && !this.
  dirRight) {
    xAdj = -xMoveSpeed;
    degrees = 270;
  } else if (this.dirUp && !this.dirDown && this.dirLeft && !this.dirRight)
{
    xAdj = -xMoveSpeed;
```

```
      yAdj = -yMoveSpeed;
      degrees = 315;
    }
    for (let i = 0; i < 360; i = i + 45) {
      webix.html.removeCss(this["frame0"], wxGame[`CSS_ROTATE_${i}`]);
      webix.html.removeCss(this["frame1"], wxGame[`CSS_ROTATE_${i}`]);
    }
    webix.html.addCss(this["frame0"], wxGame[`CSS_ROTATE_${degrees}`]);
    webix.html.addCss(this["frame1"], wxGame[`CSS_ROTATE_${degrees}`]);
    const newX = this.xLoc + xAdj;
    if (newX > 2 && newX < 756) {
      this.xLoc = newX;
    }
    const newY = this.yLoc + yAdj;
    if (newY > 0 && newY < 516) {
      this.yLoc = newY;
    }
    this["frame0"].style.left = `${this.xLoc}px`;
    this["frame1"].style.left = `${this.xLoc}px`;
    this["frame0"].style.top = `${this.yLoc}px`;
    this["frame1"].style.top = `${this.yLoc}px`;

}
```

Of course, it only makes sense to move the player when it's visible, so that's the first check done, and you abort if it isn't visible. Assuming it is, then the code needs to determine two things: which direction it's moving and how to rotate the image. There are four flags (as Picard would say, "THERE! ARE! FOUR! LI–err, FLAGS!") for up, down, left and right, and they can be set to true simultaneously, which gives you a grand total of 16 possible combinations (four "bits," 2^4=16). However, there are really only eight that have meaning here: up, down, left, right, up+left, up+right, down+left, and down+right. Any other combination won't be caught by the if block here and will result in the player not moving (and being "rotated" to its normal "up" orientation since the degrees variable defaults to zero, which effectively means no rotation). Each branch of the if statement corresponds to one of those combinations.

Whichever branch is hit, assuming any are, the values of xMoveSpeed and yMoveSpeed, either one or the other or both depending on the direction of travel, are stored as xAdj and/or yAdj. These values are negated when the values need to be decreased instead of increased.

In addition to determining these movement adjustment values, the if branches also determine the number of degrees the ship needs to be rotated. With that determination made, the rotation is performed on every animation frame <img> element for the player. Here, two new Webix functions are used: webix.html.removeClass() and webix.html.addClass(). You'll recall in the constructor of WXGAME that the CSS classes were created corresponding to each rotation amount and references stored to them on wxGame. Now, when you know the degrees to rotate, you can get a reference to the appropriate CSS class and use webix.html.addClass() to apply it, thereby rotating the ship appropriately for the direction it's traveling. However, before you can even do that, you need to ensure that only one class is ever applied. The easiest way to do this is to just clear any class that might currently be applied by looping through the possible degree increments and calling webix.html.removeClass(). Both webix.html.addClass() and webix.html.removeClass() take as arguments a reference to the DOM node to operate on and the name of the class to add or remove. Assuming the CSS class exists on the page, which it does since you created them all in the WXGAME constructor, the rotation is done.

With the rotation out of the way, the last step is to physically move the player. This just means adding xAdj to xLoc and yAdj to yLoc and then "clamping" the values on the high and low ends so that the player can't ever move off the edge of the playfield. With that done, you just need to set new left and top style attributes on the two animation frames for the player and you're all done!

Summary

In this chapter, the final one of this book, you did something with Webix that is a bit unusual: you wrote a game! In the process, you saw some new "helper"-type functions that Webix provides including ones for creating CSS classes, intercepting function invocations, and extending objects. You also got a basic flavor for how JavaScript games can be written and the fundamental architecture that goes into them.

I hope you've enjoyed this book and that you've learned about Webix and come to appreciate the power it brings to web development. Now, go forth, be fruitful, and create great web apps with Webix. Thanks *very* much for giving me the opportunity to serve as your guide on this journey of discovery!

Index

A

abslayout layout, 53–54
accordion layout, 55–57
Android devices, 350–351

B

Blossoming adulthood, 3–5
Buttons, 81

C

carousel layout, 58–59
checkbox widget, 81
Chips, 89
Code Snippet, 16
   angular, 18
   using XML, 17–18
Command-line interface (CLI), 343
Common Gateway Interface (CGI), 1–2
Components, 43
Context, 133–136
contextmenu, 133–136
Cordova, 341
CSS
   cssListItemTitle string, 219
   inline, 60
   methods, 30
counter control, 84

D

Data
   components
      bullet, 127–128
      chart, 101–102, 105
      datatable, 106, 108–109
      dataview, 109–110
      gage, 125–126
      grouplist, 113, 115
      list, 111–112
      organogram, 128–130
      pager, 113
      property, 117
      rangechart, 130–132
      tree, 118, 120
      treemap, 123–125
      treetable, 121–123
      unitlist, 115, 117
      webix.protoUI()
         method, 120
   DataStore, 98
   dynamic data
      loading, 98
   from external source, 97
   proxies, 99, 101
Data entry control widgets
   button, 81
   checkbox, 81
   code, 73

© Frank Zammetti 2018
F. Zammetti, *Practical Webix*, https://doi.org/10.1007/978-1-4842-3384-9

Get the eBook for only $5!

Why limit yourself?

With most of our titles available in both PDF and ePUB format, you can access your content wherever and however you wish—on your PC, phone, tablet, or reader.

Since you've purchased this print book, we are happy to offer you the eBook for just $5.

To learn more, go to http://www.apress.com/companion or contact support@apress.com.

Apress®

Printed in the United States
By Bookmasters